CND – Now More Than Ever

CND – Now More Than Ever

The Story of a Peace Movement

Kate Hudson

First published in 2005 by Vision Paperbacks,
a division of Satin Publications Ltd.
101 Southwark Street
London SE1 0JF
UK

info@visionpaperbacks.co.uk
www.visionpaperbacks.co.uk
Publisher: Sheena Dewan

A catalogue record for this book is available from the British Library.

ISBN: 1-904132-69-3

2 4 6 8 10 9 7 5 3 1

Cover photos: Getty Images
Cover and text design by ok?design
Printed and bound in the UK by Mackays of Chatham Ltd,
Chatham, Kent

For those who lit the flame of nuclear disarmament,
and for those who carry it forward.
We will prevail.

CONTENTS

ACKNOWLEDGEMENTS

I have received an enormous amount of encouragement and support from colleagues, friends and family members during the writing of this book, for which I would like to express the greatest appreciation. I have also had very valuable conversations and discussions with many CND members too numerous to list, but particular thanks for help with the contents of the book are due to the following: Pat Allen, Pat Arrowsmith, Tony Benn, Pam Cowan, John Cox, Sue Davis, Michael Foot, Sheila Jones, Bruce Kent, Michael Kustow, Andrew Murray, Redmond O'Neill, Duncan Rees, Rae Street, Marjorie Thompson and Walter Wolfgang. Without their insights, memories, contributions and critical comments, this book would not have been possible. Any errors are, of course, entirely my own responsibility. The proposal to write a history of CND was first put to me by Charlotte Cole. It was an inspired idea on Vision's part, and I would like to thank Charlotte and her colleagues for making its realisation possible.

Kate Hudson

INTRODUCTION

CND – now more than ever

In 1945, the United States Air Force dropped atomic bombs on the Japanese cities of Hiroshima and Nagasaki with tragic and devastating consequences. Hundreds of thousands of people died, many instantaneously, others soon after from burns and shock, and yet more from the impact of radiation in the months and years that followed. By 1950, an estimated 340,000 people had died as a result of the two bombs.

The impact of nuclear weapons – in both human and environmental terms – is widely recognised. A nuclear war would kill millions, perhaps destroying the entire human race. The radioactive fallout would render parts, if not all, of the planet uninhabitable. There would be no place to run to, no place to hide; in the event of a nuclear war, you may escape the blast but you cannot shut the door on radiation. It will poison and destroy, bringing sickness, cancers, birth deformities and death.

The consequences of nuclear weapons are widely understood by governments across the globe. So it seems incomprehensible that, 60 years after the atomic bombs were dropped, nuclear weapons still exist – and that some political leaders still contemplate their use. Today, in the region of 20,000 nuclear weapons are stockpiled – enough to destroy human civilisation and the world as we know it many times over. The US alone has over 10,000 nuclear warheads. Britain has almost 200 nuclear warheads; this perhaps seems small in comparison, but each of Britain's warheads has eight times the explosive power of the bomb dropped on Hiroshima. That is a phenomenal killing power – potentially 320 million people dead as a result of British nuclear weapons alone.

To make matters worse, political developments globally have been such over the past few years that there is an increased danger of the use of nuclear weapons – a fact that became clear in the run-up to the recent war on Iraq. But contrary to what the United States administration and our own government here in the UK would have us think, the danger does not come primarily from rogue states, terrorists or 'non-state actors'. The people developing scenarios for the use of nuclear weapons are the administration of the United States, aided and abetted by the UK government. It is extremely likely that they are actively developing a new generation of nuclear weapons for use in wars. Our own government has indicated that it would indeed use a nuclear weapon, even against a non-nuclear weapon state. All this constitutes a dangerous escalation that could have unthinkable consequences for every one of us. It is vital for the very future of humanity that we stop this drive to legitimise the use of the most terrible weapons in human history. We can all play a part in that process. In particular, here in the UK we have a responsibility to make our own government see sense.

For almost half a century, the Campaign for Nuclear Disarmament, or CND, has inspired, led and organised – and no doubt infuriated and annoyed! – many hundreds of thousands of people, and has contributed to changes in politics and society that have shaped the lives of millions. It has been in the leadership of the largest popular mobilisations in every generation since World War II. It has been remarkable for its flexibility and dynamism, embracing methods as diverse as vigils, lobbying, mass demonstrations, raising issues in elections, human chains, peace camps, non-violent direct action, theatre, letter writing, education, leafleting, street stalls, poetry and art, festivals, die-ins (lying on the ground, symbolising death), petitioning, walks, music, fasts, and a host of other imaginative forms of work. It has opposed all nuclear weapons from Polaris to Trident and before and beyond; it has campaigned against wars where nuclear weapons may be used and against illegal wars that destroy the framework of international law; against weapons in space, NATO, illegal pre-emptive attacks; nuclear power, nuclear waste transportation, the militarisation of Europe, the use of radioactive 'depleted' uranium in conventional weapons; the waste of spending on arms and much more. It champions a world of peace and social justice, free from the fear of nuclear annihilation.

The context of CND's campaigns has changed continually: from the Cuban Missile Crisis to the war on Vietnam, from the height of the Cold War to détente, from the 'evil empire' of Ronald Reagan to the end of the Cold War, through to the new nuclear aggression of Bush and Blair. Whatever the context, CND has worked with others, in Britain and abroad, to find the most appropriate campaigning forms to bring our own anti-nuclear issues to the fore, to make them central in the current political agenda. That is not to say that the process of arriving at the right position to take, or the right campaigning initiative, has always been easy. On the contrary, argument and debate have been the hallmark of CND throughout its history. Disagreements have arisen over a range of issues: how much we should get involved in anti-war campaigning; how much direct action is appropriate; what stance we should take on nuclear power; what we think about parliamentary politics.

This is because only a movement open to different views can adapt and develop in an ever-changing world, and CND members are so passionate about their goals that they are determined to get it right. As a result CND has been able to play a leading role in virtually every peace campaign since its birth. CND's most important asset has always been the accumulated experience of its members and its ability to consider different views through democratic debate. Many CND members have decades of experience in campaigning and participate fully in CND's internal democracy and decision-making processes. Our members do not hang back in expressing their views. Chairing a CND meeting has been described to me as being 'like trying to herd cats'!

The purpose of this book is to tell the story of this extraordinary organisation, from its birth to the present day. It will explain the origins and development of the atomic bomb, why something so terrible was ever created, and the circumstances of its use by the US on Japan in 1945. The myth that dropping the bomb was necessary to end the war will be completely debunked and the tragic consequences of this criminal action will be explained. The book also explains the political events surrounding and shaping each phase of CND's development and how anti-nuclear campaigning affected government policy and decision making (even if it wasn't admitted at the time). Reading government documents and diaries years later, one can see how the pressure of public opinion and mass mobilisation really does have an impact, and each generation of CND has played a part in that. The banning of nuclear tests is one very important example; another is the abandoning of the neutron bomb (designed to kill people whilst leaving property intact) or Nixon's pulling back from using nukes on Vietnam. There is a significant list of movement victories and we continue to work to add to this list.

In many respects, the history of CND is the history of post-World War II, told from the side of those fighting for humanity against the horror of war. It is the story of ordinary people's struggles to shape a world without nuclear weapons and war, based on legality and morality; to make our governments responsive and accountable over our right to stay alive, our right to breathe air free of radioactive pollution, our right to say no to the indiscriminate killing of other peoples. CND has been most successful and effective when it has related directly to people's most pressing concerns – linking our issues to the reality of what is going on in the world. Nuclear weapons are not the preserve of technological or military experts, in some specialist niche that isn't relevant to ordinary mortals. Nuclear weapons are the concern of us all, for in them humankind has created something that could end our very existence – and governments will only shift on nuclear weapons policy when enough of us demand change.

We continue to make this history and we continue with our struggle to bring our vision of the world into being. That is why we say: '*CND – now more than ever.*'

1

The origins of our nuclear world

The bombing of Hiroshima

The city of Hiroshima stands on a flat river delta on the Japanese mainland, Honshu. At quarter past eight on the morning of 6 August 1945, the US plane Enola Gay dropped an atomic bomb on the city centre, a busy residential and business district, crowded with people going about their daily business. The bomb, called 'Little Boy' because of its long, thin shape, was made from uranium-235. Unimpeded by hills or natural features to limit the blast, the fireball created by that single bomb destroyed 13 square kilometres of the city.

The heart of the explosion reached a temperature of several million degrees centigrade, resulting in a heat flash over a wide area, vapourising all human tissue. Within a radius of half a mile of the centre of the blast, every person was killed. All that was left of people caught out in the open were their shadows burnt into stone. Beyond this central area, people were killed by the heat and blast waves, either out in the open or inside buildings collapsing and bursting into flame. In this area the immediate death rate was over 90 per cent. The firestorm created hurricane-force winds, spreading and intensifying the fire. Almost 63 per cent of the buildings of Hiroshima were completely destroyed and nearly 92 per cent of the structures in the city were either destroyed or damaged by the blast and fire. The total number of deaths was hard to establish, but at least 75,000 died in the first hours after the bomb was dropped, with around 140,000 dead by December 1945. The death toll reached around 200,000 by the end of 1950.[1]

Many of those who survived the immediate blast died shortly afterwards from fatal burns. Others with possibly less-fatal injuries died because of the breakdown of rescue and medical services, much of which had been destroyed, with personnel themselves killed. Within two or three days, radiation victims who were near the hypocentre developed symptoms such as nausea, vomiting, bloody diarrhoea and hair loss. Most died within a week. Radiation victims further away from the explosion developed symptoms one to four weeks after the explosion. Many survivors – known in Japanese as *hibakusha* – still suffer to this day from the impact of radiation. Pregnant women who survived the bomb faced additional horrors, for the bomb had a terrible impact on a foetus. Many were stillborn, but those born alive faced higher infant mortality rates than normal, or had abnormally small skulls, often suffering from mental disabilities. From about 1960 a higher rate of cancer became evident, in particular of the thyroid, breast, lung and salivary gland. Radiation is known to cause many types of cancer, and Japanese scientific research has now shown a direct correlation between the distance from the atomic bomb hypocentre, the probable exposure dose of radiation and cancer rates.[2]

A survivor's story

My whole heart trembled at what I saw. There was a great fire ring floating over the city. Within a moment, a massive deep white cloud grew out of the centre of the ring. It grew quickly upwards, extending itself further and further from the ring's centre. At the same time I could see a long black cloud as it spread over the entire width of the city. What I saw was the beginning of an enormous storm created by the blast as it gathered up the mud and sand of the city and rolled it into a huge wave. The delay of several seconds after the monumental flash and the heat rays permitted me to observe, in its entirety, the black tidal wave as it approached us. I decided that I had to return to Hiroshima as soon as possible.

I looked at the road before me. Denuded, burnt and bloody, numberless survivors stood in my path. They were massed together; some crawling on their knees or on all fours, some stood with difficulty or leant on another's shoulder. No one showed any sign that forced me to recognise him or her as a human being. Nearly all the buildings in the school complex had been destroyed, leaving only one structure that faced a hill at the back of the school grounds. The area was filled with debris. Yet, the cruelest sight was the number of raw bodies that lay one upon the other. Although the road was already packed with victims, the terribly wounded, bloody and burnt kept crawling in, one after another. They had become a pile of flesh at the entrance to the school. The lower layers must have been corpses because they emanated a peculiarly nasty smell characteristic of the dead that mingled now with burnt, bloody flesh.

Finally I reached the burnt fields where the military hospital had stood. In front of the main office lay three corpses. Their flesh had been burnt black beyond all recognition. As I walked among the ruins, I saw human skeletons covered with ash lying on the melted wire of the broken beds. The crushed frames stood side by side. There were many bodies whose intestines had been forced out of their rectums.

I believe it was about a week after the bombing that an unexpected event happened. Unusual symptoms began to appear in the survivors. When patients raised their hands to their heads while struggling with pain, their hair would fall out with a mere touch of the fingers. Quite soon their heads appeared as if they had been shaven. Experiencing severe symptoms of fever, throat pain, bleeding and depilation, the survivors fell into a dangerous condition within an hour of the onset. Very few patients who came down with these sudden symptoms escaped death.

The survivors seemed to fall ill in groups of seven or eight. These same groups appeared to die together. As I look back on it now, those who were irradiated with the same dose of radiation at the same distance from the epicentre fell ill simultaneously and died together. At the time as physicians we could not know that our patients were dying because of an atomic bomb, which could kill them long after the blast.

Dr Shuntaro Hida, who was visiting a patient outside Hiroshima when the bomb was dropped. He saw the explosion over the city and returned immediately to help survivors[3]

The experience of children in Hiroshima

My father was an air raid warden and no matter how busy he was he put on a black uniform and went out. Every time my father went off to the air raid I felt terribly lonely. However, I thought this was better than if he went off to war. We were just about to eat breakfast when that terrible atom bomb fell. Just as we saw a bright flash there was a loud bang and I almost fainted. It was such a loud noise that it was really frightening. When the bomb fell, cushions and things came falling from the second floor. I caught them and tried to get outside but I couldn't get out. When Father went out some broken glass fell and stuck in his back. Father picked this glass out by himself and helped us get out of the house. Grandmother in the end collided with a post and died. She was really a kind, good grandma. Mother, while she was trying to rescue a child who lived next door, touched poison [radiation] and died rather a long time later.

When we tried to cross the trolley tracks they were so hot that I jumped back. When we came to the river there was a man who was really suffering; he was black all over and he kept saying, 'Give me water, give me water!' I felt so sorry for him I could hardly bear it. People were in the river, drinking the river water. An air raid warden was saying, 'You mustn't drink the water.' He was saying it but people didn't pay any attention to him and lots of people kept going into the water and dying. Although I said Mother died after quite a long time, it was really about the beginning of September. After we came to Rakurakuen Mother worked too hard and had to go to bed. Since Mother was in great pain day after day, we called the doctor. The doctor said, 'The baby is going to be born pretty soon.' At the end of August a baby was born. But only the baby's head was born and then the baby and Mother died together. I was terribly sad. On top of all this my little sister's thumb was almost cut right off. Fortunately, however, it got better. But even now in the winter she suffers very much. My little brother got a sore on his head and if you just touch it pus comes out. I am so sorry for my little brother and sister that I can hardly bear it. I was the only one who didn't get hurt.

Sanae Kanoh, fifth-grade girl (about nine years old), who was four years old in 1945[4]

While my friends and I are playing in the school yard, we all notice an aeroplane flying over our heads and, saying, 'How come the all-clear sounded?!' we keep on playing. And then, as there was a flash of greenish light or I'm not sure what kind of light, I covered my face with my hands. Wondering what this can be, I open my eyes and find it so pitch dark that I can't see a thing. While I am walking uncertainly around, it gets light. Thinking to go back home, I look around and find that there isn't a building left that looks like a house, and here and there flames are rising.

Crying and calling my mother's name, I hurried home. I can't tell where my house is supposed to be, and as I'm wandering around I hear the voice of my sister calling my name. The instant I saw my sister I was frightened. She is standing there dyed bright red with blood. When I look at myself I find that the skin has peeled off both arms and legs and is dangling from one side. I couldn't understand what it was all about, and with that and the terror, I burst out crying. In the meantime Mother had come crawling out from among the tiles and, dragging out an overcoat and Father's Inverness cape, she put them on the two of us, who were red and naked. On the night of the 6th we stopped at the Yasu Shrine in Gion. That night because of their burns everyone was calling to each other, 'Water, water!' We waited for the dawn.

On the morning of the 7th we were all loaded on a truck and taken to Kabe. On the night when we arrived at this place my sister died. I think that unless someone was there he wouldn't know how to express the sorrow my mother felt at that time and he couldn't make his pen describe our life at the temple. How can I find the words to tell how the burned and festering people spent day after day moaning, how people without anyone to care for them, with maggots crawling all over their bodies, died muttering in delirium? Would it be right to call this a Living Hell?

**Masataka Asaeda, ninth-grade boy (about
13 years old) who was in third grade
(about 7 years old) in 1945[5]**

The bombing of Nagasaki

On 9 August, the US dropped a second atom bomb on the Japanese city of Nagasaki. This bomb, named 'Fat Man' because of its rounder and fatter shape, was more powerful than that dropped at Hiroshima and was made from plutonium-239. Nagasaki is a city built on hills, which affected the immediate impact of the bomb. The explosion took place in the Urakami valley, which meant that the physical destruction of that area was even greater than at Hiroshima. Other parts of the city, however, were shielded to some extent by hills. Around 23 per cent of Nagasaki's buildings were destroyed by the blast and fire and over 40,000 deaths occurred in the first few seconds. 70,000 people were dead as a result of the bomb by the end of 1945, and around 140,000 by the end of 1950.[6] Virtually every living thing within three-fifths of a mile from the centre of the blast was immediately destroyed. Beyond this central area, people died in a similar pattern to Hiroshima, from the impact of fire, falling buildings and untreated burns and other injuries, depending on their distance from the centre of the blast. Deaths from atomic radiation followed in large quantities, many within a few days, but other people faced suffering and eventual death in the years that followed. Even today the effects continue, and more dead and deformed babies are born in these areas than in other places.[7]

A father searches and grieves

I threw myself into the search for my family and cast about the still-hot rubble. Before long the tips of my shoes burnt and my toes stuck out, and my hands became swollen with blisters . . . Looking along the road, I found a charred corpse that seemed to be my wife in front of our neighbour Mr Baba's house. I intuited that the dead baby on her back was our one-year-old daughter Takao. However, I was never able to find our eight-year-old son Tateki and our eldest daughter Mariko.

Tsuneo Tomimatsu, Nagasaki[8]

The story of Sadako and the paper cranes

Sadako was two years old when the atomic bomb was dropped on Hiroshima. Almost ten years later she contracted leukaemia, caused by exposure to nuclear radiation. Sadako had great hopes in the Japanese tradition of origami – that folding paper into the shape of the crane bird would help her recover. She kept folding paper cranes until she died in October 1955 after fighting for eight months against the disease. Sadako's death led to a campaign to build a monument for world peace, the Children's Peace Monument in Hiroshima, which was funded by donations from all over Japan. Around 10 million paper cranes are placed each year before the Children's Peace Monument, many made by children from throughout the world who have been moved by Sadako's tragic story.

see www.sadako.org

A priest's view

I did not hold a service of thanksgiving in St Albans today because I cannot honestly give thanks to God for an event

brought about by a wrong use of force, by an act of whole-sale indiscriminate massacre different in kind over all acts of open warfare hitherto, however brutal and hideous.
The Dean of St Albans, UK, August 1945[9]

Why was the atomic bomb developed?

Given the devastating power and destructive force of nuclear weapons – and the radioactive nightmare that they produce – how did they come to be invented in the first place? Surely it would have been better if the technology had never been developed? Many scientists working in the early years of the 20th century warned of the potential dangers of atomic power unleashed. HG Wells even wrote a science fiction novel in which a devastating war was fought with atomic weapons. Yet despite these fears and warnings, scientists did not hold back from working on atomic power. It seems obvious with hindsight that the bomb should not have been produced and, indeed, a number of scientists who worked on the atom bomb deeply regretted it afterwards. Tragically, however, the scientific breakthroughs that put atomic bomb production within the realms of fact not fiction came on the eve of World War II. During the war a nuclear weapons race was on, with the US and UK both urgently seeking to produce an atomic bomb before the Nazis produced their own.

How the atomic bomb works

An atomic explosion is a chain reaction in which more and more atoms are split, releasing colossal amounts of energy and particles that collide with more and more atoms, causing yet more chain reactions. A conventional explosion (of dynamite, for example) is a chain reaction in which energy is released as chemical bonds are broken and new chemical bonds are created. An atomic explosion is so much more powerful because in it some matter is transformed into energy. Albert Einstein calculated the amount of energy released in this way to be represented by the equation $e = mc^2$ (the mass of matter transformed into energy multiplied by the speed of light squared). Hence an enormous amount of energy is produced by the destruction of even a very small mass of matter.

This process is called 'fission' and can be produced by hitting an atom – the smallest particle of matter – with a neutron. The type of atom used in the bomb-making fission process is usually a heavy metal such as uranium or plutonium, which is unstable and radioactive. Uranium, which occurs naturally, is 'enriched' in order to create the concentration necessary for fission to take place. Upon fission the uranium atom releases energy and more neutrons, which in turn hit other atoms and cause further fission. This can trigger a chain reaction and, if enough enriched uranium is present, within a tiny fraction of a second there is an enormous release of heat, energy and radioactivity. Each bomb must contain enough enriched uranium – the amount (about 15 kilos) is known as the 'critical mass' – to sustain the chain reaction. When the bomb is assembled the critical mass is divided into parts to prevent the chain reaction happening until the bomb is actually dropped. The atomic explosion occurs when these parts are brought together.

A second and even more powerful type of nuclear weapon uses the same process as the sun – nuclear 'fusion': joining two light atoms together with the release of enormous quantities of energy. This discovery led to the production of the hydrogen, or thermonuclear, bomb, in which an atomic bomb is detonated to trigger the even more powerful fusion reaction. But at the time of Hiroshima and Nagasaki this was still some way down the road.

In 1933, the Hungarian nuclear physicist Leo Szilard (who had fled from the Nazis and was living in London) believed he had discovered the process that could lead to a nuclear chain reaction. Although Szilard had not worked out how this would happen in practice, he was sufficiently concerned about its potential impact to try to control this knowledge. He applied for a patent on his discovery and gave it to the British admiralty in an attempt to keep it secret. His attempts failed, however, because a number of other nuclear physicists, who did not see any need for secrecy, were pursuing the same line of research and arriving at similar conclusions across Europe and beyond. Soon official atomic bomb programmes were under way in a number of countries.

In 1939, on the initiative of Szilard, the great physicist Albert Einstein wrote to US President Eisenhower, alerting him to the possibility that such weapons could be produced. Einstein was well known to be a long-standing pacifist, but his concern was that the Germans would develop the bomb first. He encouraged the president to fund Szilard to work on his theory of the chain reaction. This was the origin of the Manhattan Project, which by 1945 had produced the atomic bomb.

So the initiative for the development of the bomb came from concerned scientists; not just Szilard and Einstein, but other scientists, such as Otto Frisch, Rudolf Peierls and Joseph Rotblat, who had fled from the Nazis in Europe. They had a very direct understanding of why the Nazi menace must be stopped. As Joseph Rotblat put it, 'We feared that if Hitler acquired this weapon, it would enable him to win the war. It was this appalling prospect that convinced us to start the project.'[10]

But whilst many of the scientists at the time had considerable moral scruples about the development of such a weapon, this view was not shared by all. The United States government and military leadership began to believe that possession of the atomic bomb, alongside their economic dominance, could give the US military dominance in the postwar world and should be developed for that purpose – a view that was shared by British Prime Minister Winston Churchill.

By the end of 1944, however, it was clear that Germany was not going to succeed in making an atom bomb. In these circumstances, scientists such as Joseph Rotblat, who had seen the development of the atomic bomb as a necessary evil in the arms race to defeat Hitler, now left the Manhattan Project. Others tried to alert politicians to the dangers ahead. But top politicians pressed for the rapid completion of the bomb. As Rotblat himself has later pointed out, 'There is good reason to believe that the destruction of Hiroshima and Nagasaki was not so much the end of the Second World War as the beginning of the Cold War, the first step in a fateful chain of events, the start of an insane arms race that brought us very close to a nuclear holocaust and the destruction of civilisation.'[11]

In May 1945, the Germans were finally defeated and the war in Europe ended. Many of those involved in the Manhattan Project felt that it was no longer necessary to continue and that the scientific discoveries could be turned to peaceful purposes. Although the war continued in Asia against Japan, it was known that whilst the Japanese had a small atomic research project, they had no uranium, so there was no atomic threat on that front. Nevertheless, on 16 July 1945, the US carried out the first 'A-bomb' (atomic bomb) test in the desert at Alamogordo in New Mexico. The blast was everything the scientists feared and the political and military leaders had hoped. As a result many atomic scientists signed a petition calling on the US president not to use the atomic bomb against Japan without demonstrating the power of the bomb to them first and so giving them the chance to surrender. The petition was ignored and suppressed.

Why the atom bomb was dropped on Japan

Conventional wisdom – especially in the US – about the dropping of the atomic bomb on Japan is that it was necessary in order to bring about a speedy conclusion to the war and save lives. Even today many people genuinely believe that the bomb was necessary to bring about a Japanese surrender and to avoid the need for an invasion of Japan by the US, which might have cost hundreds of thousands of lives. But extensive scholarly research in the US, using primary sources from the time, shows that this just wasn't true.[12]

By the time the bomb was ready for use, Japan was ready to surrender. As General Dwight Eisenhower said, Japan was at that very moment seeking some way to surrender with minimum loss of face, and 'it wasn't necessary to hit them with that awful thing.'[13] So if Japan was ready to surrender, why were atomic bombs dropped on Hiroshima and Nagasaki? A significant factor in the decision to bomb was the US's desire to establish its dominance in the region after the war. Those planning for the postwar situation believed that this required US occupation of Japan, enabling it to establish a permanent military presence, shape its political and economic system and dominate the Pacific region with-out fear of Japanese resurgence. But Japanese resurgence was no longer the US's key strategic concern; its main concern, above all, was the Soviet Union in the postwar world, both in Asia and in Europe.

The Soviet Union was the US's wartime ally against Germany. Ultimately, of course, their economic systems were incompatible; the US would not accept that any part of the world economy should be closed to it, and those seeking an alternative to the market economic model of the US tended to look to the Soviet Union. This looming antagonism was heightened by the increased power and prestige of the Soviet Union following its role in breaking the back of Germany's military machine. The US consequently wished to prevent a Soviet advance in Asia and subsequent Soviet influence on Japan.

One is forced to conclude that the US wanted to demonstrate its unique military power – its possession of the atomic bomb – in order to gain political and diplomatic advantage over the Soviet Union in the postwar settlement in both Asia and Europe. As eminent US historian Gar Alperowitz observes:

> *Modern research findings clearly demonstrate that from April 1945 on, top American officials calculated that using the atomic bomb would enormously bolster US diplomacy vis-à-vis the Soviet Union in negotiations over both postwar Europe and Asia. The atomic bomb was not, in fact, initially brought to Truman's attention because of its relationship to the war against Japan, but because of its likely impact on diplomacy.*[14]

Whilst many leading US politicians, diplomats and military figures thought it unnecessary to bomb Japan, the group around the US's president at the time, Harry S Truman, pressed strongly for it. Secretary of War Henry Stimson, for example, described the atom bomb as the 'master card' in US diplomacy towards the Soviet Union.[15]

By early 1945 it was clear that while the Japanese government was not offering 'unconditional surrender', it was nevertheless seeking a negotiated surrender, via the neutral Soviet Union.[16] Its condition was that the position of the

Japanese Emperor Hirohito would be maintained without loss of face. A possible scenario would have been altering his role to that of constitutional monarch and ensuring his exemption from war crimes charges, charges that could have led to his execution, as they did with many leaders of Nazi Germany.

There was general agreement amongst the Western leaders that this would be an acceptable approach, but this position was not conveyed to the Japanese government. Indeed, records indicate that President Truman kept this out of the Potsdam declaration – the postwar settlement that the Great Powers (the wartime alliance of the Soviet Union, US and UK) worked on – because the US A-bomb test at Alamogordo had just been successfully concluded. The US leadership did not inform the Japanese that its surrender terms were more or less acceptable, because it needed an excuse to use the bomb in order to demonstrate its awesome power in a world where only the US was in possession of this weapon. Its only opportunity to do so was before the Japanese surrendered.

The Soviet Union had promised to enter the war on Japan three months after the end of the war in Europe. That day was rapidly approaching and the US had two reasons for wishing to use the bomb before this took place. Firstly, there was every likelihood that Soviet entry into the war would trigger a Japanese surrender, thus removing any justification for using the atom bomb. Secondly, the US wished to prevent any possibility that the Soviet Union would occupy Japan whilst the US troops were still far away and so consolidate Soviet influence. So the US dropped the first atomic bomb on the city of Hiroshima on 6 August. On 9 August the Soviet Union entered the war in Asia, as promised. Later the same day, before Japan had had time to grasp and respond to the ghastly results of the Hiroshima bomb, the US dropped a second bomb on the city of Nagasaki. The US government got what it wanted, but at the most appalling human cost.

What the experts said

> *It is my opinion that the use of this barbarous weapon at Hiroshima and Nagasaki was of no material assistance in our war against Japan. The Japanese were already defeated and ready to surrender because of the effective blockade and successful bombing with conventional weapons . . . In being the first to use it we had adopted an ethical standard common to the barbarians of the Dark Ages. I was not taught to make war in that fashion and wars cannot be won by destroying women and children.*

**Admiral William Leahy,
President Truman's chief of staff**[17]

> *Nor were the atomic bombs decisive. It has long been held in justification that they made unnecessary an invasion of the Japanese mainland and thus saved the resultant fighting and thousands and possibly hundreds of thousands of casualties on both sides. On few matters is the adverse evidence so strong. The bombs fell after the decision had been taken by the Japanese government to surrender. That the war had to be ended was agreed at a meeting of key members of the Supreme War Direction Council with the Emperor on 20 June 1945, a full six weeks before the devastation of Hiroshima.*

**Professor JK Galbraith,
official US investigator, Japan 1945**[18]

It would be a mistake to suppose that the fate of Japan was settled by the atomic bomb. Her defeat was certain before the first bomb fell and was brought about by over-whelming maritime power.

Winston S Churchill, British wartime leader[19]

The world after the bombing

On 10 August, the Japanese government surrendered and accepted that the US would occupy Japan. The occupation would last until a number of US objectives had been achieved, including Japan's complete disarmament and the establishment of a 'peacefully inclined and responsible government'. In return, the US now accepted Japanese conditions regarding Emperor Hirohito – that they wanted to retain their Emperor without fear of war crime charges. Indeed, when the Japanese surrender was accepted, Emperor Hirohito remained on the throne until his death some decades later.

The formal surrender was signed on board the US battleship *Missouri* on 2 September. The terms of surrender were no different to those that the Japanese had offered before the bombing; exactly the same ends could have been achieved before the atomic bombing, had the US government accepted the Japanese condition to safeguard its Emperor. But now, of course, the US had secured the occupation of Japan and had demonstrated its 'master card' in the new world of 'atomic diplomacy'.[20] Washington had shown the world – and in particular the Soviet Union – in no uncertain terms that it had a weapon of unique and devastating power, and that it was prepared to use it.

Subsidiary claims made by the US to try to further justify the use of the bomb have also been shown to be false. For example, it was claimed that the citizens of Hiroshima and Nagasaki were warned, by the dropping of leaflets, what was going to happen and urged to evacuate the cities. This is simply not true. Evidence shows that the decision was taken at the highest level not to give any prior warning. Leaflets were dropped on Japanese cities, but they were dropped *after* the atomic bombings, warning that further resistance would be useless.

It was also claimed that Hiroshima and Nagasaki were legitimate military targets. Again, this just wasn't true. Hiroshima was home to the Japanese Second Army HQ, but it was primarily a big city with a huge civilian population. About 10,000 of the total 200,000 deaths in Hiroshima were military personnel. Nagasaki had no military units and, of the total 140,000 deaths there, only about 150 were military. In total, over 95 per cent of the combined casualties of the two cities were civilian.[21]

As well as securing political, diplomatic and military advantages for itself, the US had also secured the otherwise impossible opportunity of testing its nuclear weapons on human beings, and determining their impact on buildings and other materials. It was also able to monitor the impacts of radiation on humans in a way that would otherwise have been impossible. In dropping two bombs, one of uranium and one of plutonium, in different physical settings, a variety of effects could be tested. Given that it was absolutely unnecessary to drop the bombs to end the war, it seems likely that this macabre experiment was another factor in the US decision to bomb, and to bomb twice.

Research scientist Rosalie Bertell considers that there was 'a deliberate plan to study the effects of the two different types of bombs.'[22] The US occupation forces took over 85,000 feet of film footage of the post-bomb areas and in September 1945 a US research team established itself in Hiroshima, to measure the 'health effects' on a human population exposed to atomic fission.[23]

An inevitable consequence of the US development of the atom bomb and its actual use was the development of the arms race. The Soviet Union, which had made some efforts towards developing atomic weapons during the war, was now determined to break the US atomic monopoly. The view was clearly that in order to counter the threat of nuclear weapons it would be necessary to possess them oneself.

Some of the younger Soviet nuclear physicists had pressed the Soviet government for funding for atomic research prior to the war but had received little support. It was only in 1943 after it was apparent that the US, UK and Germany were all trying to produce atomic bombs, that a Soviet atomic bomb project was set up. Under the leadership of the physicist Igor Kurchatov, the project had 100 researchers by the end of 1944 (but was nevertheless much smaller than the US Manhattan Project).[24] The Soviet Union tested its first atom bomb in 1949 and Britain exploded one in 1953.

However, the US was breaking new ground. In 1952 it tested its first hydrogen bomb, or H-bomb, based on nuclear fusion. Hydrogen bombs have higher destructive power and greater efficiency than atomic bombs. The H-bomb was tested in November 1952 at the atoll of Eniwetok in the Marshall Islands in the Pacific Ocean, and was reported to have completely obliterated an island. Its destructive power was several megatons of TNT and the blast produced a light brighter than a thousand suns and a wave of heat felt 50 kilometres away. The Soviet Union exploded an H-bomb of about 1 megaton in August 1953, and the US exploded another one in the region of 15 megatons in March 1954. This one produced a fireball 4.8 kilometres in diameter and created a huge mushroom-shaped cloud. The nuclear arms race was well and truly under way and became a significant component in what was known as the Cold War between the US and the Soviet Union in the post-World War II years.

Opposition to the bomb

Reliable details about the human tragedy experienced in the cities of Hiroshima and Nagasaki were not available in the West for some time. There was massive popular opposition to nuclear weapons, but the US occupation restricted its impact both inside Japan and in the wider world through censorship of publications critical of atomic weapons.

The first widely published and accessible account came from an American author, John Hersey, who was sent to Hiroshima in 1946 by *The New Yorker* magazine to interview survivors and find out what had actually happened. In August 1946, *The New Yorker* published Hersey's 30,000-word account in a single issue. A few hours after publication the issue had sold out. Albert Einstein bought a thousand copies. Hersey's account was published in Britain as *Hiroshima* by Penguin Books in November 1946 and was also broadcast on the radio.

One of the first international statements against nuclear weapons came from the United Nations (UN), which had been founded in June 1945 and whose Charter included the primary purpose 'to save succeeding generations from the scourge of war.' The UN General Assembly met for the first time in London in January 1946. Its first resolution was to prepare proposals for 'the elimination from national armaments of atomic weapons', and it was unanimously accepted.[25]

In August 1945, British Prime Minister Clement Atlee stated in a secret memorandum, 'The only course which seems to me to be feasible and to offer a reasonable hope of staving off imminent disaster for the world is joint action by the US, UK and Russia based upon stark reality. We should declare that this invention has made it essential to end wars. The new World Order must start now.'[26] At the same time, of course, the British government was determined to acquire nuclear weapons of its own.

Immediately after the war, with only limited public knowledge of the threat posed by nuclear weapons, however, the overwhelming concern of the public was never again to go through the carnage of World War II, in which around 55 million people died. There was deep concern about the international situation but the longing for peace did not coalesce around nuclear weapons for some years. The UN was seen as an alternative to war, and some organisations at that time opposed all military options. They shared the values of many people at that time, calling for 'world government' – a popular, if utopian, idea in the aftermath of the war, when there were great hopes for a new, peaceful and just world.

In Britain, the National Peace Council, which was a coalition of primarily pacifist groups, called on the government to renounce war and support the move towards a world government.[27] Other organisations, such as Federal Union and the Crusade for World Government, also championed world government. The philosopher Bertrand Russell was a key figure in the movement (and later went on to be CND president), as was Henry Usborne, a Labour MP who organised a Parliamentary Group for World Government and got the support of nearly 100 other MPs during the course of 1947. Labour ministers such as Stafford Cripps and Ernest Bevin were also supportive.

In the early years after the war, although many scientists continued to pursue and advance nuclear weapons technology (backed by the government), others were particularly significant in highlighting the specific dangers of atomic bombs. After all, scientists were in a better position than the general public to understand the destructive meaning of $e = mc^2$. The US Federation of Atomic Scientists was enormously concerned about atomic energy and wanted it to be brought under international control. In 1946, the US government produced the Acheson-Lilienthal Plan, which proposed this. This however was subsequently watered down into the Baruch Plan, which appeared to institutionalise the US advantage in atomic energy. The Soviets certainly believed that and vetoed the Plan.[28]

Many scientists subsequently turned to other ways of raising public awareness of the dangers of the atomic bomb. In the winter of 1947, an 'atom train' toured Britain under the guidance of the devout Quaker scientist, Kathleen Lonsdale, who deeply regretted 'that scientific knowledge should have been so misused.'[29] Public meetings were held around the country, explaining the facts about the bomb.[30] In 1950, 100 Cambridge scientists petitioned the British government not to make an H-bomb. In 1955, 11 leading scientists – 9 of whom were Nobel Prize winners – signed a Manifesto, urging scientists internationally to work for peace. Known as the Russell-Einstein Manifesto, after its two most famous signatories, it was endorsed by hundreds of scientists and generated considerable public awareness of the issues and of the dangers presented by radioactive fallout from nuclear testing.

In 1957, an international conference was held in the Canadian village of Pugwash. Made up of scientists concerned about the threat of nuclear war, from that meeting an organisation and regular conference programme emerged. The Pugwash Conference was notable not least because it included scientists from all over the world, including the socialist countries. At a time of intense Cold War tension and strong anti-Soviet sentiments – Western peace activists were often abused for opposing nuclear weapons and accused of trying to 'weaken' the West – this was a significant achievement.

The Russell-Einstein Manifesto

We are speaking on this occasion not as members of this or that nation, continent or creed, but as human beings, members of the species Man, whose continued existence is in doubt...

We have to learn to think in a new way. We have to learn to ask ourselves not what steps can be taken to give military victory to whatever group we prefer, for there no longer are such steps; the question we have to ask ourselves is: what steps can be taken to prevent a military contest of which the issue must be disastrous to all parties?...

It is stated on very good authority that a bomb can now be manufactured which will be 2,500 times as powerful as that which destroyed Hiroshima. Such a bomb if exploded near the ground or under water sends radioactive particles into the upper air... No one knows how widely such lethal radioactive particles might be diffused, but the best authorities are unanimous in saying that a war with H-bombs might possibly put an end to the human race. It is feared that if many H-bombs are used there will be universal death – sudden only for a minority, but for the majority a slow torture of disease and disintegration...

Shall we put an end to the human race; or shall mankind renounce war?[31]

The pacifist movements

The vast majority of the British population initially approved of the bombings at Hiroshima and Nagasaki because it had been told the attacks had been necessary to end the war. An opinion poll shortly after the bombing showed that 72 per cent of the population supported it.[32] But there was, nevertheless, a widespread and growing unease about the threat that the new weaponry posed to human life and civilisation.

Fairly rapidly, attitudes towards the bomb began to change, but political activity tended to focus on avoiding war – whether through the schemes for world government, the UN or outright pacifism, which had been a powerful force in the run-up to World War II. A number of long-standing pacifist organisations, such as the Peace Pledge Union – which was a section of the War Resisters' International – and the Fellowship of Reconciliation, were active on peace issues, but not on specifically anti-nuclear ones. The Peace Pledge Union (PPU), whose members renounced war and declared they would never sanction another, had been founded in 1936. By 1939 it had 150,000 members, 1,000 local groups and 30 full-time staff, but it lost members during the World War II, given its anti-facist character. The war was overwhelmingly seen as a just war and support for pacifism fell away. By the end of the war, PPU membership was down to 20,000.[33]

The Fellowship of Reconciliation (FOR) was the British section of an international Christian pacifist movement. It suffered heavily during the war in terms of numbers and credibility. Its members had suffered wartime persecution through concentration camps, gas chambers or imprisonment.[34] In 1945 FOR in Britain had around 13,000 supporters, but there was quite a bit of overlap with PPU membership.[35]

In the late 1940s, pacifists were more engaged in campaigning to prevent the reintroduction of conscription in Britain than in opposing nuclear weapons.[36] Even when the development of a British atom bomb was announced by Prime Minister Clement Attlee, in 1948, there was no massive public outcry. The largest peace demonstrations in the late 1940s, which tended to be organised by the British Peace Committee and attracted tens of thousands of participants, were against German rearmament; the US and British governments were promoting its rearmament as a necessary step to counter the Soviet Union. This issue deeply divided the Labour Party (as mentioned before, many prominent Labour MPs were anti-war) and became entwined with the choice of developing the welfare state or devoting scarce resources to a new armaments drive, which included developing a British atomic bomb. But the largest specifically anti-nuclear demonstrations were only able to mobilise round about 3,000 people. At this point, there was no mass opposition to nuclear weapons and no significant campaigning against them.[37]

Responses to a more dangerous world

Within the next few years, however, the situation changed significantly. 1949 was something of a turning point. In April of that year, the North Atlantic Treaty Organisation (NATO) was founded, militarily linking North America and western Europe in an anti-Soviet alliance. This included an agreement to accept US air bases in Britain.[38] In August 1949, the Soviet Union tested its first atomic bomb. This came as a surprise to everyone, including US intelligence, which had expected the Soviet bomb to be most likely to appear round about 1953. The Soviet Union had started its atomic bomb project in earnest in August 1945, and had completed it in four years, close to the time taken in the US.

This changed the world situation completely. The US no longer had a monopoly of atomic weapons. No doubt as a result, in January 1950, the US announced plans to develop the hydrogen bomb, a bomb hugely more powerful than the atomic bomb. Now the nuclear arms race was in full swing at the front line of the developing Cold War. The world was again becoming a vastly more dangerous place. Britain could now be a target for nuclear weapons; this raised public anxieties more than the primarily humanitarian questions that had previously motivated concerned citizens. The horrific prospect of nuclear war between the US and Soviet Union shaped public attitude into the 1950s.

Combined with this, the reality of the atomic bomb began to be more widely understood as more accurate information about the impact of the bombs became available. Opposition to nuclear weapons began to develop, first on a small scale and often promoted by pacifist organisations and religious groups (although the British Council of Churches supported the atomic bomb as a deterrent and for the purpose of reprisals[39]). Both internationally as well as in Britain, many people believed that the only way to avoid nuclear annihilation was to develop responsible world government. Although the world government movement more or less faded out in the 1950s, many of its supporters retained an anti-nuclear interest and became involved in new campaigns such as the Campaign for Nuclear Disarmament, or CND.[40] Bertrand Russell continued to advocate world government through the 1950s, making a strong case for it, particularly with regard to disarmament, in his work *Has Man a Future?*, published in 1961.[41]

Further to this, in June 1950 the Korean War began – the first war since Hiroshima and Nagasaki in which there was a strong likelihood of the use of nuclear weapons. During World War II, Korea had been occupied by the Japanese. With the defeat of Japan, Korea was occupied by Soviet forces in the northern part of the country and US forces in the south. The forces met at the 38th parallel. In January 1949, the Soviet occupying troops withdrew, followed by the US forces some months later. Two separate state structures now existed, the communist-led Korean National Democratic Republic in the north, and the Republic of Korea, established by the US, in the south.

The intense and bloody Korean War that lasted for over a year involved not only the Koreans themselves, but also the US, UK and other Western forces mobilised by a UN Security Council resolution. The Soviet Union was not in a position to use its veto to prevent the action because it had refused to participate in UN agencies until the UN recognised the communist-led People's Republic of China – rather than Chiang Kai-shek's Nationalists – as China's legitimate government.

China, which had a communist government from October 1949, also became involved and received some material support from the Soviet Union. The US commander, General Douglas MacArthur, spoke openly of invading China, bombing Chinese cities and using the atom bomb. Given that the Soviet Union was now developing nuclear weapons, such an escalation would have risked nuclear war with the Soviet Union and was rejected by Washington. MacArthur was dismissed and the war remained limited to the Korean peninsula, but without doubt the nuclear threat had been a real one. This was the shape of wars to come.

A number of initiatives developed around this time. In March 1950, the Stockholm Peace Appeal was launched by Frédéric Joliot-Curie, the French nuclear physicist, on behalf of Partisans for Peace, a communist-led initiative that was subsequently renamed the World Peace Council. Launched as a petition calling for the 'unconditional prohibition of the atomic weapon', the Appeal secured 500 million signatures from 79 countries by the end of 1950.[42] The British Peace

Committee, the organisation linked to the World Peace Council in Britain, secured 1 million signatures for the petition. But despite the positive nature of the Stockholm Peace Appeal, there was considerable reserve shown, both towards it and towards the British Peace Committee, because of the communist leadership of the World Peace Council. In fact, the Labour Party added the British Peace Committee to its list of proscribed organisations: Labour Party members were not allowed to join it. When a major conference was planned for Sheffield in 1950 in support of the Stockholm Appeal, the prime minister, Clement Attlee, described it as bogus. He accused the organisers of seeking 'to paralyse the efforts of the democracies to arm themselves.'[43] Through denying admittance to many of the participants, including Joliot-Curie, the government secured the removal of the conference to Warsaw.

Hostility to communist peace activists was not restricted to the government, however. In the Cold War context, where great hostility existed towards the Soviet Union, anti-communism was rife and existed even within the peace movement. Many people found it difficult to accept that British communists genuinely wanted peace and disarmament and were not just working in the interests of the Soviet Union. With time these attitudes did change to a considerable extent as people came to welcome dedicated peace activists whatever their personal convictions.

The Stockholm Appeal

We demand unconditional prohibition of the atomic weapon as a weapon of aggression and mass annihilation of people, and that strict international control for the implementation of this decision be established. We shall consider as a war criminal that government which first employs atomic weapons against any country.[44]

A different type of initiative came from the Peace Pledge Union, which attracted new, younger members. In the early 1950s it began working on a Non-Violence Commission (NVC) to look into the use of direct action in campaigning, influenced by the Gandhian philosophy of *satyagraha*, which encompassed non-violent civil disobedience. Its intention was to consider how direct action could be effective in campaigning for withdrawal of US troops, ceasing manufacture of British nuclear weapons, withdrawal from NATO and the disbanding of the British armed forces.[45] Such new campaigning methods were also being pioneered in the US by the civil rights movement. The NVC established contact with both the US Congress of Racial Equality, which was to go on to develop mass sit-ins as a very effective technique, and Peacemakers, a pacifist group that carried out actions at missile bases.

Michael Randle and Pat Arrowsmith – who were to be direct action activists for generations – joined Hugh Brock, who had been a conscientious objector during the war, and put these new methods on the map in Britain. Pat Arrowsmith, described in the press as 'a brisk young woman' was from an upper-middle-class family. Her father was a vicar and her ancestors had been Christian missionaries. As a girl she was a border at Cheltenham Ladies' College. She has been a life-long peace activist, many times imprisoned. When she was asked what one of her early prison sentences was like, she replied that it was rather like her boarding school!

Shocked into action by President Truman's declaration in January 1950 that the US was working to develop a hydrogen bomb, this group of activists branched out from the traditional methods of the Peace Pledge Union. Bringing Gandhi's methods to the fore, it launched 'Operation Gandhi' to challenge the madness of the nuclear arms race. In January 1952, twelve activists engaged in a sit-down on the War Office steps and were eventually arrested. Subsequent protests took place during the building of the Atomic Weapons Establishment (AWE) at Aldermaston in Berkshire, at Mildenhall US Air Force Base in East Anglia and at Porton Down microbiological research centre on Salisbury Plain.

These early actions were numerically small but received significant press attention. What really changed the whole numerical framework and brought about serious mobilisations was the issue of nuclear testing.

Campaigning against weapons testing

In October 1952, Britain tested its first atomic bomb over the Monte Bello Islands in the Pacific Ocean. In November 1952, the US tested a 10.4 megaton hydrogen bomb – more than the total explosives used by all sides during World War II. This bomb, in the early stages of thermonuclear development, was enormous and unwieldy. Weighing 82 tons, it had to be housed in a huge refrigeration plant.[46] On detonation, its fireball measured 3 miles in diameter, and the giant mushroom-shaped cloud that it threw up, dropping radioactive mud and rain, measured over 100 miles in diameter.

Less than a year later, in August 1953 the Soviet Union tested a smaller, more sophisticated hydrogen bomb of around 400 kilotons at Semipalatinsk in Soviet central Asia. In response, in December 1953 in a speech to the UN, President Eisenhower proposed that atomic competition give way to co-operation, and that all countries with such weapons should participate in a UN-sponsored international atomic agency. Unfortunately this proposal, known as Atoms for Peace, didn't gain much ground, in part because US hawks such as John Foster Dulles instead proposed a more popular policy of 'massive retaliation' against anyone who attacked the US or its allies.

Shocking though the first hydrogen bomb tests had been, however, it was the US test of 1954 that really shifted popular consciousness on the question of testing. In March 1954, the US conducted a hydrogen bomb test at Bikini Atoll, in the Marshall Islands. The test was a 17-megaton blast with about 1,000 times the force of the bombs used on Japan. Although a radioactive danger zone had been identified in advance of the explosion, in the event the explosion was hugely more powerful than anticipated and large quantities of radioactive fallout – white like snow – descended on four inhabited islands, including Rongelap, 100 miles from Bikini. The islanders, who were not evacuated for some days, suffered in the short term from various forms of radiation sickness and in the long term from very serious radiation-linked diseases. As Rosalie Bertell explains:

During the first five years after the radiation exposure of the Marshallese there was a significant increase in miscarriages and stillbirths among exposed Rongelap women. It took about nine years for researchers to notice the high rate of growth retardation and thyroid abnormalities in the Rongelap children. In 1972, Lekoj Anjain, from Rongelap, died of leukaemia at the age of 19. He had been exposed to the gamma radiation cloud on Rongelap at one year and had played in the white fallout. Lekoj had suffered acute radiation sickness, beta skin burns and epilation (loss of hair) at the time of the nuclear explosion but had seemed to recover. When 13 years old, he had surgery for thyroid nodules. His mother, father and two brothers also had thyroid surgery. Lekoj died in the US at the National Cancer Institute Hospital in Bethesda six weeks after his admission. He had been the youngest child on Rongelap at the time of the bombing.[47]

The blast also caught the *Lucky Dragon*, a Japanese fishing boat 85 miles distant, in its radioactive fallout. The boat and the fishermen were heavily contaminated with radioactive fission products; all the men fell sick and one of them died. Given the distance of the boat from the explosion, the death and sickness that followed shocked many people. It became clear that the hydrogen bomb was extremely 'dirty', giving out large amounts of radioactive material.[48] This realisation considerably fed opposition to hydrogen bomb testing, raising serious fears in people's minds about the widespread health consequences of the tests.

Subsequent data indicate that these fears were well founded. The patterns of incidence of cancers were highly alarming, as Chris Busby has pointed out:

> *In other countries of the world, where people were not exposed to the acute flash of external radiation from the bombs, but were exposed to the fallout from Hiroshima and the early tests, there were major increases in cancer and leukemia. Death rates for all types of childhood cancers increased in sudden jumps in the US between 1948 and 1951 . . . trends in the UK largely followed those in the US . . . There was a sharp rise in cancer deaths of all types for the age group 5–14 years following some 3 to 5 years after the New Mexico test and the Japanese bombs . . . For all age-groups and for both sexes there were tremendous increases beginning suddenly between 1947 and 1951 with the sharpest changes in the very young and the very old.*[49]

In April 1954, on the initiative of a number of Labour MPs including Anthony Wedgwood Benn, the Hydrogen Bomb National Campaign was set up. Local groups developed and a million signatures were collected on a petition calling for a top-level disarmament conference and reform of the UN. Similar demands put forward as a Labour Party resolution in the House of Commons had won 108 votes. Tony Benn remembers the origins of this campaign:

In March 1954 the United States tested the first hydrogen bomb on the Bikini Atoll in the Pacific and a number of Japanese fishermen working on their ship the Lucky Dragon *were seriously burnt by the blast and radiation, even though it had occurred over 50 miles away. The bomb itself was 600 times more powerful than the atomic bombs dropped on Hiroshima and Nagasaki and the political shock waves went around the world, which led some of us to plan a campaign designed to bring about a summit meeting between the nuclear powers to end the threat that was posed.*

Fenner Brockway, Sir Richard Acland, Tony Greenwood, George Thomas, who was later Speaker of the House of Commons and I, met to discuss how this could best be launched and we decided to book the Albert Hall for 30 April, at which we would make our Appeal for a National Petition.

Canon John Collins [later to become CND chair] unfortunately withdrew at a late stage because he was afraid that the line-up of speakers might make it seem too political but we went ahead and the meeting was held at what became the beginning of a six-month campaign for signatures which we presented on 31 December 1954 at No 10 Downing Street, where Churchill was still prime minister, and the debate within the party began to get under way.[50]

This specific campaign was over by the end of the year, but popular opposition to testing continued to grow as the radiation risks from H-bomb testing became more widely understood and the testing programmes of the nuclear states expanded. By the end of 1958, around 307 nuclear tests had taken place, mostly in the atmosphere, conducted by the US, Soviet Union and the UK.[51]

The human impact of the tests

The tests had very damaging consequences for many British servicemen and women who were affected by radiation. Relatives of the victims are still pursuing the Ministry of Defence (MoD) for compensation. Sue Davis tells the story of her brother:

> *My brother Tony was a fighter pilot throughout World War II and stayed in the RAF afterwards because he loved flying; it was his life. In 1957, he was sent to Christmas Island to pilot the official photographers of the nuclear tests, and also the post-trial samples. In January 1964, he died of acute myelo-monocytic leukaemia. The consultant haematologist at Addenbrookes Hospital in Cambridge told us both that the only way he could have contracted this particular form of leukaemia was through the radiation dose he had received on Christmas Island. It was a shock to us both; we had no idea that his service there was life threatening.*
>
> *Afterwards, my solicitor had a lengthy correspondence with the MoD, to claim exemption from death duties since he died as a result of active service, to make them accept responsibility for his death and to admit to the danger of the nuclear tests. Of course they denied all this and claimed he was never in danger.*

In 1985, the British Nuclear Test Veterans Association was formed and it began its struggle for compensation. In 2004, the MoD was served with the case we are currently pursuing, suing the MoD for compensation, with over 1,000 witnesses. The pressing need for this now is especially for the children and grandchildren of nuclear test veterans, born with horrendous birth defects, like those among the Pacific Islanders who suffered from the tests. Apparently my brother's case is especially strong. After all these years it is good to be in this struggle alongside so many others.

Sue's lawyer suggested that a question should be put in parliament about her brother's case, but being at that time apolitical she refused, fearing the publicity. But she has no doubt that was when her journey began into anti-nuclear activism and CND via Greenham Common.[52]

The decision to test the British H-bomb on Christmas Island in 1957 was ultimately the trigger for really serious organising and mobilisation, which resulted in the foundation of CND. In February 1957, the National Committee for the Abolition of Nuclear Weapons Tests (NCANWT) was founded with Sheila Jones and Ianthe Carswell as joint secretaries. Dr Sheila Jones, herself a scientist, went on to help found CND. She has been a lifelong activist for peace and is currently CND Archivist. NCANWT pursued vigorous campaigning activities over the subsequent months, eventually bringing together the activities of over 100 local groups. Numerous eminent figures backed NCANWT as sponsors, including Benjamin Britten, EM Forster, Henry Moore and Michael Tippett, president of the Peace Pledge Union.[53]

Opposition to the tests now came from many quarters.

Following a request from the National Christian Council of Japan, the British Council of Churches condemned the tests and opposition MPs urged their postponement. The government's position, however, expressed in a Defence White Paper in 1957,[54] was that Britain's only safeguard against nuclear attack was to be able to threaten retaliation. This notion of 'deterrence' – that you can deter attack by possessing nuclear weapons – remains British government policy to this day.

Those organised around 'Operation Gandhi' now formed the Emergency Committee for Direct Action against Nuclear War and backed direct action against the tests. They included Bertrand Russell and Spike Milligan, and supported the Quakers Sheila and Harold Steele, who decided to sail a boat into the test area in an attempt to prevent the testing going ahead. Although they failed to achieve their destination, nevertheless they did attract worldwide publicity to the issue. The Emergency Committee subsequently became the Direct Action Committee (DAC), most famous for its organisation of the first march to Aldermaston in 1958.

Trying to bring change through the Labour Party

The year 1957 saw a considerable raising of the profile of anti-nuclear issues, both in Britain and around the world. A number of high-profile initiatives gave voice to popular concerns. In April 1957, the world-renowned and esteemed humanitarian and Nobel laureate, Dr Albert Schweitzer, broadcast a 'Declaration of Conscience', appealing for an end to testing. As he said, 'Not our own health only is threatened by internal radiation, but also that of our descendants . . . we are forced to regard every increase in . . . radioactive elements by atomic bomb explosions as a catastrophe for the human race, a catastrophe that must be prevented.'[55] The Nobel laureate Linus Pauling began a high-profile petition campaign amongst scientists calling for an end to nuclear testing, and the first Pugwash Conference of scientists, mentioned earlier, took place in July 1957.

Against this backdrop of intense international concern, moves took place within the Labour Party – which was in opposition at that point – to organise against the hydrogen bomb. During the summer of 1957, the Labour H-Bomb Campaign Committee was formed, joined by 30 MPs and organised by Walter Wolfgang (who has fought on these issues within the Labour Party ever since, and is a life vice-president of CND in recognition of his work). In September 1957 the Committee organised a rally in Trafalgar Square, attended by 4,000 people, against British production of the H-Bomb.

Many people felt that the best way to solve the problem of British nuclear weapons and testing was to elect a Labour government committed to abandoning them. This approach had a certain logic to it, but necessitated first of all a change in Labour Party policy. In 1957, 66 Labour Party branches put resolutions to the Annual Conference in Brighton, calling for unilateral renunciation of the hydrogen bomb by Britain. A resolution pledging that a Labour government would not test, manufacture or use nuclear weapons was defeated.[56] Aneurin Bevan, who was then shadow foreign minister, spoke against the resolution on behalf of the Labour Party National Executive. He famously asked delegates not to send him 'naked' into the conference chamber.[57] Supported by the trade unions, Bevan won the vote, defeating the resolution by a margin of 7 to 1. As Tony Benn reports:

In 1957, at the Labour Conference in Brighton, the question of Britain's nuclear weapons came up for debate on a motion from Norwood CLP and Nye Bevan rose to speak and to the amazement of his followers on the Left he denounced the Unilateralist Resolution and said that, if passed, Britain 'would go naked into the conference chamber', arguing that we had to retain our nuclear armoury in order to have any say in future international disarmament negotiations.

A few weeks later, in February 1958, I resigned my position as one of Labour's Front Bench spokesmen on Defence, explaining in a letter to Gaitskell, who had appointed me, that I could not, under any circumstances, support a policy which contemplated the use of atomic weapons in war.[58]

The birth of CND

There was a strong feeling, after the defeat of this position at the Labour Party Conference, that it was necessary to find alternative ways to campaign against nuclear weapons. Public anxieties about the dangers of the bomb were rising. The day the Labour Party Conference ended, the Soviet Union launched the first Sputnik – the first space vehicle in history. The US and its allies were stunned. The belief that a belligerent foreign policy based on nuclear weapons could backfire and result in the destruction of British cities by such weapons now gained credence. Heightened fears contributed to a move to create a powerful and coherent movement against nuclear weapons.

The final catalyst for the foundation of CND occurred in November 1957. Disillusionment with the Labour Party led to an outpouring of anti-nuclear feeling. Intellectuals articulated the views of huge numbers of concerned citizens. Bertrand Russell spoke out sharply, and the writer JB Priestley wrote an article in the *New Statesman* magazine, entitled 'Britain and the Nuclear Bomb', that captured the popular mood, calling for unilateral disarmament:

> *The British of these times, so frequently hiding behind masks of sour, cheap cynicism, often seem to be waiting for something better than party squabbles and appeals to their narrow self-interest, something great and noble in its intention that would make them feel good again. And this might well be a declaration to the world that after a certain date one power able to engage in nuclear warfare will reject the evil thing for ever.*[59]

Readers responded to such an extent that the editor, Kingsley Martin, suggested to Bertrand Russell, JB Priestley and others that a mass movement against nuclear weapons was needed. They agreed, but they were not the only ones who were thinking along these lines. NCANWT, with serious support and many groups across the country, was already planning to extend its remit beyond testing to disarmament as well. On 16 January 1958, its leaders, together with other notable anti-nuclear figures, were invited to a meeting set up by Kingsley Martin and hosted by Canon John Collins, of St Paul's Cathedral. Canon Collins, an Anglican priest with a strong commitment to social justice, became the first Chair of CND and steered it through its early years. His life was one of remarkable commitment to progressive campaigning – including the struggle against apartheid in South Africa. Among them were Bertrand Russell, the novelist Rose Macauley, biologist and writer Julian Huxley, Michael Foot, Sheila Jones and activist Peggy Duff. NCANWT agreed to transfer its resources, including funds, offices and staff, to the new organisation, the Campaign for Nuclear Disarmament.[60] NCANWT already had a public meeting planned for 17

February in the Central Hall, Westminster and agreed to hand it over to the new CND.

Although the new campaign and its planned meeting received virtually no press attention in advance, public interest was enormous. Not only was the Central Hall itself completely packed, four overflow halls were also booked and filled – probably about 5,000 people in all. The audience was militantly anti-nuclear, and the speakers from the new CND committee, who had prior to the meeting adopted a rather wishy-washy set of demands to put to the government, became militant in their turn. Everyone demanded not only multilateral initiatives towards disarmament but also unilateral nuclear disarmament on the part of Britain; disarmament irrespective of whether other countries continued to hold nuclear weapons. This was reinforced the following evening, when a meeting of supporting organisations demanded that unilateral renunciation of nuclear weapons be included in CND's policy statement.[61] Shortly afterwards, the newly founded CND issued its policy statement publicly, and it did indeed embrace both multilateralism and unilateralism:

CND's policy statement

We shall seek to persuade British people that Britain must:

a) *Renounce unconditionally the use or production of nuclear weapons and refuse to allow their use by others in her defence.*

b) *Use her utmost endeavour to bring about negotiations at all levels for agreement to end the armaments race and to lead to a general disarmament convention.*

c) *Invite the cooperation of other nations, particularly non-nuclear powers, in her renunciation of nuclear weapons.*

Realising the need for action on particular issues, pending success in its major objectives, Britain must:

a) Halt the patrol flights of planes equipped with nuclear weapons.

b) Make no further tests of nuclear weapons.

c) Not proceed with the agreement for the establishment of missile bases on her territory.

d) Refuse to provide nuclear weapons for any other country.[62]

Thus was CND established. Its original aims remain just as valid today.

2

Aldermaston and the early radicalism

The world into which CND emerged was changing rapidly. Worldwide, the colonial empires were being dismantled as national liberation movements achieved the independence of their countries. European colonial power in East Asia had been broken by the Japanese. Britain withdrew from India, partitioning the country into the two states of India and Pakistan amid a bloodbath claiming countless lives. Dutch rule in the East Indies ended. The Chinese Communist Party came to power in the world's most populous country in 1949. Ghana was the first colony in Africa to gain its independence, named the 'Black Star of Africa' in 1957, under the leadership of Kwame Nkrumah. Others followed rapidly. A revolution in Cuba in 1959, under the leadership of Fidel Castro, kicked out the corrupt dictator Batista and engaged in a programme of social and economic reform. This radical wave alarmed the US and its allies, to the extent that the largest conflicts in the postwar world occurred as the US intervened to try to prevent the colonial revolutions radicalising along the lines that had occurred in China. But major social change was not confined to the former colonies.

In Britain, the establishment of the welfare state by the postwar Labour government had brought health and education to all. Full employment brought jobs for all, a real advance in a country where memories of the poverty and hunger of the 1930s were still relatively recent. The great vision of the UN, for a world free of injustice, poverty and war, still held widespread resonance. In many ways there was a new confidence in the ability to build a new world based on science and reason, that social progress and advance for all peoples were unstoppable. This was also the time when 'youth culture' emerged as a distinct social and cultural phenomenon, as education and wider opportunities created a more affluent and articulate generation of young people. Indeed, opportunities were improved across all economic classes and social mobility was better than it had ever been before. As Harold Macmillan said, 'You've never had it so good', and for many people this was genuinely the case.

Britain's role in the world

Yet the great promise of the postwar world was blighted by continuing inequalities, uneven economic development and the threat of war and nuclear annihilation. There were also other factors specific to Britain that made for a less certain and perhaps more anxious and questioning society; firstly, with regard to Britain's role in the world. Britain emerged from World War II extremely economically weakened and very reliant on the US. One of the key goals of the US in the postwar period was to open up the world economy to US trade – the famous 'open door' policy that would access widespread markets to sustain and expand its economic position.

There were a number of obstacles to this. The Soviet Union, China and other state-socialist countries with their planned economies were outside the world market framework, so the US put considerable effort into other parts of the world that had traditionally been inaccessible. One of its main goals was opening up China and the former European colonial empires to US trade.

The consequences of this policy had struck Britain rather forcibly in 1956. Indeed, in some senses the closing months of 1956 were a watershed in British politics. President Nasser of Egypt – one of the founders of the Non-Aligned Movement, the organisation of developing countries that wished to remain independent of either super power – nationalised the Suez Canal. Britain, France and Israel invaded, intent on reversing the nationalisation and restoring British and French control of the Canal, which was a crucial route to the Middle and Far East. The US, however, had no intention of allowing these countries to restore their colonial control in the area, when it had every intention of dominating the region itself, as was to be seen by its behaviour in countries such as Iraq and Iran.

At this time, both Britain and France were dependent on the US economically and the US pulled the plug. Both the British and French economies went into crisis and their colonial adventure was defeated. A number of lessons were learnt, however. Israel learnt that the US was the most powerful ally it could have and promptly acted on that knowledge. Britain learnt that it could not afford to go against the US but, nevertheless, the sense of betrayal it experienced over Suez led the British government to start making overtures towards cooperation with other European countries. Anthony Eden was replaced as prime minister in 1957 by Harold Macmillan, and he made the first approach towards joining the European Economic Community; to which President De Gaulle famously replied, 'Non!', regarding Britain as a Trojan horse for the US. The Suez crisis was a great humiliation for the British government and disoriented the British public.

The Empire was on its way out as the 'Winds of Change' were blowing through Africa and other former colonies. Britain's traditional self-identity was changing, and there were plenty of people in Britain who were pleased to take part in shaping a new society with different values. Again, popular culture was one area where changing values and ideas were expressed. The late 1950s saw the development of a new film movement, 'social realism', where directors made films about working-class lives, and about young people and their social and economic concerns. Breaking with the traditional dominance of the portrayal of middle- or upper-class lives, writers and directors such as Shelagh Delaney and John Osborne produced path-breaking works such as *Look Back in Anger* and *A Taste of Honey*, [1] and many other plays and films shaped new ideas and perceptions of society. Mike Leigh and Ken Loach are the contemporary exponents of this cinematic tradition.

CND and social radicalisation

CND in its early years was inextricably linked to the social radicalisation of the time. The early Aldermaston Marches, to the Atomic Weapons Establishment in Berkshire, represented microcosms of the new Britain, articulating both widespread popular dissent and the social rebellion of the youth of the time. In many respects it was through the early mobilisations of the anti-nuclear movement that the radical politics of what were to become the new social movements were first expressed. In his book *Bomb Culture*, Jeff Nuttall talks of the new youth culture on the marches:

> *Beatniks . . . appeared from nowhere in their grime and tatters, with their slogan-daubed crazy hats and streaming filthy hair, hammering their banjos, strumming aggressively on their guitars, blowing their antiquated cornets and sousaphones, capering out in front of the march, destroying the wooden dignity of . . . the official*

> *leaders of the cavalcade. It was this wild public festival*
> *spirit that spread the CND symbol through all the jazz*
> *clubs and secondary schools in an incredible short time.*
> *Protest was associated with festivity. There was a new*
> *feeling of licence granted by the obvious humanitarian*
> *attitude of the ravers themselves.*[2]

Early sociological studies suggested that many of CND's early supporters had no formal faith or politics, and were more concerned about 'working for a more humane society than in finding themselves a good job.' In particular, surveys found that there was an immediacy to campaigners' concerns: 'They believed that the bomb immediately threatened the future of civilisation, that it had to be banned very quickly or Armageddon would come first.'[3]

Simultaneously, however, Cold War anxieties, fear of the bomb and fear of the unknown impact of scientific experimentation were also taking hold on people's imaginations. Political protest was one manifestation of this, but popular culture also reflected these concerns. Film, again, was a mirror of society's anxieties. This time Hollywood paved the way, with the developing science fiction genre. *Them!*, directed by Gordon Douglas in 1954, is about giant radioactive ants on the rampage, the result of an atomic test in New Mexico. Stanley Kramer's *On the Beach*, a film adaptation of Shute's novel made in 1959, was a story set after a nuclear apocalypse, as a group of people await death from radiation. This film affected audiences strongly and CND decided to conduct a campaign around it. A special leaflet with a tear-off slip for contacting CND was produced to give out to audiences as they left the cinema, and many forms were returned daily. The Lewisham CND group in London leafleted extensively and even held a public meeting on the theme. According to CND's Annual Report in 1959, there was 'no doubt that the film is having a big impact.'[4]

Other sci-fi films featured subtexts of anxiety about the spread of communism, such as *Invasion of the Body Snatchers*, made by Don Siegel in 1956. This was also the time of the McCarthyite witch-hunts of the Left in the US, not only in Hollywood, but in society more widely. Thus the late 1950s were a time of great social and political ferment, of which CND was very much a part.

The US/UK 'special relationship'

The year of 1958 – CND's real launch on society – was a year of contradictory developments for the movement. One of these was a small step in the right direction, but others helped to introduce and consolidate the 'special nuclear relationship' between Britain and the US, which has remained with us since. Challenging this relationship is a central goal for CND.

In March 1958, the Soviet Union announced a unilateral moratorium on nuclear tests. After some months of intense disputes at the highest level about whether to do the same, President Eisenhower announced, in August 1958, that the US would suspend testing for a year from 31 October. This decision seemed to indicate that mass expressions of strongly held public sentiment could indeed have an impact on government policy making. Records show that the most significant factor in the eventual US decision to suspend testing was the pressure of public opinion.[5]

However, there was a short-term negative side to this decision. Each of the three nuclear weapons states, the US, the Soviet Union and the UK, engaged in a flurry of testing prior to the cut-off date. The extent of these was such that towards the end of October 1958, the radiation level in Los Angeles was

120 times greater than usual. The mayor of that city tried to get the tests called off, but the US Atomic Energy Commission insisted that the fallout was harmless and continued testing up to the deadline.[6]

The moratorium was welcomed as a first step towards arms control, and it encouraged the movement for nuclear disarmament to campaign for further steps. Popular fear of nuclear war was widespread; an opinion poll in early 1958 showed that 80 per cent of the British public thought that less than half of the population would survive a nuclear war. This was the context of rising support for the demand to 'Ban the Bomb'.[7] The development and consolidation of the UK–US special relationship continued, with the US supplying Britain with nuclear technology and Britain acting as a junior partner in the prosecution of the Cold War. In 1957, the Soviet Union launched 'Sputnik', the first satellite. This indicated that the Soviet Union had made major strides forward in terms of weapons delivery, as the technology to put a satellite in space was closely connected to developing intercontinental ballistic missiles capable of carrying nuclear warheads. In February 1958, Britain signed an agreement with the US for the building of 15 missile bases in the UK: five each in East Anglia, the Midlands and Yorkshire.[8] These were to house US nuclear-armed Thor missiles, to be developed as part of NATO, with a range of 1,500 miles and capable of striking Soviet targets.

Opinion polls showed a majority of British public opinion opposed the creation of these nuclear bases on British soil. One of CND's founding propositions had been against these bases: 'Britain must not proceed with the agreement for the establishment of missile bases on her territory.'[9] Big rallies also took place in West Germany against the siting of US-controlled NATO nuclear weapons there.[10] The opponents argued, not unreasonably, that by hosting US nuclear bases targeting the Soviet Union, the host countries would themselves become obvious targets for nuclear attack.

In 1960, CND's annual conference voted for British withdrawal from any alliance based on the use of nuclear weapons – NATO, of course – and in 1961 voted to support the approach of 'positive neutralism' – in effect, non-alignment.[11] NATO's nuclear doctrine was based on the idea that in the event of war, the Soviet Union would be able to overrun western Europe with its huge armed forces unless nuclear weapons were used to stop it. Hence a first-use policy; the purpose of Thor. Today, around 480 US nuclear weapons – free-fall bombs – remain in western Europe, located primarily in non-nuclear weapons states. Some 110 are located at the Lakenheath airbase in East Anglia, 150 are stationed at three bases across Germany, 90 are in south-eastern Turkey, 90 in Italy, and 20 each in Belgium and the Netherlands. Britain also, of course, has around 200 of its own nuclear weapons.

Whilst there was no legal obstacle to their deployment back in 1958, since 1968, the Nuclear Non-Proliferation Treaty (NPT) has ruled out nuclear weapons states locating nukes in non-nuclear weapons states (Article I).[12] Equally, it has ruled out non-nuclear weapons states locating other countries' nukes on their own soil (Article II). So this arrangement, enshrined through NATO, is doubly illegal.

Along with the stationing of the Thor missiles in Britain, the programme of nuclear weapons development was speeded up, particularly for intercontinental ballistic missiles and the submarine-launched Polaris missile. The development of Britain's own missile project, Blue Streak, was begun at this time. The other piece of bad news in 1958 was the signing of the US/UK Mutual Defence Agreement, which was a highly secretive agreement on a whole range of nuclear-sharing activities. There are strong reasons to think that this agreement today also keeps the UK in the framework of US foreign policy, often a mistaken approach to follow, seen with such tragic effects recently in Iraq. The Mutual Defence Agreement has been renewed on a regular basis ever since, most recently in 2004, despite protest by anti-nuclear MPs, who sought a parliamentary debate on the matter. The debate was not granted.

The marches

The single event that most put CND on the public map was the Aldermaston March of April 1958. The Easter march to the Atomic Weapons Establishment at Aldermaston, Berkshire, the main location for the research, development and production of Britain's nuclear warheads, was originally an initiative of the Direct Action Committee (DAC), which formed a committee to organise the march in December 1957. This committee included Hugh Jenkins, who was later to become chair of CND from 1979–81, Frank Allaun MP, Walter Wolfgang from the Labour Hydrogen Bomb Committee and Pat Arrowsmith, who became the march organiser. The leadership of the newly formed CND was lukewarm about the project initially, stating that it would 'give its blessing to the [DAC] plans [for Aldermaston] and should publicise them, but should make clear at this stage of the Campaign they could not be very closely involved.'[13] In fact, CND members participated extensively in the event, and it was immediately, inextricably linked with the new-born CND in the public mind.

Rapidly, the Aldermaston March, which was repeated over a number of years and on and off over the decades, became synonymous with CND. Most recently, the Aldermaston March took place in 2004, raising public awareness of the likely research and development of a new generation of nuclear weapons at AWE Aldermaston.

A lasting consequence of the first march was the famous symbol produced for the march organisers by the artist Gerald Holtom, which became CND's own symbol and is universally recognised as the sign of peace. According to Peggy Duff, who worked for CND in its early years, the artist explained the symbol in the following way: 'First, the semaphore for the initials 'n' and 'd'. Second, the broken cross meant the death of man, the circle the unborn child. It represented the threat of nuclear weapons to all mankind, and, because this was new, the threat to the unborn child.'[14] Very soon thereafter, the symbol came to adorn badges, posters, leaflets, mugs, banners; and ever since has been graffitied on to walls and virtually any available flat surface all over the world.[15]

The DAC's leaflet for the march welcomed 'all who are opposed on any ground to nuclear weapons, whether possessed by the British, American or Russian Governments.' It urged people to 'walk for a weekend, a day or an hour', and remarkably large numbers did so, despite the fact that it was the wettest Easter weekend since 1900.[16] Almost 6,000 attended the send-off rally in Trafalgar Square, and around 4,000 began the 52-mile, 4-day march. Around 8,000 converged on Aldermaston on the final day, marching the last mile in silence. These numbers far exceeded the expectations of the organisers, who had thought they might get around 300.

An important mobilising group for the march was the communist-influenced British Peace Committee, which continued with a high level of activity during these years. In early 1958, it passed a resolution welcoming the formation of CND and urged its local groups to give support to the new organisation.[17] According to John Cox, chair of CND from 1971 to 1977, this backing was one of the reasons that the turnout for the initial CND demonstrations was so much higher than the organisers expected.[18] But the enthusiasm with which people from all walks of life flocked to the Aldermaston March was not confined to this single event alone. Hundreds of CND groups – over 450 by 1960 – sprang up around the country; mass meetings took place, demonstrations and rallies abounded and young people were involved everywhere in large numbers.

In 1959, CND organised another Easter March, this time from Aldermaston to London. The purpose of the route reversal was to indicate CND's intention to take its message to the heart of political power; to tell the government that a change of policy was needed. Thousands participated in the march itself and 20,000 came to the final rally in Trafalgar Square. According to an informal survey, over 40 per cent of the marchers were under 21.[19]

A year later, in 1960, 40,000 marchers arrived in London, and up to a 100,000 joined the rally in Trafalgar Square. Despite the hardship of four gruelling days of walking, sometimes in pouring rain, the marches were characterised by their good nature and friendliness. Jo Richardson, who was later to be a Labour MP, organised the catering for three of the marches and observed: 'Everyone was there to show their opposition to the bomb: organisers, caterers, drivers and, above all, marchers. That's why there really were no cross words and no problems that couldn't eventually be solved, in that marvellous spirit of comradeship which is my abiding memory of the Easter Marches.'[20]

There can be no doubt that the scale of anti-nuclear protest caused anxiety within the highest government circles. This resulted in attempts to organise against CND. In March 1958, the prime minister, Harold Macmilllan wrote to a member of the Cabinet thus:

It is most important that we should find some way of organising and directing an effective campaign to counter the current agitation against this country's possession of nuclear weapons. This is a question on which the natural emotions of ordinary people would lead them to be critical of the government's policy, and to accept without question or reason the arguments which our opponents use . . . The question is how to . . . exploit the differences between those who oppose our policy.[21]

Efforts were made not only to round up people of standing who would speak in favour of nuclear weapons, but also to kill stories in the press and to disrupt the Aldermaston Marches. The fact that the issues CND addresses are becoming more, not less, 'live' today is confirmed rather ironically by the fact that other government documents likely to contain information about covert operations against CND are marked 'Closed for the next 100 years' at the Public Record Office.[22]

As well as British government interest, the US also paid attention to what was happening in CND. In November 1959, the US Consul in Liverpool visited the secretary of the local CND group and asked extensive questions about the group and its officers. He maintained that he had been requested by the US Embassy to collect information about CND, 'as America was interested in the strength and purpose of the movement.'[23]

Various publications at the time also sought to undermine the work of CND and other peace activists in various ways. *Danger from Moscow*, published in 1960, asserted that peace actions, especially the protests at Thor bases were directly inspired by communist agent provocateurs, working on orders from Moscow. *Mud Pie*, published in 1964, suggested that CND supporters were a bunch of incompetent and gullible suckers. No one really took any notice of these types of attacks.

From its origins, CND has always been a very broad organisation, encompassing in its membership an extremely diverse range of political views, ethical and moral considerations and social backgrounds. As one campaigner put it rather humorously at an early CND conference, 'In CND I have to mix with so many odd people that the sooner we ban the bomb the better.'[24] There is no doubt that over the years CND has generally benefited from this diversity and been strengthened by the different approaches to campaigning that this inevitably brings.

CND today is very pluralistic, both in perspectives and methods. That does not mean, however, that there have not been major and heated debates between different views within the movement. The direction of CND's campaigning was often hotly contested. In the early years, debates focused most sharply on two issues: firstly, the extent to which CND should be involved in parliamentary politics and, most notably, whether working for policy change within the Labour Party could eventually translate into a government committed to nuclear disarmament; secondly, the methods that CND should employ in its campaigning, and particularly the extent to which CND should engage in direct action (usually breaking the law in doing so) as distinct from more mainstream campaigning methods such as lobbying, high-profile rallies and utilising famous and establishment personalities.

Parliamentary politics

Many have argued, then and now, that whilst CND should not formally support one party over another, it should intervene politically in the electoral arena to press support for anti-nuclear policies. Nowadays many CND groups hold peace hustings at election time to put questions to candidates about nuclear policy, war and peace. In 2004, CND held a peace hustings for the London mayoral elections, putting candidates on the spot over their attitudes towards the development of new nuclear weapons, the Iraq war, nuclear first-strike policy and many other issues. Great political debates raged around electoral politics in the post-Iraq war period, as many peace activists felt they could not, in all conscience, vote Labour after the Labour government's participation in the illegal US-led invasion of Iraq.

But a number of different approaches have been taken over the years. In 1958, London University Students' Committee suggested a 'Voters' Veto' campaign. The idea was to persuade people not to vote for candidates who did not support CND policy. The proposal was enthusiastically supported by the DAC. However, the Voters' Veto was not supported by the CND leadership, which placed its hopes in changing Labour policies. Michael Foot described it as a 'policy for hermits'. Foot very clearly articulated the view that the way forward for nuclear disarmament was through winning the policy in the Labour Party: 'Only through the election of a Labour government and the political pressure which we may exert afterwards can we succeed.'[25] The alternative view was put by Michael Craft from Colleges and Universities CND: 'The greatest tragedy for the Campaign would be the return of a Labour government with its policy unchanged. It is pious to hope that we could change their policy in office, and disillusion would spread in the Campaign. The great merit in the Voters' Veto is to force the Labour Party to think again before it is too late.'[26] However, the Voters' Veto idea did not take off. In a by-election in south-west Norfolk in early 1959, the DAC, together with the

Students' Committee, launched a veto campaign against a Labour candidate who opposed CND policies. The candidate won with an increased majority.

A major debate about CND's attitude towards elections took place at its Annual Conference in 1962. The resolution that became CND's policy was moved by Michael Foot. It upheld CND's independent campaigning role and said: 'In order to retain the character of a pressure group influencing all political parties, the campaign shall not support any one candidate.'[27]

Unilateralism and the Labour Party

The perils of the Cold War, particularly the Korean War, and the existence of a dynamic campaign highlighting the horrors of nuclear war had a significant impact on public opinion. By the beginning of the 1960s, the overwhelming majority of the public wanted to see the abolition of nuclear weapons. A poll in 1962 showed that 82 per cent of Britons favoured an agreement among all countries to eliminate the bomb. Another poll early the following year showed 84 per cent of survey respondents supporting the worldwide abolition of nuclear weapons.[28]

CND enthusiastically embraced the more radical proposal that Britain should unilaterally renounce nuclear weapons, irrespective of what any other country chose to do. This was a minority position supported by nearly a third of the public. As former CND Chair John Cox has pointed out, 'All the public opinion polls showed that the support for unilateral nuclear disarmament remained below 30 per cent throughout these years of intense and widespread campaigning.'[29] Yet in effect, this unilateralist minority influenced a very broad majority who, while not convinced of unilateralism, wanted to see the abolition of all nuclear weapons by agreement of the governments possessing them. However, though making pious speeches and declarations about disarmament, those governments were nevertheless engaged in a relentless nuclear arms race.

Unilateralism was particularly popular amongst young people and gained ground in the trade unions and sections of the Labour party membership as multilateral progress towards nuclear disarmament failed to materialise. A resolution to that effect had been defeated at the Labour Party Conference in 1957. However, far from discouraging anti-nuclear campaigners, this reinforced in their minds the need for a mass movement outside the Labour Party, contributing to the impetus for the founding of CND.

There was a modest increase in the unilateralist vote in 1958. But Labour went into 1959 – an election year – with a policy of ending all British nuclear tests and working towards an agreement where all nations other than the US and Soviet Union would renounce nuclear weapons.[30] This latter proposal, described as the 'non-nuclear club', was devised to be a kind of halfway house between unilateralism and multilateralism, and reflected the pressure brought to bear by the increasing numbers of Labour members and supporters – particularly trade unions such as the Transport and General Workers Union (TGWU) – that supported CND's unilateralist approach. CND's advice to local groups for the 1959 election was to: 'support any candidates considered to be genuine supporters of CND, but to pay due respect to, and recognise, the existence of the party allegiances of individual members.'[31] However, the Labour Party was defeated at that election. Interestingly though, instead of adopting a more cautious approach towards nuclear weapons, on that occasion it moved towards the embrace of full unilateralism.

1960 saw a real advance as a number of trade unions shifted towards unilateralism. The position that the trade unions took was extremely important, both because the unions were a major factor shaping Labour Party policy and because they represented literally millions of British workers. Trade union leaders and members alike played a significant role in campaigning for nuclear disarmament. Ron Todd, for many years general secretary of the TGWU, consistently championed the cause of unilateral nuclear disarmament and was a vice-president of CND until his death in 2005. In April 1960, Britain's so-called independent deterrent, Blue Streak, was cancelled. In the aftermath, the Labour Party changed its policy and opposed any further attempts by Britain to manufacture its own independent nuclear weapons system. The Blue Streak was intended to have been a British-manufactured missile to carry British manufactured warheads, coming into play in the mid-1960s.

As Peggy Duff points out, the whole project had been extremely expensive: '£87 million had been wasted on it. Later the *Daily Mail* revealed that £312,700,000 had been wasted on government defence projects, including the Swift Fighter, the Victor II bomber, the Avro 730 bomber, the Blue Streak missile, five known missile types and thirteen known aircraft projects.'[32] From then on, Britain was the recipient of US nuclear weapons systems such as the Polaris and Trident submarine-launched systems at Holy Loch and Faslane in Scotland, and free-fall nuclear bombs under the auspices of NATO.

In May 1960, the idea that nuclear weapons might be abolished by mutual agreement of all those possessing them was dealt a powerful blow. A summit conference had been planned in Paris, to be attended by the great powers. Huge hopes were vested in this conference, but they came to nothing. A US U-2 spy plane was shot down whilst flying illegally over the Soviet Union and the pilot, Gary Powers, was captured and tried for espionage. As a result of this violation of its territory, the Soviet delegation refused to take part in the conference. In July 1960, the Labour Party took a position against Britain being an independent nuclear power. At the Labour Party Conference in October of that year, party leader Hugh Gaitskell took the counter-offensive, denouncing supporters of unilateral nuclear disarmament as 'pacifists, neutralists and fellow-travellers'. He claimed they were destroying the party.[33] However, the conference rejected his views and voted for the unilateral rejection of nuclear weapons. Tony Benn, newly elected to the Labour Party's governing body the National Executive Council (NEC), remembers the events of that time:

We saw the first Aldermaston March at Easter in 1958 and the formation of CND and the movement grew by leaps and bounds so that at the 1960 Labour Conference a motion to commit Labour to nuclear disarmament was tabled by the TGWU and it was clear that it had great support.

George Brown MP suggested reaching some sort of compromise and, as a very new member of the National Executive, having been elected the previous year, I tried to persuade Hugh Gaitskell to accept it but he would not budge and Frank Cousins who had put forward the original motion was also determined to stand firm.

During the NEC meeting at which our position was being discussed CND marched past the hotel and the atmosphere was very tense so when the NEC refused to seek a compromise I resigned from the NEC, the Unilateralist resolution was carried by the delegates and

Hugh Gaitskell made his speech promising to Fight, Fight and Fight again to save the party.

This battle within the party went on for over a year, during which I was excluded from the Commons because of the death of my father and the peerage battle, and in 1961 Gaitskell swung the party back to his pro-nuclear position.[34]

The leadership of CND appeared to be taken by surprise by the turn of events but, as Tony Benn explained, this was only a temporary victory. In parliament, MPs simply ignored the policy of their party, and only five MPs voted in line with conference policy during the Defence Debate. CND activists in the Labour Party and trade unions worked hard to consolidate the unilateralist policy but the Labour Party leadership fought tooth and nail, with all the resources at its disposal, to reverse the policy.

In the run-up to the next conference, intense lobbying was carried out by the leadership to ensure that the policy would be changed. This activity, combined with a desire on the part of the trade unions to heal the rift with the Labour leadership over defence issues, led to a reversal of the position in 1961. This led some anti-nuclear activists to think that they should have nothing more to do with political parties. Others, such as Frank Allaun MP, took the view that 'only government could achieve unilateral nuclear disarmament, and, in British terms, that meant either a Conservative or Labour government.'[35] Hugh Gaitskell died in 1963. Harold Wilson was elected the new leader of the Labour Party, bringing with him a very different style. Based on a coalition of the centre and left of the party, his approach was to try to establish a broad consensus for an agenda of modernising Britain, and avoid any head-on confrontation with the left that had been the hallmark of Gaitskell's leadership. He attempted to defuse the issue of nuclear weapons without backing the unilateralist position. Labour won the 1964 general election amid great hopes for the future and talk of a meritocratic society developing 'in the white heat of the technological revolution'. However, on the issue of nuclear weapons, as Frank Allaun MP put it, Wilson 'carried on the Conservative administration's nuclear weapons programme almost without alteration.'[36] The new government decided to continue Britain's commitment to Polaris, which had been agreed at a meeting between US President John F Kennedy and the former UK Prime Minister Harold Macmillan in Nassau in 1962. The only difference was that there were to be only four submarines, rather than five.[37]

Direct action

One of the key debates in CND from its inception was the role of 'direct action' and whether breaking the law was a permissible way of campaigning against nuclear weapons. The first Aldermaston March, which was organised by the DAC and supported by CND, really launched the new movement into the public eye and onto the political agenda. CND went on after the march to pursue a range of campaigning and lobbying activities, building local groups and organising meetings and events. The DAC maintained its orientation towards civil disobedience, with a broader overall goal of changing society through peaceful means. Its principles, summed up by April Carter, who was a leading activist in the DAC, include a 'belief in the need for non-violent action directed against weapons and bases designed for nuclear warfare, the need for personal commitment, and reliance on popular protest rather than on working through the established political process.'[38] The position of the CND leadership, on the other hand, can be summed up by a comment from Canon Collins, who was at that time CND's chair: 'It seemed to me that for CND as such to identify itself with illegalities would be to alienate its potential supporters, not only in the Labour movement but outside it, to whom the bulk of campaigners wished to address themselves.'[39] They were concerned about the impact on the public of any form of law breaking and felt that action that lost CND public support would not be justified.

Even so, many in the ranks of CND's local groups were more sympathetic. For the first couple of years, CND and direct action activities took place side by side, often with considerable overlap. The Thor missile bases were a particular focus for campaigning in those early years and both organisations were involved in activities at these bases. Events did from time to time highlight the differences in approach between the two organisations, however. Towards the end of 1958, DAC carried out an action at the Thor base at North Pickenham in Norfolk, attempting to enter the base. On the first day of the action, it was prevented from entering the base by workmen on the site and, according to Pat Arrowsmith, active in both CND and DAC, the protestors suffered physical attack at their hands while the police looked on. On the second day of the protest, the workers were absent but Pat was thrown into an icy pond by an RAF policeman![40] The episode was given widespread media attention. One national daily newspaper, not understanding the different components of the movement, accused CND of sabotage. Canon Collins issued a statement dissociating CND from the action:

We aim to change public opinion and the policies of the political parties through the usual democratic channels . . . The National Campaign for Nuclear Disarmament is not

> *in favour of civil disobedience or sabotage so long as reasonable opportunities exist for bringing democratic pressure on Parliament.*[41]

Canon Collins' statement provoked some anger in the movement, not least because the DAC had not been engaged in sabotage. At the next meeting of CND's Executive Committee, it made the statement that in future it would not, 'as far as possible, publicly repudiate nor formally associate itself with actions involving civil disobedience.'[42]

Not long after this, at CND's first annual conference in March 1959, Pat Arrowsmith put forward a resolution that CND should undertake civil disobedience. According to CND colleague Peggy Duff, it was likely that a majority of the Conference would support the resolution. The Executive Committee strongly opposed the resolution and threatened to resign en masse if it was passed. Probably as a result of this threat, the resolution was defeated, but not overwhelmingly.[43] There was a danger though that the issue could be portrayed in an over-polarised way, which was undesirable given that activists shared the same aims, even if they sometimes differed on the appropriate methods. Hugh Brock, who was DAC representative on CND's Co-ordinating Committee in 1959 'sometimes wondered whether the activities of the DAC were rocking the boat too much. He felt that some of their friends too often exaggerated the part they had played, for example, in the first Aldermaston March, which could never have been so successful as it was without the backing of the Campaign.'[44]

In reality a fairly co-operative approach existed, for example when CND and the DAC decided to co-operate over a demonstration at the Thor missile base at Harrington,

Northamptonshire, in January 1960. The DAC planned a march and a sit-down at the base. CND organised a march led by Canon Collins 'in sympathy with civil disobedience but not supportive'[45] and that would pass the base but not engage in the sit-down. The combined event was a success and seemed a good formula for future co-operation. Generally speaking, there was not a rigid demarcation over the focus of actions; CND also conducted a range of actions at bases, but without direct action. In 1959, CND had demonstrated at the rocket bases in Yorkshire and at RAF Brize Norton, amongst others. But if course CND's great strength was that it sought to involve many people in its campaigning and to get the message out far and wide amongst the population. A major CND campaign in September 1959, was entitled the 'Let Britain Lead' week. It sounds a bit odd nowadays, but it was encouraging Britain to take the lead on nuclear disarmament. A sense of the scale of the campaign can be grasped by the fact that in one week of campaigning a million leaflets were given out all over Britain, 50 national speakers toured the country, there were marches and rallies in every region and the CND Architects' Group produced 18 exhibitions for public display. As a result, 20 new local groups were formed.[46]

Later that year, however, a new initiative was launched, which led to sharp conflict within CND's leadership – between its chair, Canon Collins, and its president, Bertrand Russell. The trouble began as Russell started to articulate and act upon the frustrations of those in the movement who found the CND leadership's approach too conventional.

The Committee of 100

In September 1960, a CND march took place from Edinburgh to London. Russell wrote to inform Canon Collins that when he spoke at the final rally when the march arrived in Trafalgar Square, he planned 'to say something in support of those who practice direct action.'[47] Russell was dissuaded from doing so, as it might have a negative impact on the decision on unilateralism at the Labour Party Conference the following month. But eventually it leaked out that Russell was planning a new movement – the Committee of 100 for Civil Disobedience against Nuclear Warfare. Russell's idea was that the new Committee would be launched – hopefully – after a unilateralist victory at the Labour Party Conference. The role of the Committee would then be to win wider public support through publicising the issue via mass civil disobedience. The composition of the Committee was designed to widen the movement's appeal. The Committee was widely drawn, including 'celebrities' from the cutting edge of the artistic and cultural world: John Arden, Shelagh Delaney, Lindsay Anderson, John Braine, Augustus John, Robin Hall, George Melly, John Neville, John Osborne, Herbert Read and Arnold Wesker.[48]

Canon Collins had not been informed by Russell of this development and was reportedly very annoyed when he found out about it from Victor Gollancz, the renowned left-wing publisher, who had been invited to join the Committee. Russell resigned as President of CND before the Committee was officially launched in October 1960.

Russell was president of CND but he had also been a supporter of the DAC and its forerunners since the mid-1950s. He simultaneously considered direct action to be a dangerous doctrine leading to anarchy, and believed that 'almost all great advances have involved illegality.'[49] Above all, though, he considered it to be a means of getting publicity for the movement:

*All the major organs of publicity are against us. It was
extremely difficult to get any attention at all until we
resorted to [direct action]. . . I have no views in principle
either for or against civil disobedience. It has always been
practiced at different times and places. With me it is
purely a practical question of whether to do it or not, a
method of propaganda.*[50]

Whilst Russell's correspondence at the time shows that he
thought the two different approaches had to remain independent of each other (although personally supporting both
during the first couple of years of CND's life), this approach
did not last long. As Russell's biographer describes it: 'Hunting
with both packs was defensible as long as both organisations
seemed to be doing equally valuable work. But by the summer
of 1960 he was beginning to feel that the voice of the church
militant, epitomised by Collins' chairmanship of CND, was
becoming little more than a whisper in the parish magazine.'[51]

In the middle of 1960, Russell was visited by a young
American called Ralph Schoenman, who proposed a new
campaigning approach: neither the mass marches and legal
protests of CND, nor the activities of the DAC, which in
Russell's words, 'were too often concerned with individual
testimony by way of salving individual consciences.'[52]
Schoenman's idea was mass civil disobedience, intending to
combine the direct action of DAC and the mass movement of
CND. Russell took up the idea, and the Committee of 100 was
formed. The role of Schoenman himself was a controversial
one, and it seems that many, during his years of influence
with Russell, 'questioned his motivation', fearing that he had
been placed there to disrupt the peace movement by elevat-
ing direct action above policy debate and campaigning. The
truth about these allegations may never be known.[53]

Much of the Committee's campaigning was in opposition to the decision to locate US Polaris nuclear submarines at a base to be established at Holy Loch, 30 miles from Glasgow. There is clear evidence that the British government was very much affected by popular opposition and campaigning against the base, in particular over public concern about US control of nuclear weapons in British territorial waters. Indeed, as the Cabinet noted in July 1960, to overcome the 'considerable political difficulty in securing public support in this country for these arrangements,' Britain 'should aim to get American agreement to full and timely consultation with us . . . and joint decision in an emergency.'[54] But that was out of the question for the US, and the government was not able to get any control for Britain over any use of US nuclear weapons in Britain. The Polaris base, therefore, presented the stark possibility that Britain could be destroyed in a nuclear war prosecuted by the United States without any British agreement to participate. Not surprisingly, therefore, protest against the Polaris base was quite considerable. Accounts from the time suggest that the physical presence and proximity of the base had an enormous impact on public opinion in Scotland. As Janey and Norman Buchan observed:

> *What gave the campaign in Scotland its strength as well as its particularity was, of course, the coming of Polaris to the Clyde. What had been a terrifying abstraction was now only too real, visible, menacing. We had a particular target which was of immediate and direct relevance. From a very early stage, therefore, it was apparent to us that the mobilisation of opinion in Scotland was more widely based; more representative of the people in general, and therefore, in a word, more working class in character than the early days of CND elsewhere in Britain . . . One's first*

sight of the sinister black hull of a nuclear submarine slowly moving up the estuary is not only the immediate revelation of an obscenity but an enormous stimulant to action.[55]

The Committee of 100's first demonstration took place in February 1961, outside the MoD headquarters, to protest the arrival of the US Polaris depot ship at Holy Loch in Scotland. Around 4,000 people sat down in protest, but there were no arrests. The DAC also took direct action at Holy Loch itself at the same time, and the events gained widespread public attention. However, the tolerant police attitude was not to last. At subsequent actions, mass arrests routinely took place. In March 1961, CND's annual conference reaffirmed its commitment to legal methods, but it also congratulated the DAC and Committee of 100 on their demonstrations. The Conference stated that the three different forms of protest should be seen as 'three techniques in a united attack on preparations for nuclear war.'[56] In other words, it was recognised that these diverse methods were all valid parts of the process of campaigning against nuclear weapons. This remains CND's position today.

In the summer of 1961, the Committee announced a new round of mass civil disobedience, in opposition to the actual arrival of the first US Polaris submarine in Holy Loch. The protests coincided with the erection of the Berlin Wall; it was a time of greatly heightened international tension. There was a massive sit-down protest in London in September, as well as more action at Holy Loch itself. In advance of this, Russell, Lady Russell and many other members of the Committee of 100 were arrested and charged with inciting civil disobedience, under the Defence of the Realm Act of 1361. Russell made a powerful speech from the dock, arguing that civil disobedience was a last resort: 'Patriotism and humanity alike urged us to see some way of saving our country and the world.'[57]

Both Russell and Lady Russell were sentenced to two months in prison, but this was reduced on medical grounds to one week each. Russell was almost 90 years of age at this point and served his term in Brixton Prison, where he had spent time as a conscientious objector during World War I. Russell's imprisonment raised the profile of the anti-nuclear movement enormously, achieving exactly the type of publicity that Russell had hoped for. Russell's age and the fact that he was regarded a one of the great philosophers of the 20th century only added to the impact of his stand. When the planned protest took place in London, it attracted over 12,000 people, in spite of the fact that the police had banned the sit-down under the Public Order Act. The ban contributed to the scale of participation, as people also came out to protest in defence of their civil liberties and to protest the draconian treatment of the Russells.

Following this massive mobilisation, the Committee decided to turn its attention to military bases. Seven protests were planned for December for bases and in town centres. The government's response to this was brutal as it set out to intimidate the movement. The Committee's six employees were all arrested prior to the demonstrations and given relatively lengthy jail sentences – the men receiving sentences of 18 months and the one woman 12 months. The turnout at these occasions fell to 7,000, influenced by the government's hard line and threat of prison. Local Committees were set up around the country, but it was hard to mobilise significant numbers outside London. Support for the Committee gradually began to wane, and it was not helped by occasional activities, by groups within the Committee, which seemed to be divisive. On one occasion breakaway civil disobedience at the end of an Aldermaston March caused division and confusion; another breakaway march organised by libertarians and anarchists – the so-called 'Spies for Peace' – had a similar effect.[58]

Canon Collins spoke sharply about anarchist interventions when he resigned as CND chair in 1964: 'There ought to be a complete repudiation of neo-Tolstoian anarchy within CND. Indeed, it should be made abundantly clear to any whose main concern is not nuclear disarmament but disruption of the body politic that they are not wanted either within CND or at its demonstrations.'[59] In January 1963, Russell resigned as president of Committee 100, depriving the Committee of much of its profile and significance, and support dropped away. Even many of the Committee's supporters felt that it had lost its effectiveness. As one leading Committee member said, as early as the end of 1961, 'We have become a public spectacle, a group isolated from the general body of public opinion and feeling, a rowdy show to be televised and reported in the press for the interest and amusement of a majority who are not with us.'[60] Canon Collins also reflected on the Committee of 100 in his resignation statement: 'Not all publicity is publicity for good. Over against whatever of value has emerged as a result of the function of the Committee of 100 must be placed the dissensions, the quarrels and the disruption of unity within the nuclear disarmament movement which have entered.'[61] After leaving CND, Canon Collins went on to play a major role in the struggle against apartheid in South Africa.

The Berlin crisis
The world situation during the early 1960s had again been conducive to an increase in protest and CND had experienced

a strong upsurge in support. One of the ways in which this was shown was through an enormous proliferation of local groups. Many of these were in London, and local activist Pat Allen was involved in setting up one in Newham:

It is not so easy now to recapture the mood of CND's early years. Following the Korean War, the Suez crisis and the Cold War tension, there was a real fear that a major conflict could erupt at any time. As not so many years had passed since the end of World War II we all knew what another war might entail. In many towns and cities the bomb damage was still there to remind us. The great unknown was what would happen in a nuclear conflict. Given the context, it was perhaps not so surprising that when a number of eminent people got together around Canon John Collins to launch CND there was a snowball effect. It seemed that just about everywhere from Land's End to John O'Groats this was what people had been waiting for. Unlike previous anti-bomb campaigns it was not confined to people with a particular political perspective; rather it appealed to all those people who had sufficient imagination to understand what a nuclear war might entail and who did not accept the tired notions of deterrents or the absurd suggestion that there was a massive Soviet Army preparing to attack us.

My own involvement was first in Gravesend and then in Newham from 1960 onwards. By this time most other parts of London already had local CND groups so we were a bit slow off the mark but nonetheless I was soon in touch with a Methodist Minister, a Co-op activist and a Labour Party activist to establish Newham CND. Very soon we had 50 or 60 members, including a number of enthusiastic young people as well as a local councillor and a representative of the Trades Council. Compared with more middle-class localities our numbers were feeble. In places like Wanstead and Woodford membership ran into hundreds. CND was based on the notion that when multitudes of people from every walk of life got involved in peaceful protest the government would have to take notice. Unfortunately, and because the war danger was so very real, many people felt that something more dramatic than peaceful protest was needed and this resulted in CND being wracked by intense internal controversy. Fortunately in Newham we were able to continue on a steady course.[62]

By 1962, there were around 900 CND groups[63] and the Aldermaston march of that year attracted in the region of 150,000 people to its final rally. There were also very big demonstrations in other parts of the country too, and also abroad; in all there were 44 demonstrations in 15 countries that Easter.[64] Looking at the international events that were taking place at the time, it is easy to see why there was such a rapid growth in support for CND and peace movements more widely. After a brief moratorium, both the US and Soviet Union had begun nuclear testing again, and this caused considerable public outrage and protest, including a continuous picket outside both Soviet and US Embassies.[65] But other events internationally also led many people to fear that nuclear war might indeed be imminent. In August 1961, the Berlin Wall was constructed, sealing West Berlin off from East Germany. The crisis that ensued exacerbated widespread concern about the possibility of nuclear war; not least because the UK foreign secretary, Sir Alec Douglas Home, asserted that, 'The British people are prepared to be blown to atomic dust if necessary.'[66]

What became known as the 'Berlin Crisis' had begun in November 1958 when the Soviet leader, Nikita Khrushchev, sent a note to the Western leaders about the situation in Germany. At the end of World War II, Germany was divided into zones of occupation, run by the four allied victors: the Soviet Union, the US, France and Britain. The Soviet zone became East Germany and the other three zones became West Germany. Berlin was also divided into four occupation zones, resulting in East and West Berlin on the same basis. The city of Berlin was located well over into the eastern part of East Germany, so access to West Berlin was either by plane or by road or rail through East Germany.

Khrushchev's basic position was that it was now 13 years since World War II and, however regrettable the division of Germany was, two German states now existed and the West should recognise East Germany. Following on from this, Khrushchev also wanted the military occupation of West Berlin to end. He was willing for Berlin to be a free, demili-tarised city, but he wanted western troops out. For his part, after six months, the Soviets were going to hand East Berlin over to East Germany, and if the West hadn't reached a recog-nition settlement by then, it would be up to them to negotiate access rights to West Berlin with the East Germans. East Germany would, of course, be within its rights to ban any western communication across its territory. In the event of any attack on East Germany, this would be regarded by members of the Warsaw Pact (the Soviet-dominated Eastern-European political-military alliance) as an attack on them all. The West rejected this ultimatum.

It is most likely that Khrushschev was motivated by a great Soviet fear – the deployment of nuclear weapons in West Germany – and the note he sent to the western leaders was clearly orientated towards the goal of preventing that.[67] As it stated: 'The best way to solve the Berlin question . . . would mean the withdrawal of the Federal German Republic from NATO, with the simultaneous withdrawal of the German Democratic Republic from the Warsaw Treaty Organisation . . . Neither of the two German states would have any armed forces in excess of those needed to maintain law and order at home and to guard their frontier.'[68] But the US was hostile to the idea of recognising East Germany, as was West German Chancellor Konrad Adenauer, who wanted a reunited capitalist Germany within NATO. With US nuclear weapons located in western Europe under the NATO framework, Soviet fears of nuclear weapons in Germany, able to strike the Soviet Union, were real. Having suffered World War II, in which 27 million Soviet citizens had lost their lives to German invaders, the Soviet position was simply never to allow a German threat to the Soviet Union to re-emerge. Khrushchev also had grave concerns about China acquiring nuclear weapons; relations between the two communist states were beginning to break down at this time. So Khrushchev was worrying about being squeezed between two potentially hostile nuclear-armed states.

Following Khrushchev's ultimatum, there was intensive diplomatic activity. Certainly the Germans didn't want war – that might become nuclear war – over Berlin. Germany could easily be wiped off the face of the earth. Khrushchev himself pulled back from confrontation, and a four-power foreign ministers conference was organised in Geneva in the summer of 1959. The Soviet foreign minister, Andrei Gromyko, indicated that the Soviet Union was flexible on the timing of a recognition agreement – maybe up to 12 or 18 months. Soon after this, in September 1959, Khrushchev went on a state visit to the US and came away with an agreement that a summit would take place in Paris in spring 1960, to resolve the Berlin Crisis. Unfortunately, this was the summit that broke down because of the U-2 spy flight over the Soviet Union, as mentioned earlier in Chapter 2, and again the negotiations over Berlin were delayed.

In the US presidential election campaign of 1960, the Democratic candidate John F Kennedy won and the two leaders agreed on a summit meeting in Vienna, four months after he took up office. In the intervening period, the Soviets put the first man in space, Yuri Gagarin, and just a few days later, in April 1961, the invasion of Cuba at the Bay of Pigs took place. President Kennedy authorised US support for an invasion of Cuba by supporters of the Batista dictatorship, which had been overthrown by the guerilla army led by Fidel Castro and Che Guevara. The invasion proved to be a disaster, causing great embarrassment for Kennedy. The US was now rather on the back foot.

Kennedy and Khrushchev met in June 1961 and failed to reach any agreement. Khrushchev insisted now on a six-month deadline to sign a peace treaty with East Germany. The consequence of a failure to achieve this was widely read to be war – possibly a nuclear war.

Tension mounted again, however, even before the six months were up. President Kennedy announced an additional $3.25 billion for military spending and a stronger civil defence programme to be ready in the event of a nuclear attack. In the middle of August, building work began on the Berlin Wall, closing off access routes between East and West and preventing the migration of East Berliners to the West. At the end of August, the Soviet Union announced that it was resuming atmospheric nuclear testing. These tests continued for two months, testing some of the most powerful devices ever exploded.[69]

Not surprisingly, there was an escalation of campaigning by CND as a result of both the Berlin Crisis and the renewed testing. In September 1961, a 'No War Over Berlin' rally was held in Trafalgar Square, followed by an intensive evening of leafleting in the West End. Many tear-off slips from the leaflets were returned to CND by the public, indicating strong public anxiety. A mass lobby of parliament was held the following month, both against the danger of war over Berlin and against the renewed testing.[70] An interesting development took place around this time: the mobilisation of women as a specific force in campaigning. Following the resumption of testing during the late summer of 1961, when the US and Britain rapidly followed the Soviet Union into renewed testing, there was an immediate and rapid increase both in the number of women supporting CND and in activities by and for women. The Women's Group of CND became very active, women's meetings and events proliferated and there was a women's delegation to meet the prime minister in March 1962. Co-operation also took place with women's organisations abroad, notably with the significant US group, Women Strike for Peace (WSP). Around this time, 3 CND women joined a delegation of 50 women from WSP to Geneva, to lobby the Disarmament Committee.[71]

Over the next couple of years, the anti-test campaigning that continued at an intensive level was to bear fruit in the form of the Partial Test Ban Treaty in 1963, banning nuclear tests in the atmosphere. There was also a gradual improvement in relations over Berlin. Tensions were high for some time across the border within the city of Berlin, but gradually the atmosphere eased. Khrushchev no longer referred to the ultimatum, and the West did not try to challenge the existence of the wall. For, as President Kennedy himself said, 'It's not a very nice solution, but a wall is a hell of a lot better than a war.'[72] Ultimately, it was clear that although neither side was prepared to give in over Berlin, neither side wanted a nuclear war.

The Cuban Missile Crisis

These were extremely tense times indeed through which to live, and it is no surprise, therefore, that these were also times of great popular mobilisations for CND. As many who were active at the time have observed, people seriously feared nuclear confrontation over Berlin.[73] But even the fear that people had over Berlin was overshadowed by the spectre of nuclear annihilation raised by the Cuban Missile Crisis.

Although the US had failed to overthrow Castro by supporting an invasion of anti-Castro Cuban exile forces at the Bay of Pigs, it did not give up there. In November 1961, a presidential directive set up Operation Mongoose, a covert-action programme against Cuba. In March 1962, plans were begun for an invasion of Cuba and an economic blockade. Khrushchev was concerned about Cuba, and he was also concerned about the fact that the Soviet Union was effectively surrounded by US troops and weaponry: 'By 1962 a million US soldiers were stationed in more than two hundred foreign bases, all threatening the Soviet Union, from Greenland to Turkey, from Portugal to the Philippines.'[74] There were also US nuclear weapons in Italy, the UK and Turkey. Putting these two concerns together, Khrushchev came up with an idea that he thought could both protect Cuba and help offset the US military advantage; he decided to install Soviet missiles in Cuba.

By September 1962, the installation of missile sites, from which nuclear weapons could be fired, had begun. In mid-October the US discovered what was going on. In their assessment the missiles could be operational within two weeks. Many in the US administration, including US Air Force General Curtis LeMay argued for air strikes against Cuba to take out the sites, thinking that the missiles had not yet arrived. Kennedy fortunately decided against this, because in fact Soviet missiles were already installed and a nuclear exchange could have followed any attack on Cuba. According to one US historian, 'If John Kennedy had followed LeMay's advice, history would have forgotten the Nazis and their terrible Holocaust. Ours would have been the historic omnicide.'[75]

Instead, Kennedy opted for a naval blockade. The Soviet Union insisted that the missiles were there to defend Cuba, not to attack the US, and complained that the US naval blockade was illegal, amounting to piracy. The US Strategic Air Command put its nuclear bomber force on alert. The Soviet leadership was now informed of the US course of action and, fearing an attack on Cuba, authorised the Soviet commander in Cuba to use tactical nuclear weapons against the US forces if they landed in Cuba. He was also told not to launch missiles that could hit the US without direct orders from Moscow. All US military forces worldwide were now put on a high state of nuclear alert, as were Warsaw Pact armed forces. The UN Secretary-General U Thant appealed to both Kennedy and Khrushchev to suspend the blockade and stop the shipments to Cuba and to refrain from any action that might lead to war. The British government also had grave concerns about the escalation towards war, and expressed its doubt about the legality of the naval blockade. The prime minister, Macmillan, even offered to 'scrap the Thor missiles in Great Britain in a trade-off for the Soviet missiles in Cuba,' if it would 'save the Russians' face.'[76]

Ultimately, neither side wanted to embark on a nuclear war. Eventually the Soviet Union withdrew the missiles in exchange for a US pledge not to invade Cuba, and a secret deal that US nuclear weapons would subsequently be withdrawn from Turkey; they were quietly removed in 1963. But it was touch and go without a doubt. As Soviet columnist

Yuri Zhivkov wrote in *Pravda* newspaper, 'We have lived through the most difficult week since World War II.'[77]

There can be no doubt at all that there was extreme fear throughout the world that nuclear war was about to take place, and this was as true in Britain as anywhere else. Pat Arrowsmith and her partner, who were both at that time working for the Committee of 100, fled to Killarney in the far south-west of Ireland, in an attempt to survive the bomb should there be a nuclear attack on Britain; they were under no illusion about the kind of world they would face if they survived. They weren't the only people to do this, but they faced severe criticism on their return to Britain after the danger had passed. They were accused of cowardice in the tabloid press and were thoroughly disapproved of by many in the peace movement, as if they had somehow 'deserted their posts'.[78] Being well aware of the impact of nuclear weapons, they felt that, as 'their posts' would have been thoroughly obliterated, to remain would be a futile gesture.

Shortly after this, Pat was involved in two new initiatives designed to prevent the actual use of nuclear weapons, both of which she helped to promote on a trip round Europe. The first built on the orientation, particularly of the direct action wing of the peace movement, towards trade unionists. Pat had been employed by Merseyside CND to make industrial links; now she spoke at meetings in the port cities of Genoa, Trieste, Piraeus and Venice, urging the setting up of a Dockers International, which would refuse to handle nuclear cargoes. The second was to set up 'Crisis Contingents', rather like the World Peace Brigades that were also under way at that time, which would organise people – using non-violent methods – to put themselves in the way of any major war that would obviously have had the potential to go nuclear. One example of this approach coming to fruition was the Non-Violent

Action Mission to Vietnam, which took place in the late 1960s as the war there appeared to be escalating towards nuclear use.[79] It can also perhaps be seen as the forerunner of initiatives such as the Gulf Peace Team, which went to Iraq during the first Gulf War in 1991, attempting to put itself in the way of fighting.

The Cuban Missile Crisis appeared to shock the nuclear weapons states into a more sensible approach. As Frank Allaun said, 'Millions of people went to bed one night wondering if they and their children would be involved in the holocaust before the morning. Both Kennedy and Krushchev learnt from the terrifying experience and began to think of co-existence.'[80] Two developments subsequently took place that were intended to ensure that the world would not go so close to the nuclear brink again. The first was the setting up of a 'nuclear hotline', to enable US and Soviet leaders to have direct contact to avoid nuclear war. The second was the signing of a Partial Test Ban Treaty in 1963, mentioned earlier, which banned all nuclear testing in the atmosphere. This was signed by the US, Soviet Union and Britain. France however, did not sign it, and the following year China exploded its first atomic bomb, followed in 1967 by a hydrogen bomb test. Nevertheless, the Partial Test Ban Treaty was a major step forward and this, together with the fact that the great powers had pulled back from the precipice at the crucial moment, contributed to a considerable lessening of fear over nuclear weapons amongst the general public.

CND had its origins in the anti-testing movement, and working to secure a Test Ban had been a major mobilising factor for a number of years. Apart from the immediate fear aroused by the crises over Berlin and Cuba, anxiety about the effects of testing on health was probably the greatest public concern. Indeed, as British Minister Sir William Penney said in 1962, 'Whenever I talk to people about disarmament, it's always the test-ban treaty they bring me around to . . . It has to do with the here and now, and they want an end to this fouling of the air they breathe.'[81]

For many people, the sense of urgency about nuclear disarmament now receded. The superpowers had pulled back over Cuba, and the Partial Test Ban Treaty removed the public's most immediate concerns about health impacts of testing. For CND, this spelt the end of the first phase of its activism.

3

From the Vietnam War to the neutron bomb

From its launch in 1958 CND had effectively articulated the rising popular concern over the danger of nuclear weapons and nuclear tests. For five years it was at the forefront of campaigning to change government policies and it significantly contributed to the worldwide concern and pressure that resulted in the Partial Test Ban Treaty. It also helped prevent nuclear war over Berlin or Cuba. These years culminated in the global realisation that any war between the US and the Soviet Union would be nuclear. In the early sixties, a new issue came to dominate the concerns of the vast majority of the peace movement – and indeed much of the wider community. The Vietnam War dominated world politics for a decade. The US became sucked deeper into a conflict it conceived as necessary to stop the rise of communism in Asia, whilst most of the Vietnamese saw it as a continuation of the struggle for national independence from foreign invaders. Indeed, their struggle against the most powerful military force in the world won the support of millions of young people throughout the world. This was the context of CND's work from the mid-1960s.

The war in Vietnam had deep roots. Vietnam had been conquered by France in the late 19th century. The French colonial regime, like other European empires in Asia, was incapable of resisting conquest by the Japanese. As in China, the resistance to the Japanese in Indochina was led by the communists, who in consequence became the leaders of the national liberation movement in each country. After Japanese defeat at the end of World War II, the Vietnamese communist leader Ho Chi Minh declared the independence of Vietnam. But the French wanted to retain their colonies in Indochina and fought to maintain control of the region. In May 1954, after eight years of fighting, the French suffered a shattering defeat at Dien Bien Phu at the hands of the Viet Minh, the national liberation movement under the leadership of the Vietnamese Communist Party. The architect of the Viet Minh's guerilla military strategy, General Vo Nguyen Gap, observed, 'A poor feudal nation had beaten a great colonial power . . . It meant a lot; not just to us but to people all over the world.'[1]

The French were beaten, but the US took the view that it had to intervene to prevent Vietnam falling to the advance of communism. Thus began the intervention that eventually resulted in the deaths of 3 million Vietnamese, 60,000 Americans, and the US's first war defeat in history. After French withdrawal from the region, Vietnam was divided into two along the 17th parallel; the Viet Minh and Vietnamese Communist Party, backed by the Soviet Union and China, led the North – the Democratic Republic of Vietnam – and a US-sponsored regime headed by Ngo Dinh Diem led the South. Elections were supposed to take place two years later, with the aim of re-uniting the country. A little more than 10 years previously the US had been through the experience of the Korean War, in which it had been fought to a standstill following the intervention of China. After that experience the US move into Vietnam was more cautious and protracted until it finally ended up with half a million troops engaged in a conflict that absorbed 3 per cent of US gross domestic product – an economic burden that ended up bringing down the entire postwar Bretton Woods economic arrangements, where economic stability had been provided by the dollar-gold standard.

The US started by trying to prop up the French colonial regime, sending considerable aid. This strategy failed at Dien Bien Phu. A reassessment followed, with Eisenhower reasoning that if Vietnam 'fell' to communism then the rest of South-East Asia could also 'go over very quickly' to communism, 'like a row of dominoes.'[2] This 'domino theory' of potential communist expansion ultimately led to the steady escalation of US engagement in Vietnam until the final ignominious collapse in 1975.

The US-backed Ngo Dinh Diem regime in the South set out to wipe out the Viet Minh and their supporters in the area. The planned elections were cancelled, as the most likely victors were the Viet Minh. Although the repression and cancellation of the elections were symptomatic of a lack of political legitimacy, the US propped up the regime with financial and military advisers. In December 1960, various opposition forces in the South formed the National Front for the Liberation of South Vietnam (NLF), known also as the Viet Cong. At this time, the US was engaged in the issues around Cuba and Berlin and would not directly commit troops to Vietnam. However, the new president, John F Kennedy, sent increased numbers of military advisers. By the end of 1961, there were around 3,000 US military personnel in Vietnam. By the end of 1962 this had increased to 11,500 and people were beginning to speak of the 'undeclared war'. In November 1963, Diem was ousted and killed in a coup by South Vietnamese generals. Later that month, President Kennedy was assassinated and was succeeded by Lyndon

Baines Johnson, or 'LBJ'. By the end of 1963, there were 20,000 US military personnel in Vietnam.

US war and atrocities in Vietnam

Open US military action in Vietnam followed in August 1964. An incident was contrived in the Gulf of Tonkin, leading to an exchange of fire between North Vietnamese patrol boats and US naval vessels. Following this, President Johnson ordered the first bombing raids on North Vietnam. The Viet Cong stepped up its anti-US activity in the South. By early 1965, the war between the US and the Viet Cong-supported North Vietnam was under way in earnest. In March 1965, the first 3,500 US ground troops landed at Da Nang. The US began the heavy bombing of North Vietnam, which they continued for eight years. The scale of US bombing, the frequent atrocities in the war and the tenacity of the Vietnamese began to turn global public opinion, including within the US, against the war. The war dominated television news for years, and much of the visual coverage profoundly shocked the world. Who from that time will ever forget the images of the My Lai massacre? The massacre took place on 16 March 1968 and became a symbol of US war crimes in Vietnam. Photographs of the massacre provoked worldwide outrage. US soldiers killed hundreds of civilians – mostly old men, women, children and babies – in the village of My Lai. Some were tortured and raped, others were herded into a ditch and executed with automatic weapons. 'A memorial at the site lists 504 names, with ages ranging from as high as 82 years to as low as 1 year.'[3]

The US also used Vietnam as a guinea pig for chemical weapons, causing great controversy and untold suffering, as Jeremy Isaacs and Taylor Dowling explain:

High explosives, napalm and cluster bombs rained down on North Vietnam from the bellies of giant B-52s and from ground-attack aircraft . . . In addition to high explosives, the United States dropped 18 million gallons of herbicides to destroy the tropical forests that hid the Viet Cong and the rice crops on which they subsisted. The United States also used a chemical defoliant known as Agent Orange, which contained small amounts of a highly toxic dioxin. It was believed afterwards that some US soldiers who handled the chemical got cancer or skin disease. Tests subsequently revealed that the South Vietnamese had blood levels of dioxin three times that of US citizens, from Agent Orange accumulated in rivers and streams. It would take years for the poisonous chemicals to be flushed out of the fragile ecosystem. In all, the United States dropped more tons of explosives on Vietnam than were dropped by all parties during the entire Second World War.[4]

Anti-war campaigning

Opposition to the Vietnam War shaped the politics of a generation of young people in the 1960s. Mass protest in the US, in Britain and across the world created large new movements with new ways of organising and thinking. The radicalisation of the protest movement against the war interacted with the vast scope of the civil rights movement in the US, the women's movement and the lesbian and gay liberation movement. So what role did CND play in this time of political ferment and activity?

Anti-nuclear campaigning continued throughout the 1960s and 1970s and there were some notable advances in international controls at this time, which clearly resulted partly from popular opposition. But mobilisation around anti-nuclear issues decreased for a number of reasons. The 'nuclear hotline' agreement between leaders and the easing of tension between the Soviet Union and the US after they had backed off over Cuba made actual nuclear war now seem unlikely. The Partial Test Ban Treaty was a great achievement that met many people's concerns about atmospheric pollution.[5]

Thus by the mid-1960s, the perception was that the nuclear danger had receded for the moment, while tens or hundreds of thousands of people were being killed each year in Vietnam. The war was an immediate issue, requiring immediate action and opposition. Many activists naturally moved their attention and energies away from campaigning against nuclear weapons to opposing the war on Vietnam. This raised for CND the issue of the extent to which it should be involved in the campaigning against the war on Vietnam. Peggy Duff, then general secretary of CND, observed in her report to the Executive Committee in 1966 that CND was highly active in two areas; opposition to nuclear weapons, certainly, but also campaigning against the Vietnam War. She pointed out: 'It is not always easy to integrate these two and there are also campaigners who feel strongly that one or the other is vitally important . . . There is no doubt that a large majority of the Campaign is extremely concerned over the war in Vietnam. It is also clear that a large number of campaigners are concerned to act on the issue of nuclear weapons.'[6]

For many peace movements around the world, campaigning over Vietnam was not a problem, because as well as supporting disarmament it was also within their remit to oppose war. CND, however, had been set up as a single-issue organisation to achieve nuclear disarmament. CND was extremely broad politically because supporters only had to agree on their opposition to nuclear weapons, not to any particular political analysis. This was a great strength, but it could also weaken and marginalise CND. Despite the misgivings of some members, CND did play a significant role in campaigning against the Vietnam War, although the degree of priority given to this varied.

As John Cox, CND chair for most of the 1970s, points out, 'CND always opposed the US intervention in Vietnam. What was in dispute, and remained a problem for as long as the war lasted, was the amount of attention CND should give to the anti-war campaign.'[7] In Britain, the movement against the Vietnam War was eventually led by the Vietnam Solidarity Campaign under the slogan 'Victory to the NLF'. This expressed the moral authority that the Vietnamese struggle came to command among a generation of young people all over the world. In the US, with its troops directly engaged, the anti-war movement campaigned on the slogan 'Bring the Troops Home Now'. CND's position was to call for US withdrawal from Vietnam.

CND has frequently had to deal with the need to take up issues related to, but not the same as, its core message against nuclear weaponry. One such issue was over the visit of King Paul and Queen Frederika of Greece to London in 1963. Independent Greek MP Grigoris Lambrakis had been on the Aldermaston March in 1963 and had planned a peace march from Marathon to Athens in Greece for April 1963, raising wider issues of peace and civil rights together. This was a controversial endeavour under what was then an oppressive Greek regime. Mass arrests at the beginning of the march prevented it from taking place, but Lambrakis, protected by parliamentary immunity, marched the route alone. The peace movement in Greece continued to grow, but a month later Lambrakis was murdered. His funeral was attended by at least half a million people and his gravestone was carved with a CND symbol.[8] The events surrounding Lambrakis' death were subsequently immortalised in the film *Z*.

Shortly afterwards, the king and queen of Greece – who were well known for their close association with Greece's repressive right-wing regime – came on a state visit to London, and much discussion took place about what action CND should take, and indeed whether it was appropriate to take any, given that the issue was not directly a nuclear one. Eventually it was agreed to hold a demonstration before the arrival of the king and queen and to hand a wreath, shaped like the CND symbol, to Buckingham Palace. The argument was that this was a protest in solidarity with CND's sister movement in Greece, which was suffering repression, and in tribute to Lambrakis who had died for beliefs and values he shared with CND.[9] The demonstration and other protests against the visit – in which the Committee of 100 played a leading role – attracted huge press coverage. But some argued that it alienated support from CND. Peggy Duff, who worked for CND at that time, said it provoked 'new and virulent hostility to the Ban the Bomb movement . . . The effect on public opinion both within and outside the movement was disastrous, mainly because the queen had been involved. This was an astonishing revelation both for CND and the committee'[10] Duff herself could never really understand why this episode frightened off a number of CND supporters.

With regard to Vietnam, there were a number of different views within CND. Some argued that the war was a 'conventional' war, and so it was not of direct relevance to CND. Even so, they accepted that CND should demand an end to US intervention. Others argued that the war could escalate into nuclear conflict between the US and the Soviet Union and therefore it should be actively opposed. The left strongly supported the Vietnamese struggle and wanted to show explicit solidarity with the Vietnamese people against US intervention. Notwithstanding these nuances, CND campaigned against the war from 1965 onwards, organising quite large demonstrations in 1966 and 1967.[11] There were local demonstrations as well as national ones, with opposition to the war and opposition to nuclear weapons intermingled in literature and on banners. For example, at the 1966 Trafalgar Square Easter Rally, there was a giant puppet show on the Vietnam War and British government complicity, scripted by Adrian Mitchell and Michael Kustow, with 20-foot puppets designed by satirical cartoonist Gerald Scarfe. Writer Michael Kustow tells the story of *Punch and Judas*:

> *For someone like me in 1966, working for the Royal Shakespeare Company, tracking down fringe theatre in the cellars and corners of the city, moved by photos of street pageants in the early days of the Russian Revolution, elated by the joy of open-air rock 'n' roll festivals, CND was a clarion call, not only because of its arguments but because of its jubilant street style. That is why so many writers, painters, actors and musicians joined the marches. And why the poet Adrian Mitchell and I proposed a mega-spectacle to CND at the end of the Aldermaston March that year.*
>
> *'Give us the terrace in front of the National Gallery,' we said, 'and we'll fill it with giant puppets. Gerald Scarfe will paint them, like blow-ups of his biting cartoons. Teams of art and drama students will operate them. We'll write you a bold, shameless satirical script, featuring Harold Wilson, Ian Smith, [US President] LBJ and the Bank of England. Actors will speak their voices, there'll be songs and happenings. In spirit, it will be a mix of*

*Shakespeare and Lenny Bruce [the American comedian
whose biting attacks on hypocrisy, religion and power had
just hit London]. We'll call it* Punch and Judas.'

*Peggy Duff, of the Dickensian face and cigarette stuck
permanently to the lower lip, gave it the go-ahead and a
tiny budget. The script came quite easily; the grotesque
politics of the times lent themselves to monster effigies in a
public space taken over by masses of marchers. We kept it
funny and cheeky. TV political anchormen Robert
MacKenzie and Robin Day turned into a music-hall
cross-talk act, the Morecambe and Wise of election swings
and roundabouts. In a mock Oscar ceremony, Lyndon
Johnson awarded Harold Wilson the prize for 'best
supporting role in the Western world.' (This was at the
height of the Vietnam War and although, Wilson, unlike
Blair, never sent British troops, he supported the US war.)
Wilson's tennis-ball eyes wobbled in gratitude. Ian Smith,
who had declared unilateral Rhodesian independence,
became a giant boot in Scarfe's imagination, with only
one, basilisk, eye.*

*We also made it as spectacular as we could within our
means. As Wilson dropped off to sleep, the top of his head
split open and a squalling baby appeared; an echo of
Shakespeare's emblem of pity, his 'naked new-born babe',
and of all the children in the world hurt by want, injustice
and fear.*

*At the climax of the piece, as Wilson chanted, 'And if
they burn, we burn too,' like a voodoo mantra, and the
roar of a thousand B-52 bombers drilled eardrums, the
baby in his head was set on fire. We launched across the
square thousands of helium balloons carrying silver-foil
missiles and bombs to the sound of sirens. Our giant
puppets were wheeled into a criminals' line-up in front of*

the National Gallery and, as orange flags fluttered round them, our production team flung buckets of blood-red paint at their faces. It dribbled across their unseeing eyes, their masticating jaws, their fickle lips.

The letter placards which had been spelling out THE WHORE GAME were now reversed and displayed the word PEACE. Folk-singer Isla Cameron sang out the keening, consoling melody of Pete Seeger's 'Turn Turn Turn'; 'To everything there is a season . . . a time for war, and a time for peace.'

There was something bigger and more affirmative in our Punch and Judas *in the square than was happening on television (the satire show* That Was The Week That Was*), in nightclubs (Lenny Bruce) or theatres (Beyond The Fringe). Looking back from the era of Rory Bremner and Michael Moore, however, there is nothing to apologise for in this rough pageant, put together in a few days. Its humour and gravity breathed human contact and determination. And that came from CND.*[12]

At CND's National Conference in 1966, there was a range of resolutions, some that strongly emphasised anti-war campaigning, others that argued that CND should only work on nuclear issues.[13] In reality, for most members these issues were not counterposed. By 1967, the Trades Union Congress (TUC), Labour Party and Liberal Party Conferences had all called for 'dissociation' of the British government from US policy and action in Vietnam. CND's 1967 conference passed a resolution welcoming these positions and urged its members to lobby MPs and work in trade union branches to press for action from the TUC General Council in support of their position.[14] CND agreed at the Conference that the themes for the 1968 Easter March should be Vietnam, Polaris and NATO.

Duncan Rees, who was General Secretary of CND from 1976 to 1979 and went on this march, comments on the interlinking of issues:

> *When I went on my first Aldermaston March at the age of 14 in 1968, the 'Britain must lead' [by giving up nuclear weapons] and 'scrap Polaris' banners were matched, if not outnumbered, by a mass of placards protesting against the war in Vietnam and denouncing the failure of the Wilson Government to oppose US policy. In London, one of the key memories was of people signing the remembrance book for Martin Luther King. There were around 20,000 people on that march [at its finish] and there was an extraordinary, vibrant and determined feel to the occasion. So it may not have mattered to some that the cause of nuclear disarmament was being somewhat submerged.*[15]

CND's Conference in 1968 strengthened its campaigning position and resolved: 'CND will campaign strenuously for British dissociation from the United States, for an immediate end to the bombing of Vietnam and for the complete withdrawal of the United States from Vietnam.'[16] In the autumn of 1968, CND mobilised for an 800-strong delegation to a meeting in Boulogne, France, with representatives of North Vietnam (the Democratic Republic of Vietnam) who were in Paris for a meeting. CND also invited Madame Thi Binh from North Vietnam to speak at the Easter Rally in Trafalgar Square in 1969.[17]

The Vietnam Solidarity Campaign
At the same time the Vietnam Solidarity Campaign (VSC) focused exclusively on Vietnam. It was able to articulate directly

the rage against the injustice and brutality of the war by taking a clear position of solidarity with the NLF. Interestingly, there was some considerable overlap in membership between CND and the VSC. The latter was very effective in mobilising young people at a time of general political ferment. There were some tensions between the two organisations; some in VSC felt that CND was 'passé and irrelevant'.[18] Tariq Ali, a leader of the VSC, had formerly been an active member of CND. However, in May 1968, the CND National Council passed the following resolution: 'In view of the statements made by Tariq Ali dissociating from CND, it was agreed that he no longer be considered a member of CND committees.'[19]

By 1969 students in CND were telling the CND National Conference that student CND organisation had effectively ceased to exist and, expressing their frustrations with CND's policy on Vietnam, offered the following advice: 'In order for CND to re-establish its presence in the Universities, it is absolutely imperative that CND itself accepts that the objective political situation has changed. It cannot disregard either the present international emphasis on national liberation and social revolution, or the internal pressures within the University structure. If CND can come to terms with these changes and recast its policies, action and "image" it could make some impact on the student body, but without this, it is lost.'[20]

Pacifist opposition to the Vietnam War

CND included a number of pacifist members, who were opposed in principle to any form of violence, including the armed struggle of the Vietnamese (although they were generally politically supportive to the Vietnamese side). There was some support from these perspectives for a kind of third force, of Buddhists or pacifists, in Vietnam. Buddhist protest within Vietnam was in fact rather significant and came to public attention worldwide in the most shocking way in 1963. Still in control of just South Vietnam, Diem was extremely intolerant of religion, and his policies – including raids on temples, smashing of shrines and arrests of monks – alienated the Buddhist population. As a result, a number of Buddhist monks drenched themselves in petrol and set themselves on fire, burning themselves to death in protest on the streets of Saigon. Buddhists also opposed the 'Americanisation' of their country through the presence of the troops with their money and the attendant leisure and vice industries that grew up in their wake. In 1966, they led a series of protests under slogans such as 'Down with the CIA', and 'End Foreign Domination of Our Country'.[21] Peaceful protestors were attacked with bayonets and tear gas and again monks and nuns set themselves on fire in protest.

Towards the end of the 1960s, as the war escalated, some attempts were made by British peace activists to take pacifist action in Vietnam, initially with a religious impetus. In January 1967, the US made its biggest ground attack of the war, 30 miles north of Saigon, totally destroying villages and forest. The following month, US General Curtis LeMay declared that the war could only be lost by negotiation – and only won by the use of atomic weapons. In March, the US fired across the neutral zone between North and South Vietnam for the first time, and in April for the first time bombed Haiphong Harbour in North Vietnam, which was not a military target. Around this time, the Christian Group of the Committee of 100 decided to try to send a group of eminent people to North Vietnam to deter US bombing. This plan did not come to fruition, but it did lead to a similar project a year or so later. Peggy Smith, a 73-year-old Quaker peace veteran, initiated the formation of Non-Violent Action in

Vietnam, which towards the end of 1968 eventually resulted in 26 peace activists travelling to Cambodia with the goal of entering North Vietnam.[22]

By 1972 it had become clear that the US could not win a ground war in Vietnam and the war had created economic crisis and serious civil unrest within the US, with worldwide repercussions. The US began to move towards a new strategy based on a combination of massive bombing, while relying on US-funded South Vietnamese troops to fight the ground war. Talks towards a peace settlement began in earnest in 1972. By March 1973 the last US troops had left Vietnam. The US continued to fund the South Vietnamese regime on a massive scale. But within two years, the South Vietnamese army started to collapse. With the final entry of the Viet Cong and the North Vietnamese army into Saigon in May 1975, one of the longest wars of the 20th century was brought to an end. Reunification of the country followed shortly afterwards. The war had been a great human tragedy. But it had also been an extraordinary triumph for a people's will to self-determination and independence. The 'grasshopper', as Ho Chi Minh termed Vietnam, had defeated the 'elephant'. In its struggle it had been supported by protestors throughout the world and by a gigantic anti-war movement in the US itself. Active since 1965, mobilising large numbers, particularly of young people, rejecting militarism and embracing a culture of peace and love, the anti-war movement redefined US values for many years. As one leading US anti-war activist wrote: 'The anti-war movement started with nothing but leaflets. But it proved that people can think for themselves if the issue touches them deeply enough, technology notwith-standing. In human affairs there is still nothing so powerful as an idea and a movement whose time has come.'[23]

It is important to reflect briefly on the fact that the US did not use nuclear weapons in Vietnam, even though it was advocated by some top-level personnel. According to McGeorge Bundy, who had been a security adviser to two US presidents, what stopped Richard Nixon, for example, from even threatening to use the bomb was his conclusion that its use 'would have totally unacceptable results inside the United States, enraging the opponents of the war and setting general opinion against the new administration with such force as to make it doubtful that the government could keep up the American end of the war ... What the American people would not accept, the nuclear-minded president could not plausibly threaten.'[24] It should be added that the Soviet Union would have regarded any use of nuclear weapons as a threat to its own security with possible consequences of widening the Vietnam War to a nuclear war between the US and the Soviet Union.

Other campaigning activities

The Vietnam War dominated this period, but there were also developments taking place in the specifically anti-nuclear campaigning arena. Membership of CND declined, and its national office staff was drastically reduced, but activity nevertheless continued. From 1966 to 1968 there were major demonstrations against the launch of each of the four Polaris submarines, three of them at Barrow-in-Furness in South Cumbria and the fourth in Birkenhead, Merseyside.[25] Considerable public discussion was raised over Polaris and questions were asked in parliament. There were also demonstrations at the nuclear bases at Holy Loch and Faslane in Scotland. Work was also undertaken to draw attention to the 'folly and danger' of the anti-ballistic missile (ABM) system that was under discussion nationally at this time.[26] In 1966,

CND urged members to write letters protesting against the French and Chinese tests and also to write to MPs and the prime minister opposing nuclear overflights.[27] There were frequent flights carrying nuclear weapons across Britain, and with the recent Palomares incident, public concern was high. In January 1966, a US bomber was being refuelled in mid-air over the Spanish coast when it collided with the tanker plane. Both blew up, setting on fire huge amounts of jet fuel. Four hydrogen bombs dropped over the village of Palomares. Thanks to safety devices, a thermonuclear explosion did not occur, but high explosives went off in two of the bombs, showering radioactive particles over hundreds of acres of farmland. The third bomb landed intact near the village and the fourth was found in the sea after an intensive eight-day search. Obviously this was not as bad as it could have been but, nevertheless, the bombs that went off leaked high levels of plutonium radiation. Around 1,750 metric tons of earth were sent to the US for burial and local crops had to be destroyed. In 1975, a Spanish report stated that because of a prevailing wind on the day of the accident, plutonium dust had been churned up and the full extent of the spread would never be known.[28] There were probably more of these accidents and near misses that we will never know about; and it is likely that they happened in Britain, too. In 1957, a US bomber carrying three nuclear bombs crashed at Lakenheath airbase; if they had exploded they would have devastated East Anglia.

CND's local groups organised a very widespread and diverse range of activities during these years. One particularly active group was Christian CND, an ecumenical group bringing together a wide range of Christian groups and churches. In 1965, for example, it held a peace pilgrimage from London to Canterbury. In the late 1960s, Whitsun pilgrimages focused on the research establishment at Porton Down, where chemical and biological weapons were being developed. Vigils were held at St Martin-in-the-Fields Church in London at the time of the launching of the Polaris submarines, and prayers and fasting were conducted to commemorate Hiroshima and Nagasaki Days.[29] Many of these events were small in terms of members attending, but they were a continual pressure that did not go away.

Towards the Nuclear Non-Proliferation Treaty

During this time there was a number of international developments and agreements toward arms control and disarmament that were linked to the US strategy towards the Soviet Union in the context of the Vietnam War. The US had continually tried to isolate Vietnam by courting the Soviet Union and China; the latter through the Kissinger-inspired strategy of recognising the People's Republic of China for the first time since the communists had come to power in 1949. The US strategy towards the Soviet Union was to woo it with relatively minor arms control moves and at the same time seek to exploit the tensions between the Soviet Union and China to strengthen its own position. Kissinger succeeded in the latter but failed in his strategic goal of reducing Soviet and Chinese aid to Vietnam. The Vietnamese made clear that they were independent of both the Soviet Union and China, whilst seeing them as important allies.

The Partial Test Ban Treaty, signed in 1963, had been a very positive step, but it had only been signed by the US, Britain and the Soviet Union. In October 1964, China exploded an atom bomb, followed in June 1967 by a 3-megaton hydrogen bomb. This meant that five countries (France being the fifth) now had nuclear weapons. Israel was moving with US help to acquire nuclear weapons. India was also seeking to become a nuclear power. Notwithstanding some moves towards arms control, the arms race between the US and Soviet Union had in reality rapidly accelerated. Both sides possessed huge amounts of nuclear weaponry, but the US had superiority in missiles able to hit the Soviet Union. In the mid-1960s, Soviet scientists began to work on a system of anti-ballistic missiles (ABMs) in advance of anything possessed by the US. These would intercept incoming missiles – the same principle we see today in the US National Missile Defense or 'Star Wars' system. The problem with it then was exactly the same as the problem with it today; it would enable the side that possessed it to launch a pre-emptive strike without fear of retaliation. In other words the whole 'mutual assured destruction' notion of deterrence – the idea that the world was 'protected' from nuclear war by the certainty that neither the US nor the Soviet Union could win a nuclear war; both would be destroyed – would cease to have any impact at all.

In 1967, President Johnson raised the question of an ABM ban with the Soviet leader Kosygin, but Kosygin was unwilling to start ABM talks. At the same time, the US developed a new system that significantly reduced the effectiveness of ABM systems. This was the multiple independently targetable re-entry vehicle. Each missile would be able to carry up to ten warheads, each of which could be separately targeted; thus one missile would carry warheads capable of destroying ten cities. This would make it extremely difficult to intercept. The arms race was clearly getting out of hand; estimates suggest that between them the US and Soviet Union were spending over $50 million a day on nuclear weaponry.[30]

Concerns about proliferation and the spiralling stocks of the nuclear states had led already to efforts by Sweden and India in the UN General Assembly to bring both of these under control. In 1965, the US and Soviet Union put forward draft treaties, but they were rejected by the non-nuclear weapons states for they did 'little more than limit the nuclear club to its existing members.'[31] The UN General Assembly sought a treaty with a strong nuclear disarmament component. As Willy Brandt put it, 'The moral and political justification of a nonproliferation treaty follows only if the nuclear states regard it as a step towards restriction of their own armaments and toward disarmament and clearly state they are willing to act accordingly.'[32] In July 1968, the US, Britain and the Soviet Union signed the Nuclear Non-Proliferation Treaty. It not only forbade nuclear technology transfer and the making or acquisition of nuclear weapons by non-nuclear weapons states, it also crucially included Article VI: 'Each of the Parties to the Treaty undertakes to pursue negotiations in good faith on effective measures relating to cessation of the nuclear arms race at an early date and to nuclear disarmament, and on a treaty on general and complete disarmament under strict and effective international control.'

Including both non-proliferation and disarmament, the Treaty was very popular and was overwhelmingly passed by the UN General Assembly in June 1968, when it received 95 votes to 4, with 21 abstentions.[33] However, Article VI requiring moves toward nuclear disarmament by the nuclear powers has remained to this day a dead letter. Parties to the Treaty had the right to peaceful use of nuclear power, with a safeguards system administered by the International Atomic Energy Agency (IAEA) designed to prevent materials produced during the atomic energy process being diverted for military purposes. In terms of non-proliferation of nuclear weapons by non-nuclear states, the Treaty has had mixed success. The US has enabled Israel to become a nuclear power. South Africa became a nuclear power but renounced its nuclear weapons. Both India and Pakistan have developed nuclear weapons. Still, as historian of the world peace movement Lawrence Wittner, in his book *The Struggle Against the Bomb: Volume Two*, has pointed out, 'Although analysts had once estimated that as many as 30 nations might develop nuclear weapons by the 1970s, very few of them chose to do so. Indeed, numerous countries quite capable of developing the Bomb – Sweden, Canada, Switzerland, East and West Germany, Italy, Australia and Japan, among others – resisted the temptation.'[34]

But in terms of disarmament by the nuclear weapons states, the Treaty has been a great failure. The nuclear weapons states have simply failed to keep their side of the Nuclear Non-Proliferation Treaty and this causes increased tension today as the US and UK rattle their sabres policing the non-nuclear weapons states. When the Treaty was launched, there was considerable optimism. Indeed, enthusiasm for the eradication of nuclear weapons took a number of forms at this time. For example, several countries at this time also took steps to make themselves nuclear-free. In January 1968, the Japanese prime minister pledged that Japan would not make nuclear weapons. That same month, Canada's Prime Minister Pierre Trudeau began the phasing out of the deployment of US nuclear weapons in Canada. Also in 1968, a nuclear weapons-free zone was established by 20 countries in Latin America, renouncing the acquisition and siting of nuclear weapons on their territories. Signatories to this treaty, the Treaty of Tlatelolco, also agreed to IAEA jurisdiction over their nuclear power facilities. In return, nuclear weapons states agreed not to use or threaten to use nuclear weapons against any of the signatory states. Two other treaties were also signed around this same time: the Outer Space Treaty of 1966, which banned the deployment of weapons of mass destruction in space; and the Seabed Arms Control Treaty of 1971, which did the same for the seabeds.

The US and Soviet Union also moved towards negotiation on the limitation of 'strategic' nuclear weapons (aimed specifically at each other). Talks took place in Helsinki in November 1969, in what became known as the Strategic Arms Limitation Talks (SALT). Richard Nixon, at this point US president, was keen to reduce tensions with the Soviet Union and cut expenditure on nuclear weapons at a time when the Vietnam War was costing huge amounts: 'The direct dollar cost to the US in South Vietnam alone was $141 billion. This was more than $7,000 for each of the area's 20 million inhabitants, whose per capita income was only $157 per year. The collateral expenditures amounted to far more. Economists correctly link the rapid inflation of the late 1960s to the large federal deficits resulting from US spending for the Vietnam War.'[35]

For its part the Soviet leadership also wanted to consolidate reasonable relations with the US at a time when it had tense relations with China and feared a Sino–US rapprochement to its own disadvantage. After more than two years of negotiation, the SALT I Treaty, as it was known, was signed at a summit meeting in Moscow in May 1972 by President Nixon and the Soviet leader Leonid Brezhnev. SALT I was not a disarmament treaty but one designed to freeze some kind of balance between the US and the Soviet Union. It placed quantitative limits on ABM systems and certain types of nuclear weapons and regulated advantages possessed by one or other superpower on others, but it did not prohibit technological advances to those weapons, including multiple warheads. SALT I also did not cover medium- and intermediate-range missiles, nor did it cover US bases in Europe. Essentially it enshrined 'mutual assured destruction'. The failure to restrict numbers of warheads and technological improvements to the weaponry meant that the destructive power of nuclear weapons continued to increase. Détente – or relaxation between the superpowers – did not equal disarmament, and the 1970s were increasingly a time of the growing realisation of this sad fact and, as the decade progressed, a time of increasing CND activity.

Environmentalism and nuclear power

CND shared a lot of common ground with the environmentalist movement that began to emerge in the 1970s through the Ecology Party, Greenpeace, Friends of the Earth and other groups. Environmentalism addressed a whole range of issues that are vital for the future of our planet. As Val Stevens, an activist in CND and Friends of the Earth, comments:

> *Population growth and the impact that was having on water supplies, fuel and energy supplies, agricultural practices, and on finite resources in general; plus the spin-off in terms of mounting pollution of air, land and sea; all these loomed as insidious, but certain means of destroying our life support systems. For environmentalists, 'the bomb' became one of the routes to destruction of the planet, but by no means an overriding one – more a nagging anxiety pushed to the back of the mind.*[36]

Many of these concerns were shared by CND members, although a minority argued that CND should not be concerned with nuclear power. Close relations were developed between CND and the different environmentalist organisations, and some common campaigning occurred. In 1977, Friends of the Earth played a major role in the Windscale power plant inquiry, opposing plans to build a massive new reprocessing plant, and CND brought to the fore the links between nuclear power and nuclear weapons.[37] Researcher at Bradford University School of Peace Studies Howard Clark wrote a pamphlet for CND, *Atoms for War*, which made the links very clear:

> *The material for the first British bomb was plutonium from the first reactors . . . at Windscale. When demand for military plutonium increased, two nuclear power stations were ordered, Calder Hall and Chapel Cross; both were to produce plutonium for weapons with electricity as a by-product. This made economic sense and also presented an opportunity for a public relations campaign about 'peaceful' nuclear power. Thus 'civil' nuclear power was actually a spin-off from a cover for the military nuclear programme.*[38]

Awareness of the health dangers presented by nuclear testing was widespread, and continuing French nuclear tests in the Pacific – it had not signed the Partial Test Ban Treaty – caused widespread anger. These fears were increasingly supplemented by concerns about nuclear power stations and the low-level radiation hazards that they produce, such as radioactive emissions and waste, as well as the risk of accidents. New scientific evidence available at the time raised the same concerns of the testing days, where strontium-90 had become a byword for public concern about radiation. The point about strontium-90 was that it is chemically similar to calcium and so is easily absorbed into blood and bones. Bone tumours or leukaemia can be caused by irradiation of bone cells or bone marrow cells. Milk from cows that have grazed on radiation-polluted grass is a great risk, particularly to the health of young children. However, whilst CND was opposed to nuclear power, and remains so today, individual CND members do not have uniform views on the question, and individuals and organisations who take a different view are welcome to participate and argue their position.[39]

Some members have indeed spoken in favour of nuclear power. The scientist John Fremlin, for example, described opposition to nuclear power as an 'irrelevant part' of CND's programme, which would deter potential supporters. He considered that the danger of resource wars in the future, resulting from a shortage of energy, was considerable, and could be offset by the greater development of nuclear power. Writing in the early 1980s, he observed: 'The risk of an all-out nuclear war will increase if a real shortage of energy appears imminent in 20 to 30 years' time. As oil prices begin their final accelerating rise, it could become clear that whoever was militarily in control of the last reserves of the Middle East could be in economic control of the world.'[40] However, most CND members continue to think that the Three Mile Island and Chernobyl disasters show that nuclear power simply is not safe and its radioactive by-products pose dangers for generations to come.

Other areas of activity

CND decided at this time to increase its opposition to chemical and biological weapons. Demonstrations took place at Porton Down biological warfare research station in Wiltshire.[41] Much of the emphasis in campaigning was now on local work, and this continued in a variety of ways, although still without huge numbers. The Polaris base at Holy Loch provided a focus for continuing action, and in 1974 a Scottish CND demonstration attracted around 1,200 protestors. Indeed, from the mid-1970s, CND was opposing plans for replacing Polaris with the new Trident system. Trident's main advance over Polaris was that each missile had a number of independently targetable warheads of great accuracy. The warheads could thus be used to destroy a much greater range of targets.

Work with the trade unions was also progressing at this time, around the question of nuclear disarmament and arms conversion. The issue of job losses in the event of nuclear disarmament by Britain was a serious matter for trade unions. This was particularly so during the 1970s, when there was an economic crisis in Britain and the whole western world, linked in major part to the oil price crises of the early and late 1970s. CND was never cavalier in its attitude towards loss of jobs in the nuclear arms or nuclear power industries and was committed to a policy of arms conversion – that is to say converting military production into civil production. Mike Cooley, who was a shop steward at Lucas Aerospace, wrote a study on the types of production that could replace military production, and Dave Griffiths, who was editor of CND's magazine *Sanity*, produced a pamphlet on arms production and the economic crisis.[42]

New dangers

As the 1970s progressed, increased concern about the arms race and its dangers for ordinary citizens raised the profile of CND. As former General Secretary of CND Duncan Rees points out: 'The development of CND in the five years from 1976 to 1981 was as astounding and remarkable as it was rapid. It was of course welcome in one sense, but it reflected an increasingly serious international situation and a growing threat posed by the increasingly bellicose nuclear policies of Britain and the US.'[43] The 1970s had been declared the 'Decade of Disarmament' by the UN, but it soon became clear that the SALT I agreement was not inhibiting huge build-ups of weaponry. Events such as the signing in 1972 of the Basic

Principles of Relations between the US and Soviet Union, which enshrined 'peaceful coexistence', and of the Prevention of Nuclear War Agreement by the US and Soviet Union in 1973, made the right noises but were not actually delivering any disarmament. Kissinger made his view of such agreements clear in his memoirs, where he described the Prevention of Nuclear War Agreement as: 'a bland set of principles that had been systematically stripped of all implications harmful to our interests.'[44]

Two issues that came to be of great concern to CND were the 'counterforce' strategy and the neutron bomb. The 'counterforce' strategy was one of pre-emptive attack on nuclear targets. Whilst at first thought this seems better than an attack on a city, on reflection it is clear that counterforce is a strategy for pre-emptive war – a strategy for undertaking a first strike against another country's forces, to knock out their missiles before they could be fired, hence rendering the deterrent role of nuclear weapons redundant. This idea gained currency in US circles and led to an acceleration in the production of highly accurate missiles. Former US Defense Secretary Robert McNamara had estimated that about 400 thermonuclear warheads were 'necessary' for minimum deterrence but, by the time of SALT I, both superpowers had vastly in excess of this number: 'At the time of the SALT I agreements [May 1972], the number of deliverable nuclear warheads held by the US and the USSR was about 5,700 and 2,100 respectively – both well above the MAD [mutual assured destruction] minimum of 400 – that is, the minimum needed for both to inflict unacceptable damage on each other.'[45] As SALT I did not prevent the replacement of old weapons with new ones, and did not restrict multiple independently targetable re-entry vehicles, which enabled the carrying of multiple warheads on one missile, the scope for acceleration of the arms race was huge, within the terms of SALT I. By 1979, strategic warhead levels had reached 9,200 for the US and 5,000 for the Soviet Union ('strategic' nuclear weapons meaning those that the US and Soviet Union could deliver directly on each other). Both sides also had large numbers of tactical nuclear weapons (those for use in a 'controlled' nuclear war, in other words not targeted between the US and Soviet Union, but at Europe, for example).

The new weapons developed by both sides marked a further escalation. The US began to develop cruise missiles, which operated on a different basis to previous missiles. 'Ballistic' missiles are propelled by the initial thrust and then proceed under free-fall conditions. Cruise missiles are to be powered during some or all of their flight, with navigation equipment to help them to their target, possibly with a mini-computer link-up to a satellite guidance system. The accuracy is considerable. For its part, the Soviet Union began to deploy new models of intercontinental ballistic missiles and submarine ballistic missile systems. In 1977, the Soviet Union began to replace SS-4s and SS-5s in eastern Europe with intermediate-range SS-20 missiles, which were more accurate than the earlier missiles and could carry three multiple independently targetable re-entry vehicles.

Even though no crisis emerged as rapidly as it had done over Cuba or Berlin, a new spiral of the nuclear arms race drove the issue up the public agenda. As one White House official observed: 'Personal activities were designed according to the time it would take a nuclear missile to fly from Russia to the United States. The rule was: The president should never be more than two minutes from a telephone. Even the White House press corps designed its daily life around the possibility that the president might push the nuclear button at any moment.'[46]

The War Game

CND took two initiatives in the mid-1970s to highlight these issues. In 1973, CND applied to the BBC to make a programme for *Open Door*, the BBC2 community access slot. Eventually this resulted in the screening in October 1976 of 'All Against the Bomb'. Although, according to Duncan Rees, the film was subject to censorship by the BBC in response to MoD pressure, it aroused much public interest. After the screening, CND received several thousand enquiries and hundreds of new members.[47] The second initiative was the widespread promotion of the film *The War Game*, made by Peter Watkins in 1965. *The War Game* had been commissioned by the BBC but had then been banned from the television. In response to enquiries from CND as to the reason for the ban, the BBC director general responded that 'some young or susceptible viewers could be harmed by the impact of "The War Game".' But the film was available for screenings at cinemas and film clubs via the British Film Institute so CND groups organised local screenings. There was an enormous response to the film, with some groups organising as many as four screenings, showing it to as many as 4,000 people.[48] Building on the success of the screenings in the 1960s, CND again set about organising countless screenings across the country during 1976 and 1977. As Duncan Rees observed: 'The effect of *The War Game* . . . was to expose the horror and futility of thermonuclear war, and, as Peter Watkins puts it, "help break the present silence existing in most forms of communication on the entire, complex subject of thermonuclear weapons – their policies and their effects." Our [CND's] experience at countless meetings with the film was that it shocks, can even cause despair, but that most importantly it helps to arouse concern about the urgent need to work for the abolition of nuclear weapons.'[49]

At CND's annual conference in Manchester in 1978, it was reported that there had been over 160 major showings of the film that year – some attracting audiences as large as 800. It was estimated that in the two years that CND had been showing the film, over 20,000 people had seen it. At the same time CND was growing quite rapidly; the number of CND local groups had risen from 60 in 1976 to 102 in 1978, and membership applications were steadily growing.

The neutron bomb

A trigger for major change in public attitudes came in 1977, with the US administration asking NATO governments to increase military spending by 3 per cent, and with the announcement by US President Jimmy Carter of his decision to build and deploy a new type of nuclear weapon – the neutron bomb. The neutron bomb was an advanced radiation warhead, which had a higher emission of radiation as opposed to the other impacts of a nuclear explosion. It would be proportionately more damaging to living things than it would be to buildings. A bomb had been developed that killed people but protected property. Not surprisingly, this seemed to millions of people to be the most appallingly barbaric and immoral approach to warfare. There could be no pretence that civilians were not going to die in droves from radiation, and that they were intended to die. What particularly galvanised European opposition to this new weapon was that it was a tactical weapon to be deployed in Europe, and that it was to be under the control of battlefield commanders. This confirmed people's worst fears that nuclear weapons were now intended for use, and that nuclear strategy had evolved to think that fighting a nuclear war was possible. It was clear that the US was seeking the means to fight a 'limited' nuclear war – limited to Europe in this case. This provoked outrage and major campaigning across Europe; first in the Netherlands, then, amongst others, in Britain, West Germany, Belgium, Sweden, Norway, Denmark, Greece and Turkey. CND launched a dynamic campaign against the neutron bomb, holding public meetings and demonstrations, producing posters and leaflets, and in the process having quite an impact on public opinion. In 1978, following the example of the Dutch campaign, CND launched a petition against the neutron bomb, collecting around quarter of a million signatures in the space of a few months. Nor was it surprising that so many signatures should have been gathered. Opinion polls taken in Britain in May 1978 showed that of those who had heard of the neutron bomb, 72 per cent were opposed to its deployment in Britain.[50]

European-wide campaigning against the neutron bomb was highly effective. In April 1978, President Carter announced that he was putting off production of the neutron bomb. The US administration had put some effort into trying to gag the huge opposition to the neutron bomb: 'In early 1978, to counter such opposition in western Europe, the administration worked through the CIA to initiate a covert programme of financial and other incentives to encourage the Western European press corps to provide favourable coverage of the weapon.'[51] Clearly this gambit had been unsuccessful and, under pressure from massive popular opposition, the governments of western Europe had been unwilling to go along with it. Apparently, on 23 March 1978, British Prime Minister James Callaghan had told Carter that it would be 'the greatest relief in the world' if the neutron bomb was scrapped.[52] Carter was not willing to press forward with the neutron bomb alone, so victory was achieved.

SALT II and superpower tensions

Various diplomatic initiatives continued through the mid to

late 1970s. The Final Act of the Conference on Security and Co-operation in Europe was signed in Helsinki in August 1975. The agreement had three main components: firstly, the confirmation of existing borders within Europe – an agreement of the postwar status quo – and agreement that disputes should be settled peacefully; secondly, to encourage scientific and industrial co-operation between countries, together with trade and cultural links; and thirdly, to guarantee the free movement of peoples, ideas and information. It was signed by 33 European countries, Canada and the US.

At around this time, tensions also began to re-emerge between the superpowers elsewhere in the world. Communist movements advanced to government in Africa, in Angola and Ethiopia, with Cuban and Soviet support. President Carter had been pressing for a summit with Brezhnev, at which the Soviet leader wished to sign SALT II. Now with what were seen as Soviet advances in Africa, the US administration insisted that any advance on the SALT agreement should be tied to restraint on Soviet policy towards the third world. In the post-Vietnam War situation, whilst talking about arms limitation and reduction, President Carter in reality was engaged in a new arms build-up in the US and Europe. He authorised the development of the cruise missile, pressed for an increase in European expenditure on NATO and approved a global rapid deployment force. SALT II was eventually signed in June 1979 and both sides agreed to limit their arsenals to 2,400 missiles, reduced to 2,250 by 1981. There were also limits on intercontinental ballistic missiles, submarine-launched ballistic missiles and multiple independently targetable re-entry vehicles. However, the US Senate never ratified the Treaty.

A positive development came from the UN in July 1978, with the UN Special Session on Disarmament. It produced a

Final Document, which was adopted by consensus, outlining how an end to the arms race could be achieved. Its commitment to nuclear disarmament was absolutely explicit: 'Nuclear weapons pose the greatest danger to mankind and to the survival of civilisation. It is essential to halt and reverse the nuclear arms race in all its aspects in order to avert the danger of war involving nuclear weapons. The ultimate goal in this context is the complete elimination of nuclear weapons.'[53] The document made it clear that enduring peace and security could not be 'sustained by a precarious balance of deterrence and doctrines of strategic superiority', and welcomed all steps towards disarmament, 'whether unilateral, bilateral, regional or multilateral'. The Final Document gave strong backing to work for public peace education, urging governmental and non-governmental organisations to prepare and distribute material on the dangers of the arms race for the mobilisation of world opinion for disarmament. This strong support from the UN gave renewed impetus to the nuclear disarmament movement in its work.

4

Campaigning against cruise missiles

The US defeat in Vietnam had a profound impact on the nuclear arms race and US policy towards the Soviet Union. The 'Vietnam syndrome' was the name given to the political inability of future US administrations, due to domestic public opinion, to garner support for other military interventions, risking large – or sometimes not even so large – numbers of soldiers. No one wanted to see another 'Vietnam'. As a result the US was unable to intervene to stop the deployment of 50,000 Cuban volunteers to assist the MPLA government of Angola against a military intervention by the South African army. This led to the spectacular military defeat of the apartheid army by the Cubans and Angolans. This was a key event that triggered the Soweto uprisings, which ended with the fall of the apartheid regime – the key ally of the US in Africa at that time. In Nicaragua in 1979, the US-backed Somoza dictatorship was overthrown by a popular uprising led by the Cuban-influenced Sandinista National Liberation Front. A major civil war unfolded in El Salvador, following the murder of the Roman Catholic Archbishop Romero by the US-backed dictatorship in that country. On the Caribbean island of Grenada, a corrupt regime was overthrown by the radical New Jewel Movement.

The US had responded to its failures in Vietnam by trying

to use détente with the Soviet Union and China to put pressure on the Vietnamese. This failed. With the rise and success of new struggles under the impact of the US defeat in Vietnam, the US now comprehensively rethought its strategy. It concluded that even if it wished to do so, the Soviet Union could not control radical movements in other parts of the world, but its military and economic assistance could be decisive to their success. The US therefore decided to confront the rise of national liberation and other political struggles after its defeat in Vietnam through a massive new nuclear arms race designed to put still greater pressure on the Soviet Union, with the goal not of fighting an unwinnable nuclear war, but of breaking the Soviet economy (at that time half the size of the US, through the economic cost of the arms race). This started with President Carter's neutron bomb, the increase in NATO countries' military budgets, the deployment of cruise and Pershing missiles in Europe and Ronald Reagan's 'Star Wars' programme. This turn in US policy provoked the biggest demonstrations against nuclear weapons in history – in Europe the biggest demonstrations since World War II. CND played a decisive role in the movement.

This scale of protest was provoked by the agreement of Western leaders to a new type of missile that could lead to nuclear war in Europe. Although the western European leaders had not backed the neutron bomb, in 1979 they did back the new generation of US missiles: Pershing II ballistic missiles and intermediate-range, ground-launched cruise missiles. Following discussions throughout 1978, in January 1979 both British Prime Minister Jim Callaghan – without parliamentary consultation – and West German Chancellor Helmut Schmidt accepted that the missiles could be sited in their countries from 1983. Eventually Italy, the Netherlands and Belgium also agreed. The decision was made public after a NATO meeting on 12 December 1979, by which time Margaret Thatcher was leading a Conservative government in Britain. After the meeting, US Secretary of State Cyrus Vance commented: 'I believe that our governments can be proud of this memorable achievement and that the free people of the alliance will show overwhelming support for the decisions made here today.'[1]

Vance was shown to be very wrong about this. Even as the decision was being announced, 40,000 people were gathering at the NATO headquarters in Brussels to protest; the anti-missile movement turned out to be the greatest wave of protest that had taken place in western Europe since World War II.

Missiles in Europe

A total of 572 new missiles were planned; 108 Pershing IIs would replace West Germany's existing 108 Pershing IAs, and 464 cruise missiles would be sited across western Europe. Of these, 160 would go to Britain, 112 to Italy, 96 to West Germany, and 48 to both Belgium and the Netherlands. Of the missiles to be sited in Britain, 96 were scheduled to arrive at Greenham Common in Berkshire in December 1983, and the other 64 at the Molesworth base in Cambridgeshire by the end of 1986.[2]

The deployment of cruise and Pershing would mark a massive escalation of the arms race because they would greatly reduce the time it took to hit Soviet cities such as Moscow from bases in western Europe, without any equivalent siting of state-of-the-art missiles closer to the population centres of the US. The siting of Soviet SS-20s was used as a justification for the siting of cruise and Pershing, but they did not have the capacity to strike the US. It was for the Soviets exactly the kind of threat that the US had argued it faced from

Soviet missiles if they were based in Cuba. To counteract that threat would have required a vast technological advance and the spending necessary to achieve this.

During the first years of the 1980s, hundreds of thousands of people mobilised across these countries to try to prevent the siting of the missiles. During this time, the peace movement had strong public support in addition to those who actually turned out to protest; across the five countries that would receive the new missiles, approval of the peace movement ranged between 55 and 81 per cent.[3] The driving force for this popular support was straightforward. Since the Cuban Missile Crisis, it had generally been assumed that the ability of the US and Soviet Union to annihilate each other many times over meant that no government would be mad enough to actually start a nuclear war. The prospect of 'mutual assured destruction' was believed to mean that deterrence worked and that meant, coupled with détente and arms-limitation talks, that popular fear of nuclear war had receded. Cruise and Pershing missiles changed all that. The possibility of a 'limited nuclear war' in Europe, with western and eastern Europe, and the European parts of the Soviet Union in the battleground, produced a reaction of extreme alarm, not only amongst the inhabitants of the countries where the war was likely to take place, but also where the missiles were to be deployed. They would equally become obvious targets.

The argument from NATO leaders was that the missiles were a necessary response to the Soviet SS-20 missiles being stationed in eastern Europe since 1977. For their part, the Soviets argued that the SS-20s were permissible under SALT I, being replacements for existing missiles. SS-20s were more accurate and reliable than earlier systems, but the real significance of the new NATO missiles was that they made feasible the prospect of 'limited nuclear war' confined to the European theatre. As Owen Green wrote in a CND pamphlet in 1983, 'Only the argument that cruise is part of a programme to enable NATO actually to fight a nuclear war makes sense . . . Out of all the various categories of nuclear war that NATO's esoteric nuclear doctrine identifies, ground-launched cruise missiles are only suitable for two; a nuclear war initially limited to Europe in the hope of preserving the territories of the two superpowers, and as part of a massive nuclear strike on the USSR designed to destroy Soviet military facilities before they can be used against us.'[4] In fact, this analysis was rather borne out by the government's own glossy publication, entitled, *Cruise missiles – a vital part of the West's Life Insurance*. This stated:

> *Ultimately we need the most powerful long-range nuclear weapons such as Polaris to convince the Russians that however much force they used they could not win. But if we only had nuclear weapons like Polaris, and were in danger of defeat, we could be faced with two stark choices – surrender or all-out nuclear war. Having smaller medium-range nuclear weapons could give us another choice in those circumstances – allowing us to bring home to the Russians the appalling risks they would run if they pressed us further. The aim of using them would be to persuade the Russian leadership – even at the eleventh hour – to draw back.*[5]

In other words, this promoted the idea of using cruise within Europe to avoid the superpowers attacking each other with long-range missiles! This idea of 'limiting' nuclear war to Europe provoked horror in the countries where it would take place.

The missiles were also expensive. In December 1979, Carter had called for an increase of 5 per cent on defence spending, raising the budget to $165 billion in 1981, but under Ronald Reagan, who became president in January 1981, the US military budget was increased by over 40 per cent and was funded by inflows of capital from Japan, the third world and, to a lesser extent, western Europe.[6]

The international context

For the peace movement, the advance notice of the deployment of cruise and Pershing was a real challenge, because it presented the opportunity to build so great an opposition that the governments would be forced to change their minds. After all, production and deployment of the neutron bomb had been prevented. But the international political context had changed significantly, even in those few years since Carter reversed the neutron bomb decision. The US had been on the back foot since the end of the Vietnam War, and domestic opinion in the US was fiercely against US troops being sent to war. From the point of view of the US leaders, the only way to prevent more reverses was a further attempt to break the power of the Soviet Union – by putting an ever-increasing strain upon the Soviet economy through arms spending. The smaller Soviet economy required a far higher proportion of output, more than double, to be allocated to match US spending on defence. So every increase in military spending by the US required effectively more than double the effort from the Soviet Union. Reagan was well aware of this situation. In fact, just a few months before his election he told the *Washington Post*, 'Right now we are hearing of strikes and labor disputes [in the Soviet Union] because people aren't getting enough to eat. They've diverted so much to military spending that they can't provide for consumer needs.' Convinced that the way to defeat the Soviet Union was through arms spending, he concluded, 'So far as an arms race is concerned, there's one going on right now, but there's only one side racing.'[7]

The arms race that Ronald Reagan initiated, which included the Strategic Defense Initiative (also known as Star Wars because of its sci-fi characteristics, using infra-red sensors and lasers to track and destroy missiles) and finally broke the Soviet economy, would not have been possible for the US alone. It would have placed an unacceptable burden on the US population. But Reagan drew on the resources of Japan, western Europe and the third world as never before, with capital inflows rising to more than $120 billion a year during the 1980s. The US also ruthlessly exploited the division that had occurred between the Soviet Union and China since the 1960s. By the late 1970s, the US had established a de facto alliance with China, thus enabling it to focus its energies on the isolated Soviet Union. As Fred Halliday has pointed out, 'Had the US faced even a low-key Peking-Moscow alliance, Washington would have felt much less confident about launching the Second Cold War than it did.'[8]

President Reagan always made his views absolutely clear. At his first press conference he announced that, 'Détente is a one-way street the Soviet Union has used to pursue its own aims.'[9] Ferociously anti-communist – he had been a champion of McCarthyism in the 1940s – he had no qualms about designating the Soviet Union 'the evil empire' and pledging to lead the free world in its struggle against communism. Of course he found a willing ally in Britain's new Prime Minister Margaret Thatcher. Together they redefined conservative politics into a militant crusade to impose their version of free-market politics and democracy. Reagan received widespread support for his approach in the US. Even though Carter had increased military spending and initiated the deployment of cruise and Pershing missiles, his presidency was characterised as a period of US weakness: there had been a long-drawn out crisis over US hostages held in Iran. Whatever the later consequences, at that time the Soviet Union had sent troops into Afghanistan, and US citizens were facing an economic squeeze as OPEC oil price rises hit the consumer at the petrol pumps. Reagan's gung-ho approach won many hearts and minds amongst the US population.

British plans for Trident

In Britain, not only did the government announce that it would accept cruise missiles, it also announced in July 1980 that it was going to buy the US Trident C4 missile system as a replacement for Polaris. Polaris was due to reach the end of its life by the early 1990s, and if it was to be replaced a decision was due. (Much the same situation currently exists with Trident: a decision is due in parliament as to how or whether to proceed with a replacement.) In 1977, Jim Callaghan set up a committee to look into the Polaris replacement question, which did much of the leg work before Thatcher's government actually took the decision to go ahead with Trident. As had been the case with Polaris, the missiles would be supplied by the US, and the submarines and warheads would be British-made. This was to cost between £4.5 and £5 billion. In fact, in March 1982, the order was changed to the Trident D5 missile system; a new development announced by the US in October 1981 as part of a consolidation of the shift towards 'counterforce' weapons, to give the US nuclear war 'winning' capabilities. The move from the C4 order to the D5 was justified by the need to retain 'commonality' with the US. The D5 – a submarine-launched ballistic missile system – gave the US, according to Malcolm Chalmers writing for CND in 1984, 'the capability of destroying almost all Soviet land-based nuclear weapons missiles (ICBMs [intercontinental ballistic missiles]) in a "disarming first strike": a capability which threatens to add a new, and dangerous twist to the superpower arms race."[10]

Chalmers argued that Trident would not merely be a replacement for Polaris, it would actually be a major expansion of its nuclear force, in contravention of its stated commitment to multilateral disarmament. Trident was particularly dangerous because it was both a quantitative expansion of Britain's nuclear force and a qualitative one; it marked a change in the type of targets that Britain could attack.[11] The Polaris system had three 200-kiloton warheads on each missile and had been modernised to have a number of dummy or decoy warheads on each missile as well. (This modernisation – the Chevaline programme – had actually happened secretly during the 1970s, at a cost of £1 billion. It had only emerged during a debate in parliament about nuclear weapons in January 1980.[12]) But each missile could only be used against one target. The multiple warheads were designed to confuse ABM systems and would scatter over a specified area, perhaps ten miles apart; particularly suitable for targets such as cities. The major advance of Trident, however, was that the warheads were multiple independently targetable re-entry vehicles, which could be independently aimed to achieve the destruction of a much greater range of targets and would be accurate enough to destroy specific military targets such as missile silos and military command bunkers. This underlined Trident's first-strike capacity. Each missile would be able to carry up to 17 warheads, although under the unratified SALT II agreement, they should be restricted to 14. So the possible number of warheads on the Trident system was considerable: 4 submarines, with 16 missiles on each submarine, with 14 warheads per missile – a total of 896 missiles. If the maximum number of warheads was placed on each missile, the system would be able to destroy 14 times as many targets as the Polaris system. The range of delivery was also to be hugely increased, from the 2,500 miles of Polaris to 6,000 miles, which would cover the whole of the Soviet Union. The estimated cost now rose to £7.5 billion.

Protest and Survive and END

Another significant area of campaigning for CND was around the issue of civil defence. In February 1980, the BBC current affairs programme *Panorama* had revealed the realities of British civil defence planning. This included the government's *Protect and Survive* films that had been prepared for showing in the run-up to a nuclear war, giving the public instructions about what to do in the event of nuclear attack. The public reaction was one of major concern. In response the government produced a book of the same name, which became a by-word for government crassness in the face of widespread and genuine public anxiety. Following on from this, in August 1980, the government decided to increase 'home defence' spending by 20 per cent a year for the next three years. Bruce Kent, the catholic priest who was general secretary of CND at this time, called *Protect and Survive* 'ludicrous' and observed: 'Not only were the recommendations in themselves ridiculous (hide under the stairs for fourteen days, etc) but the message was clear. The nuclear deterrence that we were told was fool-proof was not so foolproof after all. If it was, then why all the concern for civil defence?'[13] In response, CND produced a pamphlet entitled, *Civil Defence: The Cruellest Confidence Trick*, which became a huge best-seller. It described *Protect and Survive* as 'a mass confidence trick, a public fraud of the most heartless kind because it deals in human lives.'[14] CND also, together with the Bertrand Russell Peace Foundation, published a pamphlet, written by the historian EP Thompson and others, entitled *Protest and Survive*. Later that year, a further version was published as a book by Penguin.[15] The basic argument of *Protest and Survive* was that use of the US-controlled missiles in a 'limited' war would mean 'the complete destruction of the "theatre" of western Europe and of Great Britain in particular.'[16] Through *Protest and Survive*, Thompson publicised the *Appeal for European Nuclear Disarmament* that had been launched on 28 April 1980. The *Appeal*, written by Thompson and others, was an initiative of the Bertrand Russell Peace Foundation together with CND, Pax Christi (the international Catholic peace organisation), the International Confederation for Disarmament and Peace and others. It called for a Europe free of nuclear weapons from Poland to Portugal, urging the peoples of each European country, east and west, to demand disarmament of their rulers. The *Appeal* made specific requests:

> *In particular, we ask the Soviet Union to halt production of SS-20 medium-range missiles and we ask the United States not to implement the decision to develop cruise missiles and Pershing II missiles for deployment in western Europe. We also urge the ratification of the SALT II agreement, as a necessary step towards the renewal of effective negotiations on general and complete disarmament.*[17]

Many well-known political, cultural and religious figures signed up to the *Appeal*, along with many thousands of people within the first few weeks, giving rise to the European Nuclear Disarmament movement, or END as it became known. Whilst there was clearly some overlap in support between

CND and END, as EP Thompson himself observed, 'END and CND are not identical, and although their policies complement each other, they are not the same.'[18] END decided not to build itself as a mass membership organisation that would have competed with CND; Thompson described END as 'a resource centre serving the British peace movement, and in close association with CND.'[19]

Mobilising against the missiles

Although END attempted to link up movements and intellectuals across Europe, its main effect was to add to the impact on public awareness about the missiles in Britain, and of course on public opinion – thereby putting pressure on the government – influenced by the mass demonstrations of CND. The peace camps at the bases – most notably the women's peace camp at Greenham Common – also played a significant role in this process.

Public concern about the threat of nuclear weapons was rising. Even by April 1980, an opinion poll showed that over 40 per cent thought a nuclear war was likely within 10 years.[20] This concern led some to take individual action to try to protect themselves: 'By that summer *New Scientist* estimated that there were already 300 firms in Britain marketing fallout shelters, radiation suits and the like.'[21] These futile efforts were encouraged by the home secretary, William Whitelaw, who commented: 'Most houses in this country offer a reasonable degree of protection against radioactive fallout from nuclear explosions and protection can be substantially improved by a series of quite simple do-it-yourself measures.'[22] Many were unconvinced by the government's absurd assurances and turned to protest in order to ensure their survival.

As Bruce Kent experienced at the time, CND was on 'the receiving end of this new interest . . . Week by week arrived more letters, more membership applications, more callers, more journalists, more requests for speakers, more orders for badges and leaflets . . . Our two small office rooms, which can't have amounted to more than 300 square feet in total, were jammed with volunteers, Council members and existing staff . . . By the end of 1980 we were in new offices, themselves soon becoming too small. New memberships poured in by the hundreds every week. The graph which we had on the wall outgrew the wall and had to be taken across the ceiling.'[23] Between 1979 and 1984, CND's national membership grew from 4,267 to 90,000. Local membership increased to 250,000, and rallies and protests attracted enormous numbers.[24] Other initiatives also developed around nuclear disarmament, reflecting the extremely broad nature of the support for it. The Medical Campaign against Nuclear Weapons was launched in 1980, as was the World Disarmament Campaign (WDC). WDC was founded by Lords Fenner Brockway and Philip Noel-Baker, two eminent and very long-standing veteran peace activists. Emphasising multilateralism, the WDC put great hopes in the second UN Special Session on Disarmament in 1982, after the success of the first Session in 1978, but were sadly disappointed by its failure to achieve positive outcomes.

The growth of local groups

As protest began in 1980, in many areas no CND group existed. Many local activist groups grew up rapidly, and later joined themselves to CND. Joan Ruddock, who became chair of CND in 1981, became involved in this way:

> *I helped to launch an anti-cruise group on 17 June 1980, the day the government announced that it would allow 96 cruise missiles to be sited at Greenham Common. Our*

small Newbury group was able to respond to the consider-
able media interest in the base, actively contribute to
what became Southern Region CND, and later provide
substantial support for the women's peace camp. In
common with many other groups, we campaigned for
over a year before we decided to become a CND group.[25]

Across the country during the early 1980s there was a huge
proliferation of groups that worked in many ways on many
different issues, stimulating campaigning and raising the
issues in the local communities. Rae Street, a dedicated CND
activist and currently a vice-chair of CND, describes how the
Littleborough Peace Group was developed and its range of
activities:

Back in the days of demonstrations against the US
nuclear-armed submarines at Holy Loch, in 1960, a
CND group was formed in Rochdale, a Lancashire town
with a long tradition of social justice movements; indeed,
the home of the Co-operative Movement. Rochdale CND
kept going through the 60s and 70s. It even had a
member from India who was so impressed that, when he
returned to India, he formed a CND group there. At the
end of the 70s, with the announcement of the arrival of
cruise missiles and the general repressive climate which
started with the Thatcher government, the group had an
increase in membership. At the same time there had been
new younger people coming into the town, but living in
the areas outside the centre near the moorland, for exam-
ple, the industrial village of Littleborough. A group of
those got together and decided to form a separate group in
June 1981. There was much discussion at the first meet-
ing as to whether it should be Littleborough CND, but

Littleborough Peace Group was agreed upon, following a strongly made argument that the group should have a positive face: for peace but against war and weapons of mass destruction. But from the beginning everyone wanted to be affiliated to CND; the members thought of themselves as CND-ers and the local public certainly saw no distinction. The symbol by the early 80s was so well known. At the first meeting there were nine women and two men. This was to be significant as in the next years these women were to be the core group of the Pennine Women for Peace and the local Greenham Women. The whole Greenham Women's movement had a huge impact on campaigning for nuclear disarmament. Women did feel empowered and, even though the US nuclear base, outside Newbury, was a long distance from Littleborough, they would join to visit the base, camp for weeks at a time or arrange fundraising to support the Camp. From the great surge of feeling against the dangers of nuclear weapons, being imposed from the UK government colluding with the US government, came a well spring of energy for campaigning. There were local vigils, street demonstrations, leaflets – such as 'What is Trident doing in Rochdale?' There were demonstrations at bases in the north of England; Burtonwood, Menwith Hill, Fylingdales. Many members took part in wider groupings, either through women's networks or international links. For example in 1985, one member became interested, through a Greenham Women's meeting held in Manchester Town Hall, in working with the US anti-nuclear and peace movements and still works closely with them to this day. Similarly, there was a link with the newly formed European Nuclear Disarmament, and a member who went to their second meeting in Berlin in 1983 took an

top left: Pat Arrowsmith and Guy Wilson on the campaign for Crusade for World Government demonstration, Torquay late 1940s

left: DAC North Pickenham demonstration, 1958

below: First four-day 50-mile march from London to Aldermaston, 5 April 1958

above: Aldermaston march, 1959

left: Preparing for Polaris protest, Holy Loch, 2 March 1961

below: Game of tag with police, Polaris protest, Holy Loch, 3 March 1961

above: Anti-Vietnam protest in
front of London Premises of
Elliott Automation Ltd,
3 November 1968

right: Non-Violent Action in
Vietnam volunteers meeting,
Phnom Penh 1968
(Graham Keen)

left: Arrest of protester at Greenham Common, early 1980s (Ed Barber)

below: Protesters blockading at Greenham Common, early 1980s (Ed Barber)

bottom: Embrace the base, Greenham Common, December 1982; 30,000 women link arms around the base and decorate the fence (Ed Barber)

above: Bruce Kent speaking at CND rally,
Barrow-in-Furness, 27 October 1984 (Melanie Friend)

below: Hiroshima Day, Brighton, 1985 (Melanie Friend)

above: CND protest against
  Trident, 1990s

left: 50th anniversary of
  Hiroshima, Parliament Square,
  6 August 1995 (Paul Aston)

above: 'Non' to French testing: President Chirac announced the resumption of tests in the Pacific, 1995

below: CND protest at MoD: the world's nuclear weapon states are shown to be bringers of death and destruction, 1998 (Sue Longbottom)

above left: Mayor of London Ken Livingstone and Rev Jesse Jackson lead the biggest ever anti-war demonstration in London, 15 February 2003 (Sue Longbottom)

above right: Don't Attack Iraq demonstration, 15 February 2003 (Sue Longbottom)

left: Stop Bush cavalcade: while the US and UK search for mythical WMD in Iraq, Kate Hudson points the finger at British nukes, 19 November 2003 (Sue Longbottom)

active part until the last meeting in 1992. Another member became involved in non-violent direct action and has repeatedly challenged the legality of the Trident base at Faslane in Scotland (not an easy journey from Littleborough) and been fined. The work goes on.[26]

The great strength of CND at this time, coming out of the 1970s as a relatively small organisation, was to embrace this spontaneous upsurge of groups and activities, to share its knowledge and experience, its ability to articulate public concerns, and to give direction to the mass mobilisations that followed. The wisdom of the CND leadership in responding in this way was considerable.

The mass demonstrations

Throughout 1980, many demonstrations took place across the country, numbering in the thousands, but still small compared with what was to come. Of considerable importance at this time was the shift to the left of the Labour Party. This was demonstrated very significantly in the summer of 1980, when the Labour Party NEC organised the first large London demonstration against the missiles. This was the time when Tony Benn was almost elected as deputy leader of the Labour Party, being narrowly defeated by Denis Healey. The Party conducted strong campaigning against the missiles and unemployment, and that autumn the Labour Party Conference took up a unilateralist position.

But the first really major demonstration was held by CND under the slogan 'Protest and Survive' on 26 October 1980. Participants numbered over 80,000 at the final rally in Trafalgar Square. By the end of the year, CND had set up or revived loose regional structures to help support groups and increase communication and coordination. Throughout 1981, protests and demonstrations throughout the country were increasing in size: 16,000 protested in Sheffield; 10,000 went on a Trans-Pennine march; 20,000 attended a march and rally in Clydeside; the Glastonbury festival was run in aid of CND. This is to mention just a few of the enormous range and diversity of events throughout that year. October 1981 was the time of a remarkable mobilisation throughout Europe. Within a six-week period, massive demonstrations took place in many countries across Europe: 250,000 in Bonn, 10,000 in Oslo, 50,000 in Paris, 50,000 in Potsdam, 80,000 in Helsinki, 120,000 in Brussels and hundreds of thousands in Rome.[27] In London the turnout was in the region of 250,000. As Bruce Kent described it: 'The park was full. It was, from the platform, an amazing spectacle, with moving crowds of people as far as the eye could see, right down to the edge of the Serpentine. We claimed 250,000 and that seemed a modest guess to me.'[28] Similar numbers mobilised in June 1982, when President Reagan visited Britain at the height of the Falklands War.

Nuclear-free zones

An early and very important initiative began in November 1980 when, inspired by the encouragement of nuclear-free zones in the UN Special Session on Disarmament report, Manchester City Council declared itself a 'nuclear-free zone' and invited other local authorities to declare themselves nuclear-free too. Within two years, over 140 had followed Manchester's example. According to Philip Bolsover, 'They opposed the manufacture, deployment or use of nuclear weapons within their boundaries, and they rejected civil defence.'[29] The test of the nuclear-free local authorities movement came in 1982, with the government's planned nuclear civil defence exercise, called Hard Rock. Home Secretary

William Whitelaw was forced to cancel the exercise when 24 out of 52 county councils in England and Wales refused to co-operate and another 7 were only partially co-operating. The government made some attempts to force local authorities to comply but eventually gave up. By 1984, the Nuclear-Free Zone movement had become truly international, with nuclear-free zones in Australia, New Zealand, Ireland, the Netherlands, Belgium, West Germany, Norway, Denmark, Italy, Greece, Japan and the US.[30] CND followed up the failure of Hard Rock by introducing its own campaign, called Hard Luck. This was designed to inform local authorities of the real implications of a nuclear attack on their locality, with detailed information researched by Scientists Against Nuclear Arms.[31]

Greenham

From this period of campaigning, one of the most exceptional initiatives was the women's peace camp at Greenham Common, which is vividly remembered, even today, by peace activists around the world. In August 1981, a group of 36 women from South Wales, called Women for Life on Earth, together with a few men, walked from Cardiff to the US air force base at Greenham Common, where the first UK delivery of cruise missiles was due to be received in 1983. When they arrived, they demanded a discussion about nuclear weapons with the British government. As it was not forthcoming, the women decided to set up a peace camp at the base. In 1982, the camp became women-only, with a strong feminist emphasis, publicising the slogan 'Take the toys away from the boys'. Widespread support for the camp developed, although there were numerous ongoing debates from outside about whether actions should be women-only, and the protests and actions at the base again raised the issue within CND of direct action. In any case, the camp was an independent initiative, unrelated to CND – although CND did support it with fundraising and publicity – but many CND women supported and participated in the camp. On 12 December 1982, around 30,000 women linked arms to embrace the base, around its 90-mile perimeter fence, decorating it with symbols of life, children's toys and pictures. Many women undertook radical changes in their lives in order to participate in the protest. Christine wanted to act to protect her children:

> *My husband didn't understand and didn't like me getting involved outside the home. When I wanted to go to Greenham it was the last straw. He said, 'You either stay at home and be a proper wife and mother, or you go to Greenham, but not both.' After learning all about nuclear weapons I couldn't pretend they didn't exist: we're on a brink of another Hiroshima all the time. I've got to go to court for custody of the children soon, and my lawyer said, 'Whatever you do, don't tell the judge you've been to Greenham and you're in CND, or he might not let you keep the kids.' Since going to Greenham, my own family have rejected me and feel I've disgraced them, but my friends have been very supportive.*[32]

Lawrence Wittner describes in *The Struggle Against the Bomb: Volume Three* the activity thus:

> *In the ensuing months and years, thousands of women activists settled at Greenham Common to continue resistance efforts – blocking the gate with their bodies, cutting or pulling down the perimeter fence (including four miles of it on October 29, 1983) painting peace symbols on US planes, and even dancing and singing defiantly atop the cruise missile silos. Buffeted by icy storms in winter,*

> *evicted from their tent colonies repeatedly (and some-*
> *times brutally), assailed as bizarre and disreputable by*
> *the mass media, the women of Greenham Common hung*
> *on tenaciously.*[33]

The creative approach to protest by the Greenham women often left the authorities nonplussed, as was the case at the time of the first major trial of the women in Newbury, in February 1983. Sarah Benton reported at the time:

> *The magistrates had left the court to consider their deci-*
> *sion. Inside, 44 women were on trial; at the back of the*
> *room sat a score of women supporters. As the magistrates*
> *walked out, 30 police officers unexpectedly filed in and,*
> *standing shoulder to shoulder, lined up in front of the*
> *supporters, preventing them from seeing the defendants*
> *and, presumably, from engaging in one of those willful*
> *and anarchic gestures against authority which have been*
> *the women's hallmark so far. Reacting in unspoken*
> *accord, defendants and supporters rose, stood on their*
> *chairs and, leaning over the police officers' heads, held*
> *hands. Then they began to sing, and continued to sing*
> *after the magistrates had returned, banged their gavels*
> *and cried in exasperation 'Ladies, please.'*[34]

CND also found new forms of protest, linking with the Greenham women at Easter 1983 when, instead of the more traditional march from Aldermaston, or even a march from Aldermaston to Greenham, a 14-mile human chain was formed, linking Aldermaston and Greenham, via the Royal Ordnance Factory at Burghfield, which was the final assembly point for Britain's nuclear weapons. Tens of thousands participated. Other peace camps, some mixed, grew up at other bases, such as Molesworth, Upper Heyford, Fairford, Welford, Burtonwood and Bridgend.[35] Yet more were initiated around the world, in the US, Canada, Australia and Holland. The women remained at Greenham even after the siting of the missiles and stayed until they had finally been removed. Writing in 1985, Caroline Moorehead reported, 'They have . . . no intention of leaving; their presence, their witness, is undefeatable. Furthermore there are few surprises left: pigheaded, perhaps, but also courageous, the women have survived four winters; they have been cold, hungry and frightened; repeatedly manhandled by police.'[36] The courage and commitment of the Greenham women is now legendary, and they continue to be an inspiration to peace activists today.

Molesworth and other actions

CND's Christian activists focused much of their campaigning on the bases too, in particular at Molesworth, which was due to receive the second installment of cruise missiles, after Greenham Common. In 1982, the Fellowship of Reconciliation established a peace camp there. Christian CND, a specialist section of CND founded in 1960, gave it considerable support and, according to Valerie Flessati, it was the focus for a number of controversies:

> *The first concerned an All Faiths Peace Chapel, 'Eirene', which peace campers had started to build on part of the base. This chapel became a symbol of resistance to the military use of land at Molesworth, especially after the rest of the peace camp was evicted and the base was fenced. Daily requests were made for access to pray by the unfinished chapel behind the wire, but they were always refused. Although it was not consecrated the chapel had been blessed. The Ministry of Defence consulted the*

Church of England about its status before deciding to destroy it. Eventually the chapel was bulldozed.[37]

Another issue arose over a piece of land that the Church was intending to sell to the MoD for expansion of the base at Molesworth. Christian CND tried to buy the land instead and went to the High Court to try to get an injunction to stop the sale to the MoD. Eventually the Church withdrew the sale. Polls showed that 23 per cent of CND's supporters were church members[38] and they were extremely active throughout this period, holding services, pilgrimages, vigils, a Peace Pentecost at Upper Heyford base in 1983, holding hands round the MoD, linking up with faith groups across the world, having dialogue with decision makers – a huge range of activities.[39]

During the early 1980s, huge numbers of protestors were arrested, going some way towards indicating the scale of opposition to the missiles throughout the country, although of course hundreds of thousands more protested in non-arrestable ways. In 1984, the *New Statesman* magazine began to keep a 'peace protests roll call', listing the numbers of those arrested in peaceful direct action against cruise missiles. Their first roll call, between 1981 and March 1984, listed the following locations and numbers – and no doubt there were many more that went unrecorded – arrested for a wide range of different actions:

Upper Heyford United States Air Force (USAF) base: 1000
Greenham USAF base: 1775
RAF Waddington: 5
Brawdy US tracking station: 3
Leeds: 17
London: 666

High Wycombe RAF base: 183
Molesworth/Alconbury: 51
Little Rissington USAF Hospital: 7
Boscombe Down Action Group: 3
Porton Down: 12
Bude, Cornwall: 10
RAF Cottesmore, Leics: 5
Bishopscourt Peace Camp, Co. Down: 12
Scotland: 176
Brighton: 11
Southampton: 13[40]

The campaign against CND

The sheer scale of protest did begin to have an impact on governments. As Canadian Prime Minister Pierre Trudeau observed in 1982, 'Only the deaf cannot hear the clamour arising all over the world against the arms race.'[41] When Reagan ordered production of the neutron bomb in 1981, no western European country agreed to have it deployed on its territory. Production of the neutron bomb, designed to be used against Soviet tanks in Europe, was eventually banned by US Congress in 1984. But having no intention of capitulating further to the protesters, the British government also carried out its own attempts to counter the growing strength of CND and anti-missile opinion. During 1981, this was more or less confined to encouraging the media to limit CND's access and coverage. But as public support increased, the government put more energy into its anti-CND campaign, much of it focused around suggesting that CND was funded by the Soviet Union. Bruce Kent's response to this was to offer a prize of £100 to anyone who could produce evidence of Soviet funding. No one came forward to claim the prize, but wild accusations abounded, such as that from Lord Chalfont that the Soviet Union were funding the European peace movement to the tune of £100 million a year. 'If they were', said Bruce Kent, 'it was certainly not getting to our grotty little office in Finsbury Park.'[42] From the beginning of 1983, Michael Heseltine was defence secretary and established DS19, a team within the MoD, to organise the campaign against CND. Heseltine's main angle was that CND's aim was the advancement of communism. This also tied in with the general election that was in the offing; the Conservatives did much to try to link CND and the Labour Party's support for unilateral disarmament – still not popular with the voters – as a way of distracting attention from the major issue of cruise missiles. Attention also came from MI5 and Bruce Kent commented that they spied on CND efficiently:

> *But for brave Cathy Massiter, who left the Service and blew the whistle, we might never have known that nice old Harry Newton, who stuffed envelopes as a volunteer, was actually a government informer. Not that there were many secrets to reveal. I used to chat with him over the sink at 11 Goodwin Street, and for my pains he reported me to his superiors as a pseudo-marxist, which sounds even worse than being a real one.*[43]

A number of attacks came from an organisation called the Coalition for Peace through Security, which disrupted events, sent a spy into the CND office and tried to link Bruce Kent with the IRA. The Coalition opted for slogans like 'Disarmament equals surrender', and was endorsed by leading Conservative politicians, who were at pains to make out that there were links between CND and the Soviet Union. 'One of its multicoloured brochures, adorned with a nuclear disarmament symbol blending into a red hammer and sickle, spelt out the acronym CND as "Communists, Neutralists, Defeatists".'[44]

Pressure on the US

In spite of these rearguard actions against anti-missile campaigns, the protests remained a source of increasing concern to western European governments, which in turn put pressure on the US to resume negotiations about intermediate nuclear forces (INF) – in other words, cruise and Pershing missiles. There was considerable disagreement about this within the Reagan administration, but eventually Reagan decided to make moves toward arms control talks. As Reagan himself said, 'My proposal of the . . . zero option sprang out of the realities of nuclear politics in western Europe. Now that I was in office and the American-made INF missiles were being scheduled for shipment to Europe, some European leaders were having doubts about the policy . . . Thousands of Europeans were taking to the streets and protesting.'[45] The US put forward what was known as the 'zero option' proposal. This meant that the Soviet Union should withdraw its intermediate-range nuclear weapons from Europe and Asia, and in return the US would not put cruise and Pershing into western Europe. There was considerable criticism of this proposal – which was stated to be non-negotiable – as many thought it was cynically designed to be unacceptable to the Soviets. This would give the US the propaganda advantage of having made an overture towards disarmament that had been rejected.

Yet in spite of the zero option supposedly being non-negotiable, the US was under such pressure from Europe that it was forced to move on INF talks. In March 1983, Reagan announced what was described as the 'interim solution' on the way to the zero option. The US would reduce its planned deployment of missiles into western Europe in exchange for the Soviet Union cutting back its missiles to a comparable number. It soon became clear, however, that this was mere gesture politics to defuse opposition. Events rapidly showed that Reagan had no real interest in arms control. Political changes in the Soviet Union brought this fact out into the open. In November 1982, Soviet leader Leonid Brezhnev died after a long period of ill-health. The new Soviet leader was Yuri Andropov, who had been head of the KGB. Andropov was a moderniser, committed to increasing the efficiency and productivity of the Soviet Union, and also to improving relations with the West. In March 1983, he called for an East-West summit, urged arms reduction and offered to cut back SS-20s in Europe. He also proposed nuclear-free zones in parts of Europe and the Mediterranean, together with a ban on arms sales to the third world. This was a major shift in the Soviet approach and represented a programme of actions that could have created an entirely new situation in Europe. Andropov also came up with another idea that was of major significance. At a meeting of the Warsaw Pact earlier in January 1983, he had proposed that NATO and the Warsaw Pact should agree not to use force against each other – but also that they should not use force against members of their own blocs. This would have overturned the so-called 'Brezhnev Doctrine' in eastern Europe, which had been defined in 1968 when the Soviet Union intervened in Czechoslovakia – the concept that the Soviet Union reserved the right to use force to maintain its sphere of influence in eastern Europe.

Reagan's 'Star Wars' initiative
A few days later, Reagan described the Soviet leaders as 'the focus of evil in the modern world'.[46] This was a president

determined to confront and try to break – not make – agreements with the Soviet Union. Two weeks later, Reagan announced his Strategic Defense Initiative (SDI), which was designed to eventually give the US the ability to make a nuclear attack on the Soviet Union and protect itself from Soviet retaliation. This was guaranteed to provoke a massive acceleration of the nuclear arms race and was a real slap in the face to Andropov. Clearly the US administration was not interested in détente and peaceful coexistence with the Soviet Union. It was set on systematically upping the ante in the arms race until the Soviet economy cracked. The SDI proposal had the advantage that it could be presented as being 'defensive'. In the US the newly-formed Nuclear Freeze Campaign, which worked to halt further testing, production and deployment of nuclear weapons, had developed extremely broad support. Reagan had gained some support for his militaristic policies by claiming that a 'weak' US was threatened by the Soviet Union. But there was still profound unease about the threat of nuclear weapons. A survey conducted by the Public Agenda Foundation in 1984 showed that: '96 per cent of the sample believe that "picking a fight with the Soviet Union is too dangerous in a nuclear world" and 89 per cent that "both the USA and the USSR would be completely destroyed" in an all-out nuclear war; indeed 83 per cent – who had by then followed the reports on the nuclear winter – said that "we cannot be certain that life on earth will continue after a nuclear war."'[47]

By November 1982, the demand for a freeze had been balloted in 11 US states and had been carried in 10 of them. Catholic bishops had spoken out but, most worryingly of all for Reagan, the majority of Republican voters supported a freeze. SDI gave Reagan the opportunity to change the rhetoric by shifting the emphasis to defence and security. EP

Thompson commented thus on Reagan's speech in which he launched SDI: 'He offered to change the course of history, and to provide new hope for our children in the 21st century. The very idea of deterrence through the threat of retaliation was "immoral". He out-homilied the bishops and he stole the freeze movement's clothes while it was bathing. The human spirit must be capable of rising above dealing with other nations and human beings by threatening their existence.'[48] Thompson described Reagan's speech as a work of genius and no doubt it contributed to his re-election in 1984.

Initially, however, little attention was paid to SDI in Europe, as the focus remained on campaigning against the deployment of cruise and Pershing missiles. It only hit the headlines in a big way in Europe when Reagan gave it a huge plug in his inaugural speech in January 1985. Reagan was well aware that such a system would contravene the Anti-Ballistic Missile Treaty (ABM Treaty) signed by the US and Soviet Union in 1972, which had been designed to ensure that neither party would risk attacking the other, through fear of retaliation. SDI was not well received in Moscow. Andropov described Washington's rhetoric towards the Soviet Union as 'flippant' and 'irresponsible' and objected to Reagan's failure to engage properly in the new Strategic Arms Reduction Talks (START) and the INF negotiations. Although Andropov had made positive overtures towards the US, he made it quite clear that he would take a strong stand if necessary: 'All attempts at achieving military superiority over the USSR are futile. The Soviet Union will never let that happen. It will never be caught defenceless by any threat, let there be no mistake about this in Washington. It is time they stopped devising one option after another in the search for the best ways of unleashing nuclear war in the hope of winning it. Engaging in this is not just irresponsible. It is insane.'[49]

The 1983 general election

At the general election of June 1983 the Conservative Party was re-elected and the vote of the Labour Party was reduced from 36.9 per cent in 1979 to 28.3 per cent. Labour had gone into the election under the leadership of one of CND's founders and longstanding supporters, Michael Foot, committed to British unilateral nuclear disarmament, and the media and the right wing of the Labour Party rushed to make Foot's defence policy responsible for the defeat. According to Michael Foot, Labour MP Gerald Kaufman – who was elected on the basis of the Labour Manifesto – described it as the 'longest suicide note in history', but it was Kaufman that was out of step. The bulk of the Party was committed to unilateral nuclear disarmament. Foot intended to advance this and also to take broader initiatives:

> We put forward an intelligent approach to CND's issues in the Manifesto. What we were proposing if we had won the election on that issue would be to put forward measures not only for abolishing nuclear weapons here – and we were not departing from unilateral disarmament – but we would also be putting forward proposals for securing nuclear disarmament internationally: to open discussions on getting rid of nuclear weapons across the whole field.[50]

But it was not just Labour members who took this kind of view. In fact, there were clear majorities in opinion polls against cruise, Trident and US nuclear bases in Britain. The key factor in the Labour defeat was the split of the Social Democratic Party from Labour, which succeeded in massively cutting the Labour vote and splitting opposition to the Tories. Although the Conservative vote fell, and they were outpolled by Labour and the SDP combined, they won the election. As Lawrence Wittner has observed, this election 'was not an endorsement of the government's nuclear policy.'[51]

At the same time, Labour was not helped by ineffective explanations of its policy and attacks on it from within the Labour Party leadership itself. Walter Wolfgang, a longstanding CND activist in the Labour Party, accused James Callaghan and other prominent Labour figures of trying 'to sabotage that policy during the election campaign,' and there can be no doubt that this played some role in the defeat. Bruce Kent also supports this view: 'James Callaghan, as disloyal as any Militant and just as dangerous, finally torpedoed Michael Foot's attempt to defend a non-nuclear policy by making it clear in the middle of the election that he did not agree with what was then Labour policy.'[52] Michael Foot himself corroborates the unwelcome nature of Callaghan's speech.[53]

Labour's early unilateralist position had been defeated at the Labour Party Conference in 1960, under the leadership of Hugh Gaitskell. However, the issue kept coming back onto the agenda, and unilateralist motions were passed at a number of party conferences. In 1973, such a motion was carried by 704,000 votes.[54] In the 1974 general election, Labour's Manifesto had pledged not to develop a new generation of nuclear weapons to succeed Polaris, but in government this was ignored by both Wilson and Callaghan. At each Labour Party Conference between 1974 and 1977, attempts were made to reaffirm the 1973 position, but each time the party's National Executive Committee recommended that it be remitted, and this was accepted with trade union support.[55]

However, the situation changed with the anti-missile campaigning. As Walter Wolfgang observed: 'In 1980 the first large London demonstration against cruise and Trident was in fact sponsored by the Labour NEC . . . The subsequent Labour Party Conference in 1980 committed the Party to unilateral nuclear disarmament. This commitment was reaffirmed by the 1981 and 1982 party conferences.'[56] The shift in attitude was also evident in the trade union movement. At the TUC Conference in 1981, a resolution calling for British unilateral nuclear disarmament was passed, as were resolutions calling for the removal of all nuclear bases from Britain in 1982 and 1983. By 1985, around 28 national trade unions were affiliated to CND. Foot also pursued multilateral initiatives towards disarmament, and during the election campaign itself, Labour focused on cancelling cruise, Trident and the development of all new nuclear weapons. But the Conservatives made great play, along with most of the press, about the claimed weakness of Labour's defence policies that would supposedly leave Britain at the mercy of Soviet aggression. Thatcher argued that, 'The only alternative to nuclear deterrence is surrender or capitulation.'[57] A dirty tricks campaign was also conducted against Foot to undermine his campaign. A group called The 61, partly funded by the CIA to operate against peace movements, 'helped to plant disparaging stories about Foot in the press and to produce a poster comparing Foot to Neville Chamberlain, returning in 1938 from Munich.'[58] Other factors in Labour's defeat included the Falklands War of 1982, where the victory had been popular with many of the electorate.

The Korean Air Lines tragedy

After the election, Michael Heseltine announced that CND was dead and buried, but this was far from true. CND's membership continued to grow, from 75,000 in 1983 to over 100,000 in 1985, with a paid staff of 40. CND held the largest demonstration in its history in October 1983 with 400,000 in Hyde Park. This continued increase in membership and support was not surprising, given the increasingly tense global situation.

In August 1983, a South Korean Air Lines jumbo jet was shot down over Soviet airspace by a Soviet fighter plane, killing all 269 passengers. The plane, which was flying from New York to Anchorage in Alaska, via Seoul in South Korea, had gone 365 miles off course and was flying over a sensitive Soviet security zone. At the same time a US surveillance plane was also in the area, and it has never been made clear whether the two events were linked and the jumbo jet was connected in some way to a US intelligence mission. Whatever the reasons for the terrible incident, the US leadership made the full mileage out of it. President Reagan called it a 'terrorist act' and 'a crime against humanity'. But certain evidence gave rise to suspicions that all was not as simple as it looked. Tapes of the conversation between the Soviet fighter pilot and the ground control station revealed that he had 'followed all the international protocols for warning a civilian airliner that it was off course. Having gone through all these manoeuvres, the Soviet pilot, as a final warning, then fired tracers across the bow of the airliner. When, astonishingly, this still failed to get a response, Soviet military ground control concluded that the Korean jumbo jet must be a US military reconnaissance plane on a spying mission and ordered the shoot-down.'[59] These tapes were in the hands of the US authorities but they only produced edited selections and did not reveal this part of it. Following this, US-Soviet relations became even worse than ever, and Andropov, who was ill at this time, took a hard line towards the US. Whilst apologising for the loss of life, he stated that the airliner incident was a deliberate US provocation and accused the US authorities of 'extreme adventurism' in a 'criminal act'.[60] President Reagan took the opportunity of heightened tension with the Soviet Union to increase military spending.

In October 1983, the US invaded Grenada, an island in the Caribbean with a radical left-wing government. The US claimed that the island was about to be taken over by the Cubans with Soviet backing. There was no evidence to suggest this. There were 43 Cuban military advisers there, but Grenada was also a member of the British commonwealth, and a new landing strip was being built by a British company to promote tourism. Mrs Thatcher had to complain about the invasion of a Commonwealth country, but a condemnation of the invasion by the UN Security Council was vetoed by the US.

The missiles arrive

Notwithstanding vast public opposition, in November 1983, the deployment of cruise and Pershing missiles began in western Europe. The British government began to take a harder line towards those protesting at the bases. In November, Defence Minister Michael Heseltine told parliament that protestors who got too near to the missiles would be shot. The Labour spokesperson responded, 'There are gradations of defence. You don't defend missiles against unarmed women by shooting them.'[61] None were shot, but they were treated increasingly brutally by the police. In April 1984, police attempted to close down the camp at Greenham Common, tearing down the shelters and making numerous arrests. But the women came back and remained there in their hundreds until ultimately the missiles were removed. In February 1985, 3,000 soldiers and police arrived at Molesworth in the middle of the night to evict around a hundred, mostly Quaker, peace protestors. Denis Healey MP subsequently mocked Michael Heseltine, in parliament, for turning up to this eviction operation in a flak jacket!

Nevertheless, pressure mounted on the US from governments in western Europe who were feeling the squeeze from their electors over fears of the arms race and the possibility of nuclear war, in particular with cruise and Pershing missiles in Europe. An additional concern was over how the peace movements would react to the looming SDI. The Soviets had withdrawn from the INF and START talks when cruise and Pershing deployment had begun, and pressure was on the US to get them back to the negotiating table. Reagan was also under pressure domestically to make some move towards peace as he would be hard pressed by the Democrats on this issue in the forthcoming presidential election. In January 1984, Reagan made a very conciliatory speech, stating, 'My dream is to see the day when nuclear weapons will be banished from the face of the earth.'[62] Soviet leader Andropov died in February 1984, succeeded by Konstantin Chernenko, and Reagan's softly-softly attitude towards the Soviet Union continued throughout 1984 and his re-election that autumn. The Soviets indicated a willingness to go back into arms-limitation negotiations, and senior Soviet official Andrei Gromyko met with Reagan in the White House. A small thaw had begun.

5

Towards the end of the Cold War: the Gorbachev era

The election of Mikhail Gorbachev as general secretary of the Soviet Communist Party represented a fundamental policy change, following the deployment of cruise and Pershing missiles; namely that the Soviet economy could no longer sustain the arms race and therefore concessions should be made to US foreign policy. Mikhail Gorbachev brought a new approach to world politics. Elected as Soviet leader in March 1985, in August of that year he was quoted in *Time* magazine: 'Our countries simply cannot afford to allow matters to reach a confrontation. Herein lies the genuine interest of both the Soviet and American people. And this must be expressed in the language of practical politics. It is necessary to stop the arms race, to tackle disarmament, to normalise Soviet–American relations. Honestly it is time to make these relations between the two great peoples worthy of their historic role. For the destiny of the world, the destiny of world civilisation really depends on our relations. We are prepared to work in this direction.'[1]

Gorbachev had hard work ahead of him. Following the deployment of cruise and Pershing missiles in Europe in 1983, the Soviet Union had, in protest, refused to participate in arms negotiations. Talks between the two superpowers had restarted in January 1985, under the framework of Nuclear and Space

Talks. This included Strategic Arms Reduction Talks (START) and INF (ie cruise and Pershing missiles) talks. It also included so-called defensive weapons in space, posed by the SDI (aimed at enabling the US to make a nuclear attack on the Soviet Union and protect itself from Soviet retaliation), which Reagan had first raised in March 1983. Reagan was determined to go ahead with the development of the system and its deployment in outer space, even though it contravened the ABM Treaty. This made negotiations on START and INF even more difficult than they otherwise would have been.[2] Nevertheless, Gorbachev pressed ahead with his intentions.

In his speech upon election as party leader, Gorbachev spoke of the need for peaceful and co-operative relations with the capitalist world, and the need for an agreement to eliminate all nuclear weapons. In a subsequent speech he also spoke of the need to preserve military strategic parity with NATO to guarantee security for the socialist countries, but he made it clear that there was no 'fatal inevitability of confrontation' between the Soviet Union and the West.[3] Gorbachev's words were not empty rhetoric. In April 1985, he froze deployment of SS-20 missiles in Europe until November of that year, and offered to reduce those already deployed to 243, the number they had stood at before the INF negotiations were broken off. On 6 August 1985 – the 40th anniversary of the bombing of Hiroshima – he declared a moratorium on all underground nuclear testing, supplementing the Partial Test Ban Treaty of 1963. This came in response to a proposal to both the US and the Soviet Union by anti-nuclear retired US admirals LaRocque and Carroll. Reagan refused to comply, but Gorbachev took the proposal seriously and went ahead with it unilaterally.[4] In the autumn of 1985 he proposed a 50 per cent reduction of Soviet strategic nuclear forces in exchange for a ban on developing, testing and deploying space weapons, including SDI.

The US did not respond in kind to these initiatives. However, there was agreement to hold a summit meeting between Reagan and Gorbachev in Geneva in November 1985. This was an event of enormous global significance. Reagan rehearsed well for it: 'Reagan prepared for Geneva by speaking with former presidents Ford and Nixon, and by viewing videos of Gorbachev's visits to Britain and France. He even went through a full-dress rehearsal, with US Soviet specialist Jack Matlock playing the part of Gorbachev.'[5] As a result of the summit, both leaders agreed to co-operate in preventing a nuclear war and to begin the process of reducing their nuclear arms. They agreed that 'a nuclear war cannot be won and must never be fought.'[6] They both stated that they were willing to halve their countries' nuclear weapons.[7] Whilst the dialogue between the leaders was a very positive step forward, nevertheless, these were general statements of intent rather than concrete agreements. In addition, the US had made no concessions on SDI, the most threatening development of all for the Soviet Union.

Gorbachev was determined to bring about actual change and strode ahead with a visionary leadership for nuclear disarmament. In January 1986, he called for the elimination of all nuclear weapons by the year 2000, and included this commitment in the new Party Programme. Gorbachev outlined two phases of very detailed proposals to achieve nuclear disarmament over the 15-year period. The first phase, taking five to eight years, included the elimination of all ground-launched long-range intermediate nuclear forces in Europe and a freeze on British and French nuclear weapons. The second phase included the staggered elimination of all remaining nuclear weapons. In addition to this comprehensive proposal, Gorbachev also advanced changes in policy within the Soviet Union and the socialist countries. Backed by the

Soviet Communist Party in his disarmament initiatives, he adopted a new military doctrine of 'reasonable sufficiency', which was also embraced by the Warsaw Pact. But as Stephen White has pointed out, these were not simply doctrinal changes: 'There were substantial cuts in Soviet military spending and troop numbers from 1989 onwards, and much more information was made available on the structure and size of the military budget and on troops and weapons deployments, which themselves became more defensive in character.'[8]

Gorbachev came from the reforming wing within the Soviet leadership. The majority of the Soviet leadership believed that the Soviet Union could not afford the new spiral in the arms race that the second Reagan term would bring – most notably the deployment of cruise and Pershing missiles and the SDI initiative. So they elected Mikhail Gorbachev to reach a new accommodation with the West. His primary objective was to reform and regenerate the Soviet economy, and to gain the breathing space to do this, he had to ease tensions with the West and ease the drain of money into arms. In his book *Perestroika*, published in 1987, Gorbachev was very frank in his view that the US was using the arms race to damage the Soviet Union. He referred to the US's 'immoral intention to bleed the Soviet Union white economically, to prevent us from carrying out our plans of construction by dragging us ever deeper into the quagmire of the arms race.'[9] Gorbachev described these intentions as 'naïve' and a delusion. 'Nothing', he said, 'will come of these plans.' Gorbachev was proved to be right about the intentions of the US leadership. But his own confidence in the delusional nature of the US plans was misplaced. Seven years after he came to power, the Soviet Union no longer existed, which is why he is one of the least popular politicians in the former Soviet Union today, even though he has such a good press in the West.

Gorbachev rapidly became very popular in western capitals as he set about seeking to reduce tension with the US. British Prime Minister Margaret Thatcher famously announced that Gorbachev was a man she could do business with. But Gorbachev's initiatives were not limited to those around nuclear disarmament. Firstly, he reduced Soviet intervention into various regional conflicts; secondly, he indicated that the Soviet Union would not intervene to back the communist governments in eastern Europe (which significantly contributed to their collapse); thirdly, he acceded to German unification; and finally, he embarked upon full-scale Soviet withdrawal from eastern Europe.

Washington's response to Gorbachev was logical; every concession was accepted, without for an instant relaxing the pressure for more. The unification of Germany, which overturned the entire postwar settlement in Europe, was a case in point. The original Soviet position – that any unified Germany should be neutral – was rejected out of hand by Washington and Bonn. The Soviet Union ended up withdrawing from a Germany that became united within NATO, and that inevitably then went on to decide, for the first time since World War II, that its forces could be deployed outside its own borders. The Soviet strategic position in Europe collapsed.

Gorbachev championed 'new ways of thinking', as he put it, and wanted open and constructive dialogue between nations. He wanted to remove the 'ideological edge from interstate relations'[10] and spoke frequently of the common humanity of peoples, the need to recognise universal human values and overcome conflict in the interests of all. But Gorbachev's idealism was not shared by the leaders of the US. The real situation was clearly spelt out by EP Thompson in CND's magazine *Sanity* in September 1990. Commenting on plans for the reunification of Germany, under the heading 'Lop-sided "settlement"', he wrote:

> *The American idea of a 'settlement' is for a reunited Germany – and its military forces – in NATO, and the withdrawal of Soviet forces (or 'roll-back') from eastern and central Europe and the Baltic States. Meanwhile, the Truman doctrine remains in place, US nuclear-armed navies patrol the Mediterranean and the Persian Gulf, and US bases – with their Tridents and their aircraft armed with nuclear-tipped cruise missiles – remain everywhere in the West and South, from Oxfordshire to the Turkish border with the USSR . . . The object of this settlement must be a truly symmetrical dismantling of both blocs, in which NATO at long last makes concessions which match the concessions made in the East . . . What kind of 'settlement' would it be that evicted one side and left the other fully armed and holding onto all its stations?* [11]

Some 15 years later we know exactly what type of settlement it was. Not merely was one side evicted but the other side moved to occupy its positions. We face the new world order of one superpower. Thompson's vision during the 1980s, which he pursued through END, had been based on the notion of 'exterminism': that certain characteristics within a society 'thrust it in a direction whose outcome must be the extermination of multitudes.' [12] He took the view that, unless Europe could be made nuclear free, the deadly logic of the weapons systems themselves would prevail, and exterminism would be 'the last stage of civilisation'. Exterminism, as an analysis, was fundamentally flawed because, as one critic of the analysis, Fred Halliday, observed at the time, exterminism rested in particular 'on the view that the arms race now under way is essentially irrational, impermeable to the normal methods of historical investigation and the political judgements which may follow from this.'[13]

The result of Thompson's logic was the idea that the nuclear arms race had acquired an autonomous dynamic which was out of control and irrational, and that distinctions between US and Soviet policy were secondary compared to their common involvement in exterminism, that they had somehow become mirror images of each other because of their commitment to nuclear weapons. Because he held this view, Thompson said that the origins of the Cold War were irrelevant, and that the historical responsibility of the main protagonists was 'beside the point'. 'To argue from origins,' he wrote, 'is to take refuge from reality in moralism.'[14] But if Thompson had looked at the origins and development of the Cold War – the different events, policies, initiatives and motives that had led up to the 1980s, rather than just trying to equate the two superpowers in some kind of cataclysmic theory – he would not have expressed surprise when the US and NATO did not just roll-back and disarm when the Soviet Union did. The US goal had always been victory in the Cold War and the defeat of the Soviet Union. Once it had achieved that it pressed forward its advantage in every possible way, politically, economically and militarily. That the US is not a humanitarian organisation is shown not simply by Hiroshima and Nagasaki and the millions of slaughtered in Korea and Vietnam but by much that has happened since 1991.

Campaigning continues
Despite the failure to prevent the deployment of cruise and Pershing missiles in western Europe, the anti-nuclear movement continued at significant levels of activity, in Britain and

across Europe. Membership of CND fell in the second half of the 1980s. National membership peaked at 110,000 at the beginning of 1985, but dipped to 70,000 in 1988, supplemented by around 130,000 local members[15] (local group members do not have to be national members, but if they aren't they don't have democratic rights at the national level), following the deployment of the missiles. Later, the arrival of Gorbachev reduced the fear of nuclear war in the public mind, as the superpowers began to make progress on nuclear disarmament.

Nevertheless, large mobilisations took place. In October 1985, CND organised a circular demonstration under the slogan 'Human Race, not arms race', highlighting unwillingness to contribute to the disarmament process. It drew around 100,000 participants, starting and finishing in Hyde Park and linking the Soviet and US Embassies. Considerable thought was given to follow up to the demonstration. The next day was prioritised for 'Dear Neighbour' leafleting, explaining to neighbours and members of the public why the demonstration had taken place and what CND was hoping to achieve. The week after the demonstration was designated 'CND badge week' and everyone was encouraged to wear the CND badge to show support publicly for nuclear disarmament.[16] In 1987 a similar number turned out for an anti-nuclear demonstration called by CND and Friends of the Earth, under the slogan 'No nuclear weapons, No more Chernobyls' (see section below on Chernobyl).

Lawrence Wittner has observed that many of the anti-nuclear organisations in Europe had become more co-ordinated and better organised during the 1980s, and that CND found a variety of ways in which to pursue anti-nuclear campaigning at times when mass mobilisations were not so possible. The lobbying of parliament, as well as local government was developed, and by 1987, local councils covering more than half of the population had declared themselves nuclear free.[17] (Indeed, today in 2005, around 80 councils across the United Kingdom support the work of the Nuclear-Free Local Authorities organisation.) In May 1988 alone, Wittner remarks, CND 'was able to distribute some 2 million anti-nuclear leaflets, contrasting Britain's Trident nuclear submarine programme with nuclear disarmament negotiations between the superpowers.'[18] Interestingly, Gorbachev had tried to insist that British and French nuclear weapons should be included in the INF agreement, but the western powers would not agree to it, and Gorbachev eventually dropped it.[19] So near and yet so far!

Tracking and monitoring groups

As well as an enormous range of activities by local groups in the 1980s, initiatives such as 'Cruisewatch' were also developed. Cruise missiles were designed to be fired from mobile missile launchers in the event of war, and would be driven out from Greenham, where they were stored, to the designated launch site. Every so often the forces would have to practice for this eventuality, and so missiles would be driven around the countryside. Michael Heseltine asserted that these convoys would 'melt into the countryside', and Cruisewatch was founded to make sure that they didn't. Cruisewatch tracked, publicised and disrupted the convoys: 'Alerted to convoy preparations by women encamped at Greenham or by local residents, thousands of grassroots activists in southern Britain made it a point of pride to harass every convoy – blockading the roads, adorning the trucks with peace symbols, painting the windshields, and cutting the airbrakes.'[20] Between deployment of cruise at Greenham in November 1983 and August 1985, cruise had been out on convoy exercise 14 times. Each one had been tracked by Cruisewatch, and the details of each were published in *Campaign!*, CND's internal campaigning newspaper. The destinations were usually in the vicinity of Swindon, Oxford and Salisbury Plain. Cruisewatch tracked each of the 68 convoys before the last missiles were shipped back to the US in March 1991. 'With the help of the Greenham peace camps, extensive telephone networks and Citizen Band radios, Cruisewatchers in cars and on foot followed and kept a close eye on every missile convoy that left the airbase over the six years during which the USAF practised dispersals.' [21] This was a truly remarkable achievement. Another monitoring campaign, Nukewatch – with an emphasis on public information rather than direct action – was also developed, which drew attention to the road transportation of nuclear weapons, 'alerting people to the fact that these hazardous materials travel past their schools, hospitals and homes and that the only thing separating them from a live nuclear bomb or other hazardous radioactive material is a few inches of armour plating.' [22] Sea Action also developed to monitor nuclear weapons at sea and to draw attention to their arrival in British ports.

CND's specialist sections

CND's numerous specialist sections carried out a wide range of autonomous campaigning as the 1980s continued, reporting back on their activities to CND's national council. Specialist sections included Christian CND, Ex-Services CND, Labour CND, Trade Union CND, Liberal CND, Green CND and Youth CND. Youth CND regularly produced *Protest!*, an insert in *Campaign!*, and worked hard to promote CND's issues in schools, petitioning for education without a pro-nuclear bias, and especially working with and promoting Schools Against the Bomb (SAB). SAB was an independent organisation that encouraged information and debate within schools, led by the school students themselves. Bruce Kent described it as 'the David against the Ministry of Defence's Goliath in the world of genuine Peace Education.'[23] During the early 1980s, SAB spoke at an average of two schools a week throughout Britain, often helping to set up debates with the Peace through NATO organisation, to enable school students to hear both sides of the argument and arrive at their own judgements.

CND Cymru

CND's development of its regional structures from the early 1980s resulted in a high level of coordination of campaigning, with many regional and local initiatives taking place. Scotland and Wales also had separate memberships, offices and autonomous campaigns. CND Cymru was relaunched in 1981, coinciding with the declaration that year of Nuclear-Free Wales. All eight county councils in Wales declared themselves nuclear free, with many town and community councils following suit. By 1985, CND Cymru had 3,500 members, with many more affiliated through local groups. (CND Cymru had – and still has today – a bi-lingual policy, with all materials being produced in both Welsh and English.) CND Cymru also gave active support to mining communities in Wales during the Miners' Strike of 1984–85. While some CND Cymru members questioned whether this was appropriate for CND, CND Cymru's annual conference in 1985 overwhelmingly endorsed the position: 'The miners' strike gave us the ideal opportunity to make public the connections between the expansion of nuclear power and the increase in nuclear weapons manufacture – and we were able to identify with another section of the population which has suffered the might of the State and the Law, as the Peace Movement has.

The miners' wives listened to us, as we listened to them, and now we shall work together for a nuclear-free future.'[24]

Campaigning at the bases

Work at the bases continued during this time as well, not only at Greenham Common, where the cruise missiles had arrived, but also at Molesworth, where they were still awaited. CND held a national demonstration at Molesworth at Easter 1985, supported by thousands of protesters, and also promoted a Pledge Campaign to help support the peace camp. This was based on CND regions pledging to participate in the camp rota on specific days, so that the camp would always be supported; London Region CND and South East Region CND pledged participation on Mondays, East Anglia Region CND on Tuesdays and so on. A peace camp also continued at USAF Alconbury near Molesworth, which gave rise to the trial of the Alconbury 9. Nine activists were tried at the Crown Court in Northampton, accused of conspiracy to commit criminal damage whilst living at the peace camp.[25] Five were subsequently found guilty but on the following day, to indicate defiance to the sentence, thirty members of Greater Manchester CND walked onto the base, risking arrest with a maximum sentence of 14 years:

Some danced on the grass, two took over a 'dug-out', while others posed in front of the Northrop F-5 fighter, the symbol of Alconbury. Afterwards the dancing continued blocking the entrance to the base. The American soldiers on the main gate and personnel coming in and out of the base looked bewildered. One of the group said afterwards: 'Despite the recent showcase trials, peace campaigners are not intimidated by the threat of heavy sentences and will continue the active fight to rid Britain of American nuclear weapons. This action has proved that American bases in this country are dangerously unsafe.' [26]

Civil defence

Campaigning around the question of civil defence arose again in the autumn of 1985. The Minister of Defence, Michael Heseltine, announced home defence exercise 'Brave Defender' to take place that September. Around 65,000 troops took part, including regular troops, part-time territorials and reservists, in a mock defence of around 200 vital installations – such as ports and airfields – against a conventional attack by the 'Spetsnaz', Soviet special forces. CND took up the slogan: 'Grave Defender – Training to defend the dead!' CND took the view that Brave Defender was being used to divert attention away from the main threat facing Britain, that of nuclear war. The Home Office had recently changed its assessment of the most likely scenario for any future war from nuclear to conventional. It would seem probable that the obstacles it had faced when it had last tried to organise civil defence practices against nuclear attacks – which it had to abandon – may have had something to do with the change.

Campaigning against Star Wars

Significant in terms of international developments was CND's campaigning against Star Wars, the US's SDI project. First mooted by Reagan in the early 1980s and then brought to the fore again at the beginning of his second term of office in 1985, SDI was a major obstacle to an international arms agreement. By the summer of 1985, CND had launched an information campaign about the system. CND challenged the enormous amounts of money that were being put into research for Star Wars, and the tempting of the government with lucrative contracts:

> *The former US arms negotiator Paul Warnke has*
> *commented that '"Star Wars" has been rapidly converted*
> *from "stardust and moonbeams" to that great pork barrel*
> *in the sky.' CND is urging the British government to keep*
> *its fingers out of the pork barrel. The promise of fat*
> *contracts rarely comes true, as the Trident system has*
> *shown. Research money should be put where it is really*
> *needed – and currently being cut – into medical care,*
> *agriculture and peaceful uses of science.*[27]

The military dangers were spelt out clearly in CND leaflets: that it would provide the opportunity for the US to make a first strike; that it would create increased tensions and hostility, making war more likely; that it would unleash a new round of arms escalation; that it would threaten the ABM Treaty and the Geneva Arms Talks; and that it was an obscene waste of resources.

The Chernobyl disaster

But while protest and campaigning continued apace, the catastrophe at Chernobyl in April 1986 gave a terrible indication to the world of the devastating force of nuclear power; and the very real danger of nuclear accidents. Many nuclear accidents had occurred over the years, both with nuclear weapons and at nuclear power stations, but generally they had been played down or covered up. The first major accident was a reactor fire at Windscale (later renamed Sellafield) in Cumbria. The reactor that produced plutonium for the British weapons programme caught fire in October 1957 and burned for two days, dispersing radioactive smoke over Britain, Ireland and Northern Europe. According to Dr Chris Busby, a physical chemist who is also Green Party national speaker on nuclear issues, the most immediate problem identified was the short-lived iodine-131, which would concentrate in human thyroid glands. Ingestion via the milk of animals that had eaten contaminated grass was one way of it affecting humans. So over 2 million litres of contaminated milk were withdrawn from distribution and milk restrictions were put in place. Sellafield's most recent crisis was the revelation in May 2005 that 83,000 litres of highly radioactive liquid from used nuclear fuel was left lying on the floor for nine months. Another major accident took place in the US in 1979, when a pressurised water reactor underwent a partial core meltdown at Three Mile Island, in Pennsylvania. Children and pregnant women were evacuated from nearby Harrisburg, but not immediately. The findings of Sternglass and Gould, who studied the health effects of the disaster, 'have shown persuasively that significant increases in infant mortality and other morbidity in states downwind of the releases did occur.'[28]

On the occasion of the Chernobyl disaster, the impact was so enormous there was no possibility of a cover-up. Chernobyl was a nuclear power station in the Ukraine, 65 miles north of Kiev. On 26 April 1986, number four reactor exploded. At the time of the accident, the emergency water-cooling system had been turned off, while an experiment was being carried out on the reactor. The impact of the explosion blew the steel lid off the reactor. The reactor burned for ten days, releasing 3–4 per cent of the reactor core's total radioactivity into the atmosphere. Radioactive debris was scattered over a huge area. Immediate casualties numbered 31 people dead and 500 taken to hospital. The radioactive impact on the atmosphere was enormous and strong winds carried it beyond the Ukraine to other parts of the Soviet Union and over western Europe, but the likelihood is that it affected all parts of the globe. How many people have been affected by radioactive pollution from Chernobyl will never be known, but indications are that it will be huge numbers. Disturbing reports have come from Belarus, bordering on the Ukraine, near Chernobyl: 'In an area where Chernobyl fallout was greatest, the incidence of thyroid cancer under the age of 15 has increased by a factor of over 80 times.'[29] In Britain, the impact of Chernobyl radioactive pollution was most severe in North Wales and Cumbria, where the radioactive cloud passed in May 1985, and heavy thunderstorms caused radioactive rain to fall – 1,600 miles away from the explosion. Sheep restrictions were put in place in these farming areas, and some of them were still in place 10 years later.

The CND leadership of that time did not make the Chernobyl disaster a core campaign of CND, but it had a considerable impact on campaigning in other countries, for example in eastern Europe, and also gave a major impetus to growth of the peace movement in India.[30] The Chernobyl Children's Project was set up in Britain in 1995 – launched by the Lord Mayor of Manchester – owing much to the initiative of Greater Manchester and District CND, which had been inspired by the campaigning in this area by Irish CND. The Project has focused on providing recuperative holidays in Britain for children from Belarus and humanitarian aid to affected communities.[31] Many people drew the links between the damage caused by the Chernobyl disaster and the potential impact of a nuclear war. As Gorbachev himself said, 'Chernobyl mercilessly reminded us what all of us would suffer if a nuclear thunderstorm was unleashed.'[32] Later that year, under the pressure of Gorbachev's initiatives, negotiations led to Gorbachev and Reagan meeting in Reykjavik in Iceland in October 1986. Unfortunately no progress on disarmament was made.

Afghanistan and Nicaragua

The obstacle to progress between the two superpowers was the US attachment to the Star Wars initiative. Gorbachev's proposals for the Reykjavik summit were: that all US and Soviet intermediate-range missiles should be removed from Europe; US and Soviet strategic nuclear weapons should be reduced by half over five years; and the Soviet Union would continue its moratorium on nuclear tests and explosions. But Gorbachev also wanted the US to agree to comply with its commitments under the ABM Treaty and pledge not to go ahead with the research, testing and deployment of the Star Wars system (with the exception of laboratory research, which was acceptable under the ABM Treaty). Reagan, for his part, was completely unwilling to compromise on Star Wars. Gorbachev's own view about the failure to make progress at Reykjavik was accurate: 'The stumbling block proved to be the American stance on the ABM Treaty. After Reykjavik I asked myself time and again why the United States had avoided an agreement on strengthening the regime of this Treaty . . . And each time the conclusion I came to was one and the same: the United States is not ready to part with its hope of winning nuclear superiority and this time wants to get ahead of the Soviet Union by speeding up SDI research.'[33]

This refusal to compromise on steps that would give it superiority was indicative of the whole US approach, and was also manifested over Afghanistan. By early 1986, Gorbachev had decided to withdraw from Afghanistan and proposed a timetable to do this, in exchange for US support for a coalition government between the Soviet-backed Afghan communists and the US-backed Mujahedeen. The proposal was rejected out of hand. Around the same time, Reagan 'privately approved $300 million of covert military assistance to the Afghan Mujahedeen. He authorised efforts to drive

Soviet forces from Afghanistan "by all means available". By 1987 Washington was spending $630 million in Afghanistan, the largest covert action funded by the United States since World War II.'[34] The US was sponsoring, in conjunction with Pakistan, the forces that would eventually create Al Qaeda and the Taliban. Issues such as the rights of Afghan women had no place in their strategy. US sponsorship of extremist Islamic fundamentalist forces as proxies against the Soviet Union was to have momentous consequences where these groups turned against the US.

After the Reykjavik summit, there was an increase in tension again between the two sides. Gorbachev criticised the US for rejecting any constructive way forward on disarmament. At the same time, revelations were appearing on how Reagan's administration funded the illegal Contra War in Nicaragua via illegal arms sales to Iran, which it treated officially as a 'pariah state'. Reagan's poll rating fell by 20 per cent. Gorbachev had far more difficult domestic issues to face. Unlike the very different economic reform programme in China, his programme of economic reform, *perestroika*, was disorganising the Soviet economy. His policy of *glasnost*, or openness, was opposed by conservatives and used by internal and external enemies to campaign for an end to the Soviet political and economic system. Gorbachev needed international progress to balance his difficulties at home so, in the spring of 1987, he announced that he was prepared to negotiate separately on intermediate-range missiles in Europe, and would no longer insist on linking them to Star Wars. Negotiations moved forward on the INF Treaty, without agreements on SDI and START.

The INF Treaty

The INF Treaty was signed by Reagan and Gorbachev at a summit meeting in Washington, in December 1987. This was a historic step – the first nuclear disarmament treaty. It is also worth noting that the Treaty was fully implemented. All shorter-range missile systems had been eradicated by the end of 1989, and all long-range INF systems by the middle of 1991.[35] CND described the INF Treaty as 'just the beginning' of the disarmament process, rightly claiming a role in its achievement. Writing shortly before the Treaty was signed, the CND General Secretary observed: 'CND has played an important role in the marked change in public opinion and thus has helped to create the popular demand which has brought the US and the USSR to the point at which they may give up part of their nuclear arsenals. If the collective peace movement had not protested so loud, long and consistently, Reagan and Gorbachev would not be talking now.'[35] On the other hand, *The Times* observed: 'The objective of the Geneva talks should have been reduction not elimination . . . The power blocs are safer with nuclear missiles than without them – and this applies to INF as much as any other weapons category.'[36]

British Prime Minister Margaret Thatcher was unaffected by Mikhail Gorbachev's 'new thinking', and went strongly on the offensive against Labour's anti-nuclear policies during the 1987 election. Unilateral nuclear disarmament was backed by successive Labour Party conferences between 1984 and 1987[37] and under Neil Kinnock's leadership, the Labour Party went into the general election on a unilateralist policy. Thatcher vigorously attacked the policy: 'Labour's non-nuclear defence policy is in fact a policy for defeat, surrender, occupation, and finally, prolonged guerrilla fighting . . . Never before has the Labour Party offered the country a defence policy of such recklessness, a defence policy of the white flag.'[38] The CIA-backed group The 61, which had operated against Labour and CND before the 1983 election, began its work again. It 'produced and distributed to Conservative candidates a little booklet, *The Vision of St Kinnock*. Covered in red, it was filled with pictures showing the Labour Party leader "playing the fool . . . or in earnest conversation with Fidel Castro, or addressing a CND rally." Other operations included exposing "'loony Left' activities in the councils", producing a study of the mass media showing its supposed "left-wing bias", and distributing useful material to "politically compatible columnists".[39] Labour lost the election but CND General Secretary Meg Beresford argued strongly that unilateralism was not to blame: 'Although some have tried to scapegoat Labour's non-nuclear defence policy and the strong sympathy for "unilateralism" in the Liberal Party as "vote-losers", it seems clear that the election was decided on appeals to economic self-interest in the prosperous South. This time, nuclear disarmament was not a vote-loser: that is what we have achieved since 1983.'[40]

The one-way street of superpower relations

Progress occurred on other fronts. As anti-Star Wars campaigning continued, good news arrived from the US that the project had been set back by the Democrat-controlled US Congress. Reagan's budget request for it was cut by one third, and work on SDI was mandated to remain within the constraints of the ABM Treaty. This was a significant block on the project. But during a visit by Reagan to Moscow in the summer of 1988, no further joint progress on disarmament was made. Gorbachev, on the other hand, announced the ending of military support to Namibia and Angola. He had already announced withdrawal from Afghanistan. The one-way street in superpower relations continued. Moving even further, in December 1988, Gorbachev made a very significant address to the UN General Assembly. Implementing his earlier policy of 'reasonable sufficiency', he announced unilateral cutbacks in the armed forces, in particular of offensive weapons. This included the reduction of the armed forces by half a million personnel over two years and the withdrawal of 10,000 tanks, 8,500 artillery pieces and 800 combat aircraft from eastern Europe. There were also withdrawals in the Far East and on the border with China. It was obvious, Gorbachev said, 'that the use or threat of force no longer can . . . be an instrument of foreign policy.'[41]

Gorbachev also emphasised his support for the UN and stressed his view that the problems faced by the international community were global, rather than regional, in character and should be addressed as such. As well as disarmament, he expressed concern about third world development, environmental issues and the peaceful use of outer space. He spoke strongly in favour of understanding the world as an interdependent whole, where universal human values should be prioritised and ideological prejudice cast aside. This new stage of world history, he asserted, 'requires the freeing of international relations from ideology'.[42]

Gorbachev's policies were to have a significant impact on the countries of eastern Europe, and ultimately brought about the collapse of the communist governments there. He had indicated that he would not intervene in those countries to maintain the regimes – that they had to 'do it their way'. It was humorously observed that the 'Sinatra Doctrine' had replaced the Brezhnev Doctrine. He was now also embarking on a full-scale military withdrawal from eastern Europe. By the end of 1989, most communist governments in central Europe were no longer in power and, within a couple of years, communist rule had ended throughout eastern Europe. Frequently the communist governments reformed away their own powers. The most significant question was what was going to happen to the two Germanies. The question of Germany was a crucial security issue for the Soviet Union, for obvious historical reasons; 27 million Soviet citizens – mostly civilians – had been deliberately killed by the Germans and their allies during World War II, many in systematic massacres – war crimes on an appalling scale. In the summer of 1990, Gorbachev went to the US and met with President George Bush senior, who had now replaced Reagan. Gorbachev abandoned the Soviet position that a united Germany should be neutral and accepted its likely membership of NATO. As he said in July 1990, 'Whether we like it or not, the time will come when a united Germany will be in NATO, if that is its choice. Then, if that is its choice, to some degree and in some form, Germany can work together with the Soviet Union.'[43] Germany was united in October 1990.

Change in eastern Europe

Within the Soviet Union, Gorbachev now faced the results of the domestic policies that he had been pursuing. His economic reforms had failed. They had taken the country from stagnation to crisis, and they deeply divided his own party. His political liberalisation created the space for the emergence of political forces that were finally able to exploit the incompetence of the communist hard-liners' attempted coup as they tried to turn back the clock. The ensuing crisis enabled Boris Yeltsin to depose Gorbachev and dissolve the Soviet Union. During his last year in office Gorbachev faced the break-up of the Soviet Union, as many of the republics, most notably the Baltic states, voted to declare themselves independent. Gorbachev was very popular in the West and appreciated for his extraordinary achievements in the field of nuclear disarmament. At home, the relaxation and opening up of Soviet society that he initiated was very popular, but his overall record was not judged favourably. After all, he had started out as leader of the second most powerful state in the world, yet when he left office, that state no longer existed. The verdict of Russian voters was clear; when he stood for election shortly after the dissolution of the Soviet Union, he polled between 1 and 2 per cent of the vote.

The impact of these cataclysmic and world-changing events was of major significance for the peace movement. The impact on CND would depend on whether, as many thought, the dissolution of the Soviet Union would lead to a new era of peace among states, or, whether the US would respond to the elimination of its main rival by more voraciously pursuing its own interests. Enormous arsenals of nuclear weapons still existed, but how much concern would they cause if international conflict was sharply reduced? Meg Beresford reflected on this in her report to the CND Conference in 1989: 'Regularly, throughout the last year, assorted journalists, media persons and self-appointed pundits have suggested that CND's work is done. "The Cold war is over," they tell us. "Disarmament is breaking out all over. Other environmental issues are more pressing." Would that they were right . . . The sense of imminent danger is fading but more than ever the job of CND is to make clear the difference between hopes, hype and reality.'[44] She went on to observe that Britain's Trident system was moving ahead, and that Mrs Thatcher greeted NATO plans for new nuclear weapons with enthusiasm.

The Gulf War

A sign of what was to come was one of the last major events before the demise of the Soviet Union, and the first war of the post-Cold War era: the Gulf War. On 2 August 1990, Iraq invaded its neighbour Kuwait. The dispute hinged around the oil-pricing policies of Kuwait and the Gulf states, which were having a very negative impact on the Iraqi economy, already devastated by its long war against Iran. There is some evidence that US diplomacy may have encouraged Saddam Hussein to believe that the US would not respond militarily to an invasion, effectively encouraging the dictator to take the risk. Once Hussein was committed the US began assembling a coalition for war. The rhetoric of the US and its allies was about freedom and democracy, but the US had armed and supported Saddam Hussein and backed his war against Iran. The invasion was a clear breach of international law. But the war had nothing to do with democracy. Kuwait was ruled by a royal dictatorship, which trampled on the rights of women, in particular. The proposal for war was a further test of the Soviet Union's changed policies and commitment to peaceful collaboration with the West. Iraq was an ally of the Soviet Union, and many thousands of Russians worked there. But the Soviet delegation to the UN Security Council cast its vote in favour of the resolutions that authorised the Gulf War – the biggest US military action since Vietnam.

This was the first major indication of how the US would operate in the world when it became the only superpower. But it was by no means the only indication of what was to come. The US had already invaded Panama and Grenada, deployed troops in Bolivia, Peru and Columbia, intervened in Liberia and the Philippines, and run the Contra War against Nicaragua. The new relationship with the Soviet Union under Gorbachev had reduced the constraints on Washington's ability to carry out such interventions. There was going to be no holding back.

Meanwhile, CND attempted to work out an appropriate response to events in the Gulf. Bruce Kent, writing to the *Guardian* on behalf of CND, condemned the invasion of Kuwait and urged Iraq to withdraw its forces and submit its dispute with Kuwait to the UN, to seek a peaceful resolution under the terms of the UN Charter. But Kent also drew attention to the fact that, while the British government had condemned Saddam Hussein's invasion of Kuwait, it had for years been supplying Iraq with weapons technology and financial credits. 'It is an untenable position to provide a belligerent dictator with the means of waging war either directly or through support for his country's economy and subsequently to appear outraged that the same country should use these resources to mount an illegal invasion.'[45] But Mrs Thatcher had no such qualms. She was keen on military action and made it clear that the British government would not be limited by any UN decision that fell short of war (for example, to impose economic or other sanctions) and that it would be prepared to carry out military action even without UN backing. Of course, US President Bush also took this position.

On 13 August, CND and the Green Party issued a joint statement condemning the decision to send British forces to join US troops in the Gulf. The statement supported the UN decision to agree economic sanctions against Iraq but said that the presence of foreign troops representing countries with vested interests in the region was destabilising.[46] The Labour Party leadership backed Mrs Thatcher's support for war. In a parliamentary debate on the Gulf on 6 and 7 September, 37 Labour MPs voted against this position. At the Labour Party Conference, the Fire Brigades Union put an emergency resolution, urging the government not to take action outside UN decisions. But the resolution was defeated. Opposition to a military solution to the Iraqi invasion of Kuwait came from a wide range of forces, although taken overall it was far less numerically strong on the ground than the opposition to the war on Iraq in 2003. MPs such as Tony Benn from the Labour Party, and from Plaid Cymru (the

Party of Wales), together with the Green Party, many trade unions, CND, a range of different peace, political and campaigning organisations, and academics and cultural figures, formed the basis for the Committee to Stop War in the Gulf, which was to coordinate anti-war campaigning over the next few months. CND played a significant role in the Committee, primarily through the work of Marjorie Thompson, who was CND vice-chair when the Committee was founded and was elected as CND Chair in November of 1990. Thompson was an American from a Republican background, who had been profoundly affected by the Vietnam War – the backdrop to her childhood – and she worked energetically to develop and maintain the unity of the anti-war movement. There was some opposition within the CND leadership to participation in the anti-war campaigning, as had been the case initially in the campaigning against the war on Vietnam. Some thought that CND should stick strictly to anti-nuclear activities, but CND Council voted overwhelmingly to support the Committee and it received enormous support from the CND membership.

The Committee was organised on the basis that its only aim was to stop war in the Gulf, in order to build the broadest possible support, and that any positions further to that would be decided by majority vote. The Committee organised a number of demonstrations. The first was in September 1990 and mobilised 7,000, but the second in November had a turnout of around 20,000. Shortly afterwards, UN Resolution 678 was passed by the Security Council, with support from the Soviet delegation. This authorised the use of force if Iraq had not withdrawn from Kuwait by 15 January. The way was open for war. A national demonstration was organised for 12 January, virtually on the eve of the planned war. More than 100,000 people participated, indicating a surge of opposition to war. Support for the Committee began to grow, and around 100 local committees were set up across the country. CND reported on the massive shift in public opinion away from support for the war: 'In November, polls showed in excess of 60 per cent support for military action. Now the figure stands at 47 per cent, with 42 per cent opposed and 11 per cent uncertain. Among women opposition to war stands at 47 per cent with only 38 per cent favouring military action and 15 per cent undecided.'[47]

The first air attacks began on 16 January. On 19 January, with only 48 hours notice, an emergency demonstration attracted 17,000 supporters. The key demand of the Committee was now changed to immediate and unconditional ceasefire. Over 40,000 turned out in support of this demand on 2 February. Eventually, Iraq accepted a Soviet peace initiative, which included withdrawal from Kuwait, the supposed purpose of the war being fought. But this led to the most shocking event of the whole episode. As Iraqi forces withdrew from Kuwait, they were attacked from the air as they retreated on the road to Basra, resulting in the most terrible and sickening carnage imaginable. In that slaughter, together with the land war, between 100 and 200,000 Iraqis were killed. The face of the post-Cold War US had been revealed.[48]

In one of its early statements, prior to the beginning of the war, CND had emphasised the importance of achieving a worldwide ban on weapons of mass destruction: 'The lesson that should be drawn from the whole situation is not that the peace dividend should be abandoned and military spending increased, but that stronger mechanisms must be set up to control the sale of arms and the transfer of nuclear technology and that genuine attempts must be made to achieve a worldwide ban on all weapons of mass destruction at the earliest possible date.'[49] The issue of Iraq's weapons of mass destruction was a matter of great concern at that time. In 1988, the Iraqi authorities had used chemical weapons against the Kurdish minority in Halabja, killing an estimated 5,000 and injuring 10,000 more. There were also suspicions that Iraq was developing nuclear weapons, although the IAEA had found no evidence of this at that point. Because of the record of Halabja, there were fears that Iraq would use chemical weapons against invading forces in 1991.

What seems clear though, is that the US and Britain were considering the use of nuclear weapons in retaliation to any use of chemical weapons: 'Junior ministers spoke of "massive retaliation" against Iraq if CWs [chemical weapons] were used and this surely could only have meant a nuclear response since Britain did not have CWs. In a report in *The Observer* on 30 September, a senior army officer of the 7th Armoured Brigade, which was on its way to the Gulf, confirmed that any Iraqi chemical attack on British forces would be met with a tactical nuclear response.'[50] A CND Defence Briefing produced in January 1991 estimated that the US had in the region of 1,000 nuclear warheads available for use in the Gulf, and that some British nuclear weapons were also available. The US had tactical nuclear weapons capability via aircraft carriers in the region, as well as free-fall nuclear bombs and nuclear artillery shells at US bases in Turkey. For Britain, the likely deployment was probably either on the *Argus* auxiliary vessel – it was in the Gulf, but it is not known if it carried nuclear weapons – or through the use of nuclear bombs from Britain or Germany, to be dropped by Tornado strike aircraft. CND also suspected that nuclear weapons were carried on board the British aircraft carrier Ark Royal. Again the parallels with the 2003 war on Iraq are striking: two nuclear-armed powers were prepared to use nuclear weapons against a non-nuclear weapons state. The ending of the Cold War had not ended the danger of the use of nuclear weapons. As CND's 1991 Annual Report stated:

Our hopes for a world order based on the principles of global security and the peaceful resolution of conflict have been set back. The Bush administration has used devastating force as a tool of diplomacy. Whatever else may be said about the present juncture, one thing is clear: the world is not a safer place. Preparations for the Gulf War, scheduled in October 1990, gained an unstoppable momentum with the doubling of troop deployment and it began as planned on 16 January with the most violent 24 hours in human history. The objective of the war proved not to be the defence of Saudi Arabia ('Desert Shield') or the liberation of Kuwait ('Desert Storm'), but rather the protection of Western, principally US, economic and political interests through the re-assertion of US military superiority.[51]

6

The post-Cold War world

The 1990s presented a particular challenge for CND. The end of the Cold War had done a huge amount to relieve public anxiety about the possibility of nuclear war. Whilst nuclear weapons continued to exist, their use seemed less likely and thus people were less inclined to demonstrate about them. The deployment of Trident during the early 1990s only really moved the committed activists. For the majority of people, nuclear weapons ceased to be of great interest and, as their presence dropped down the political agenda, many people assumed that we no longer had them. As one CND activist commented in 1993, nuclear disarmament was no longer 'flavour of the month'.[1] The consequences of the victory of the US in the Cold War rapidly became clear, with successive UN reports chronicling the largest peacetime economic contraction ever in the former Soviet Union, the war on Yugoslavia, the expansion of NATO and the development of the US National Missile Defense system (successor to Reagan's SDI). CND increasingly took up the issue of the National Missile Defense system, particularly in Yorkshire where bases that the US wished to use for the system were located.

Within CND, the recurrent discussion about CND's focus continued; should it concentrate solely on anti-nuclear campaigning, or should it attempt to understand and situate

183

nuclear weapons in the wider context of the kind of international conflict – war – in which the weapons would be used?
Once again there were some false debates. Nuclear weapons
do not exist in a vacuum, they are part of a war-fighting
machine – of a military arsenal – and they are also part of a
political arsenal that enables nuclear weapons states to maintain their extraordinary leverage over world affairs. It is no
accident that every permanent member of the UN Security
Council possesses nuclear weapons.

CND's conferences in the early 1990s gave a flavour of the
breadth of concerns. Resolutions covered Britain's role in
nuclear proliferation through Trident, opposition to the
opening of the THORP nuclear reprocessing plant, support
for the early completion of a Comprehensive Test Ban Treaty,
and support for the renewal of the NPT, with the ultimate
goal of global abolition of nuclear weapons. But resolutions
also stressed the importance of campaigning for a 'peace dividend', reducing the defence budget and diverting the money
into civil manufacturing and public services.

The question of a peace dividend had become an important one in the context of the end of the Cold War. After all,
the justification for the nuclear and other arsenals had been to
defend the country against possible Soviet attack. A campaign
had been planned for the autumn of 1990, calling for worldwide cuts of £100 billion in defence expenditure by the end of
the 20th century. This had been put on ice because of the
onset of the Gulf War but, in the following years, work did
progress in this area. Trade Union CND, the CND specialist
section for trade unionists, undertook much of the work,
producing a pack on how to convert companies producing
arms to peaceful purposes. In some cases, nominal amounts
of shares were bought in the main military industry companies to enable CND members to attend AGMs. The aim was

'asking embarrassing questions or generating other disruptions.'[2] In fact, this issue motivated many in their support for CND. When asked why he supported CND, top barrister Michael Mansfield QC said: 'I wish to redistribute the obscene amounts of money that are spent on nuclear weaponry towards welfare needs such as education, health, employment, housing.'[3]

Other CND members had concerns about Britain's role in the wider world, in particular its policies towards the third world. One conference resolution in 1993 foresaw some of the developments that have taken place more recently: 'CND must act to prevent the rise of a new generation of British nuclear weapons. This conference calls for a major campaign against any new British tactical nuclear weapons, whether TASMs [Tactical Air to Surface Missiles] or modified Trident missiles. Special emphasis should be placed on the declared anti-third world role of such weapons.'[4] One of the proposers of this resolution, Milan Rai, pointed out, 'As a movement we must accept and digest the fact that British nuclear weapons have been used and continue to be used to threaten non-nuclear third world countries . . . Our campaign's particularly against the new generation of British nuclear weapons and against nuclear proliferation must be based on this new understanding.'[5] In an interview in *CND Today* – which replaced *Sanity* – in the summer of 1992, the poet Adrian Mitchell observed: 'Some of the most important issues today include the ending of the long war between the rich nations of the North and the poor nations of the South. We must share out the wealth of this planet or face a prolonged series of wars.'[6] This perspective had common ground with the earlier analysis of Marjorie Thompson, chair of CND during the first Gulf War, who saw that war as the first of the 'North–South' wars that would succeed the Cold War as the US attempted to consolidate its global domination, and bolster its economy by controlling access to key raw materials, especially oil.[7] The current development of new nuclear weapons for use in 'pre-emptive wars' – in peacetime, on its own authority – against third-world supposedly 'rogue states' shows that the US is again trying to make the possible use of nuclear weapons 'acceptable'.

A changing world

This was a period of intense change. This is particularly obvious with regard to US foreign policy, as the US became the world's sole superpower. At the end of the Cold War there was much talk about 'the end of history' – an end to conflict and the establishment of a new world order. But rather than initiating a new world order based on peace, equality and justice, the US moved towards political, economic and military domination of the globe, a process we are still experiencing. As CND observed at the time, '1992 has brought forth developments in nuclear disarmament which were almost unthinkable not so long ago . . . Yet the long shadows cast by British nuclear proliferation, the huge US and Russian strategic arsenals that remain untouched by their bilateral agreements, nuclear targeting of the third world and the spectre of an entire epoch of interference and military interventions all seem to confirm the view that the Cold War has been superseded by an ever more dangerous period in human history.'[8]

A longstanding CND activist, Pat Allen observed, in the early 1990s, that CND must 'recognise the links between nuclear issues, peace issues and environmental and development issues. The alternative is to see CND increasingly marginalised.'[9] The importance of working to bring the anti-nuclear issues centrally into the wider political and campaigning framework was clearly understood by the early 2000s and was shown by CND's shared leadership of the massive movement against the invasion of Iraq and its leading role in bringing the European Social Forum to Britain in 2004. The latter linked the issues of neo-liberalism, third-world debt, racism and war in a way that had wide resonance against the backdrop of the US war drive against Iraq. This represented a convergence of the peace movement with trade unions, non-governmental organisations (NGOs) addressing issues like the environment and third-world poverty, and other popular movements developing a common under-standing of the relations between the unjust workings of the international economic institutions led by the US and the increasing use of military force by the US to impose its inter-ests. The European Social Forum is the European part of the World Social Forum movement, which – under the slogan coined by the great Indian peace activist Arundhati Roy – declared 'Another World is Possible'. The social forum move-ment brings together hundreds of thousands of people across the world, engaged in campaigning on peace and disarma-ment, the environment, debt and development, social justice and human rights and much more.

The new world order reflected the profound changes in the relation of the US to the rest of the world since the world recession at the beginning of the 1970s. After World War II the US had created an international economic order around the dollar. US capital assisted the economic reconstruction of Germany and Japan, while both remain to this day countries with large US capital and military forces stationed in them. US capital and military spending on bases all over the world stimulated economic growth. From the 1970s, the US econ-omy became less and less competitive (manifested in a vast balance of payments deficit), to the order of $400 billion as this book goes to press. That deficit has to be financed by equivalent outflows of capital from the rest of the world.

From being the world's paymaster in the 1940s, 1950s and 1960s, the US is today by far the world's greatest debtor state.

Capital devoted to the US economy cannot be used for investment in the states from which it originates. Thus the US economy has become a gigantic parasite on the world economy, exacting an annual tribute of literally hundreds of billions of dollars for the last two decades. That outflow to the US creates enormous strain on the rest of the world. It creates an economic order in which inequality between states and classes has reached the highest levels in history. Entire continents have been thrown backwards, not – as the apologists for so-called progressive colonialism claim – because their peoples are unable to govern themselves, but because of the exactions and pressure they face from the world economic order designed to maintain the flow of that annual tribute of hundreds of millions of dollars upon which US stability depends.

Sub-Saharan Africa, the Middle East, the former Soviet Union and eastern Europe have all literally seen absolute falls in living standards, with millions and millions more deaths than would otherwise have occurred. From the 1980s Latin America experienced two decades of stagnation. Even relatively rich western Europe and Japan have seen their previous situation, of growing far more rapidly than the US during the 1950s and 1960s, transformed. The European Union has slower growth and higher unemployment than the US. The Japanese economy has stagnated since the beginning of the 1990s under the strain of sustaining not only its own investment, but also a significant part of that of the US. The US economy grows relatively rapidly, not because it is competitive, but because it is subsidised – at extraordinary cost – by the rest of the world.

Why does the rest of the world put up with this burden? For the same reason that a respectable shop or club may pay 'protection' to the mafia. The US may be in relative economic decline, but it is by far the most militarily powerful state in the world and the largest economy. That is why the US seeks to turn each major problem it confronts into a military question. The message of the first and second wars on Iraq was: only the US can maintain western dominance of Middle East oil. The message of the bombing of Yugoslavia was: only the US can ensure the integration of eastern Europe and as much as possible of the former Soviet Union into the western economic order. The message of all these interventions, and others, like the Contra War in Nicaragua, is: if you try to stand up to the US you will be crushed. The problem with this approach is very clear. As Iraq shows today, for example, not all problems are susceptible to a military solution and millions of people throughout the world increasingly see that they have an interest in resisting the new international order. US exactions are so great that they also lead to more and more conflict with its allies in western Europe. Indeed the creation of the Euro is an attempt by the EU to protect itself from US exactions. Strategically its existence is intolerable to the US because it threatens the supremacy of the dollar. Such divisions between NATO states create further openings for the anti-war movement; as was seen in Iraq, the establishment, including the media, is no longer able to maintain a virtually monolithic bloc. Information seeps out, debates ensue and as a result the public understands better the utter cynicism of those in the White House or Downing Street who speak of wars for democracy or wars to stop the spread of weapons of mass destruction.

Further initiatives in disarmament

The massive changes that were taking place as the Cold War ended did allow the US to reorganise and to some extent reduce the size of its military, now oriented to fighting colonial, rather than world, wars. In July 1991, Bush and Gorbachev signed the START I Treaty, which was the first Treaty to make reductions in strategic nuclear weapons. This included intercontinental ballistic missiles, submarine-launched ballistic missiles and air-launched ballistic missiles, and was expected to be implemented by the end of 1999, by which time it would have reduced US strategic warheads from around 12,000 to around 9,000 and Soviet warheads from around 11,000 to 7,000.[10] In the last few months of Gorbachev's leadership of the Soviet Union, further cuts were agreed. In September 1991, Bush announced that 'all US ground-based tactical nuclear weapons would be destroyed, all sea-borne tactical nuclear weapons would be removed from US warships, and the number of air-delivered tactical nuclear weapons in Europe would be cut by 50 per cent.'[11] There was a strong mood in the US towards cuts in nuclear weaponry, and the US Congress increasingly turned down funding for the administration's weapons programme. In particular it continued to restrain the Star Wars initiative, cutting Bush's request for $4.9 billion to $3.8 billion and to $2.9 billion in 1992. Most importantly, the Congress prohibited Star Wars tests that would violate the ABM Treaty.

With the dissolution of the Soviet Union at the end of 1991, a number of the successor states held nuclear weapons. Not only Russia, but also Belarus, the Ukraine and Kazakhstan held nuclear weapons totalling in the region of 27,000 strategic and tactical nuclear warheads.[12] Subsequently, however, the latter three republics all signed up to the NPT as non-nuclear weapons states and transferred their nuclear weapons to Russia. Russia itself stated that it had become the legal successor to 'the former Soviet Union's obligations and rights under international arms control and disarmament agreements.'[13] Boris Yeltsin, the president of Russia, began negotiations with the US and signed START II with Bush, in January 1993. START II committed the two countries to eliminating all multiple-warhead intercontinental ballistic missiles and reducing deployed strategic warheads to between 3,000 and 3,500 each by the year 2003. Bill Clinton succeeded Bush as US president later that month, and there were high hopes that disarmament would continue under his leadership. In his presidential election campaign, Clinton had stressed the need to cut back military spending, including that spent on nuclear production and testing, and SDI. 'In their place he urged preservation of the ABM Treaty, ratification of the START treaties and negotiation of a comprehensive test ban treaty.'[14]

US militarism develops

These positions were strongly welcomed at the time, but within a few years it was clear that the US administration had rejected this framework. By the end of the decade, the US had shunned the Comprehensive Test Ban Treaty, was preparing to withdraw from the ABM Treaty and Clinton's request for the 1999–2000 Pentagon budget was $268 billion. In an era where its global rival no longer existed, and the Warsaw Pact had been dissolved, why did the US pursue a militaristic line? One possible analysis was put forward by US Disarmament expert Haralambos Athanasopulos. Writing at the end of the 1990s, he observed:

> *Although the United States has no strategic enemy in the post-Cold War era, the American industrial and military complex for its own narrow economic interests has already begun a campaign to foist new scare tactics and fears on the American public. To this end, the American*

> *military-industrial complex argues that, although the potential danger of global thermonuclear war with Russia has essentially been eliminated, a particular future threat to the United States' security interests will be posed by the horizontal proliferation of nuclear weapons and ballistic missiles of third-world countries, leading to possible regional conflicts.*[15]

Certainly the issue of nuclear proliferation came to the fore in the early 1990s and has been used, particularly in recent years, as a means of policing third-world nations and, in the case of Iraq, as a justification for war and regime change. Back in 1992, CND produced a Defence Briefing entitled 'Nuclear Targeting of the Third World', which addressed some of the contradictions presented by US and UK attitudes towards proliferation, particularly in the light of their commitment under Article VI of the NPT to genuinely pursue nuclear disarmament. The Trident programme, it observed, 'blatantly disregards' Article VI. Referring back to the 1991 war on Iraq, the Briefing stated: 'The semi-public nature of the nuclear threats against Iraq, the leaks from the Pentagon and the MoD in Britain, and the use of third-world enemies to justify nuclear escalation, all suggest a policy of legitimising nuclear threats in the future. Policy makers are anxious to avoid any real debate on the issue because the public appears strongly opposed to such policies. In fact, public and international opinion are often cited as the main obstacles to the use of nuclear weapons.'[16]

British nuclear proliferation

Campaigning against the Trident system was CND's key focus throughout this period, with a particular emphasis on the fact that it was Britain's own nuclear proliferation contravening

Article VI of the NPT. Without a doubt there was widespread concern about the dangers of nuclear proliferation at this time. There were a number of reasons for this. Firstly, with the break-up of the Soviet Union there was a possibility that nuclear technology could be sold or stolen and make its way outside the former Soviet republics in the economic crisis that was taking place there. It was also feared that Soviet nuclear scientists might sell their skills elsewhere as their employment collapsed. In fact, none of these fears appear to have been realised, but at that time no one could be certain. Secondly, in March 1993, President FW de Klerk announced that South Africa had embarked on a nuclear weapons programme in the early 1970s and had made a number of weapons before demobilising them all.

This was a cause for celebration, especially when South Africa joined the NPT; a country had unilaterally disarmed, and Africa was now a nuclear-free continent. This was formalised in 1996 by the signing of the Treaty of Pelindaba, making Africa a nuclear weapon-free zone. But it was also a cause for concern. The weapons had been disarmed, but they had been made. Furthermore, although de Klerk claimed that 'at no time did South Africa acquire nuclear weapons technology or materials from another country,' South African anti-nuclear campaigner Abdul Minty correctly pointed out: 'This contradicted the extensively published information of its long period of nuclear collaboration with the US, Britain, West Germany and, in later years, Israel.'[17] This raised major issues about the passing on of nuclear technology and know-how. When South Africa joined the NPT, the IAEA went in to make its inspections and apparently found 350-kilogramme stockpiles of weapons-grade uranium, which was enough to make 70 nuclear warheads.[18] Clearly there could have been other cases of this sort; added to these concerns, North Korea threatened to pull out of the NPT. If it pulled out, North Korea would no longer be bound by the NPT's constraints so could develop nuclear weapons, for which it believes it has a deterrent need. US hostility to the North Korean regime such as more recently labelling it part of the 'Axis of Evil', contributes to this ongoing sentiment.

So CND placed its hope for the future in a renewed and strengthened NPT and its campaigning emphasis on the role that Britain, through Trident, was playing in undermining the NPT. 'The simple fact is,' stated CND's Annual Report in 1993, 'that Britain's record on proliferation is abysmal. Trident is not only an increase in fire-power, but also an increase in range, accuracy and the number of targets that can be hit ... It is disappointing that whilst the US and Russia have taken large steps towards disarmament in the START II agreement, Britain has consistently refused to allow its nuclear weapons to be part of disarmament negotiations.'[19] With the end of the Cold War, Britain decommissioned tactical weapons designed to fight Soviet tanks and ships, whilst maintaining its strategic arsenal and starting research on weapons for use in the new wars in the third world. After the Gulf War, naval tactical nuclear weapons were withdrawn from service, along with half of its air force tactical weapons by 1994. The rest were withdrawn soon afterwards. At the same time, to deal with the British lack of tactical weapons, 'the government decided to reduce the number of warheads on some of the Trident missiles, these thus becoming few or single-warheaded sub-strategic missiles.'[20] The government was clearly keeping its options open about where it wished to target its nuclear weapons.

The Trident submarines were relentlessly rolled out over the next few years. There were continual protests against the Trident submarines and the Faslane Peace Camp was estab-

lished at the Faslane base, near Glasgow in Scotland, in opposition to them, with strong support from Scottish CND.
Concerns were also strong about the increased transportation
of nuclear weapons by road, as warheads for the Trident
submarines were taken from their place of manufacture – AWE
Burghfield, near Aldermaston in the south of England – to the
Coulport base in Scotland. CND and local authorities worked
together to put pressure on the government to issue guidelines on what to do in the event of a nuclear accident with one
of these warhead convoys. Eventually the Home Office issued
guidelines. CND assisted the Nukewatch network (see
Chapter five), organised to monitor, track and oppose the
convoys, distributing posters, leaflets and activist briefings.
Very serious work, in particular by Di McDonald and
Nukewatch South, ensured that most convoys were tracked
successfully. Other activities to publicise the link between the
convoys and Trident included the Stop Trucking with Trident
day of action in June 1993, as well as producing informative
briefings on the convoy movements.[21]

In 1994, CND produced a *Blueprint for a Nuclear Weapon-Free
World*, aimed primarily at opinion-formers and decision-
makers, in the run-up to the Nuclear Non-Proliferation
Treaty Review Conference in 1995. It argued that the only
alternative to proliferation is disarmament and stated that,
'With relations between the nuclear powers better than they
have been for decades there would appear to be no obvious
reason why we cannot build on these historic but limited
deals [INF Treaty, START I and II] to really move towards the
complete elimination of nuclear weapons.'[22] The Blueprint
outlined 12 key steps for a nuclear weapon-free world,
presenting a strong programme of campaigning demands.
They included the drafting of a Global Treaty to Ban All

Nuclear Weapons, the cancellation of Trident, the agreement of the Comprehensive Test Ban Treaty, the agreement of a treaty to halt the production of all fissile materials, and the setting up of a fund to research safe and sustainable alternatives to nuclear power. The central demand was that the NPT, which was up for review the following year, should not be extended indefinitely – as the nuclear weapons states wished – but should be extended for a limited period only, conditional on a treaty to ban nuclear weapons being agreed, signed and ratified within 10 years. But there clearly was an obvious reason why progress was not going to be made: namely, the fact that the world's sole superpower intended to retain its nuclear weapons, using them in new political ways in relation to the third world and in its self-appointed role of global policing. However, CND went on to organise its first national demonstration in London for a number of years, in October 1994. Under the theme of 'Nuclear-Free World or Nuclear Free-for-All', 5,000 – mostly young – people participated. According to Lawrence Wittner, 'Featuring music, giant puppets and speeches by movement leaders, British MPs and youth activists, the Trafalgar Square event evoked much of the spirit of the past.'[23]

Campaigning against nuclear testing

The following year was to bring a greater focus on nuclear issues, as a number of events coincided. 1995 was the 50th anniversary of the atomic bombing of Hiroshima and Nagasaki. It was also the NPT Review Conference, and a year that saw a new bout of French nuclear testing. In the early 1990s, a testing moratorium was in place, but it became clear that the nuclear weapons states were interested in resuming tests, particularly the US, Britain and France. In this situation, anti-nuclear organisations began to campaign vigorously, not only to extend the moratorium, but also to achieve a Comprehensive Test Ban Treaty. This would add to the conditions of the Partial Test Ban Treaty of 1963, by making all tests illegal, not only the atmospheric ones outlawed by the Partial Test Ban Treaty. CND worked to establish a coalition of organisations, the British Nuclear Test Ban Coalition, which drew together peace, environmental and development groups to work for a ban through a variety of campaigning and lobbying activities, including a nation-wide petition. In July 1993, under strong public pressure, President Clinton extended the US moratorium on testing until at least September 1994, on condition that no other country resumed testing. He also indicated that the US would work towards a full Comprehensive Test Ban Treaty by September 1996.[24]

The bad news was that fairly rapidly, other nuclear weapons states began to move towards the resumption of testing. In October 1993, China began testing again. Whilst the US did not itself begin tests, it indicated a desire to have a watering down of a possible Comprehensive Test Ban Treaty – allowing perhaps for small explosions, and limiting the Treaty to 10 years' duration. Then in June 1995, President Chirac of France announced that although it would in the future sign a Comprehensive Test Ban Treaty, France was going to start testing again in September 1995 in the Pacific. The response to all these developments was absolute outrage across the world, but in particular against the French tests. Centre-stage in the anti-testing campaign was a consumer boycott of French goods, which CND strongly promoted. There was also great support for the boycott in other parts of the world: 'Irate citizens poured French wine into the gutters, and Australian unions refused to handle French cargo or French postal and telecommunications services. "You should not underestimate the sense of outrage here," declared New Zealand's prime minister. Sales of French wines and champagne dropped by a third in Australia and New Zealand, and polls in the latter nation found the public opposition to the resumption of French nuclear tests hit an astonishing 98 per cent.'[25]

CND campaigned vigorously against the French tests, producing a range of campaigning materials under the slogan 'Non', protesting at the French Embassy and lobbying parliament. Widespread public concern was apparent from the thousands of enquiries about nuclear testing that poured into the CND office. Protest against the Chinese testing was also organised: Youth CND had three activists charged with 'invading China' when they painted shadows – symbolic of those obliterated in nuclear explosions – outside the Chinese Embassy in London.[26] As had been the case in the late 1950s and early 1960s when popular hostility to nuclear testing had resulted in the Partial Test Ban Treaty, so now in the 1990s this massive worldwide opposition led to a rapid development towards the Comprehensive Test Ban Treaty. The French government, which had been planning to continue testing until May 1996, actually stopped in January 1996. It had also been holding out for the exemption of small or 'low-yield' tests from the Treaty. It gave up that position and accepted the principle of a 'zero-yield' treaty – one with no exemptions at all. The US also accepted the zero-yield position. In July 1996, China gave up testing. Obstacles arose however, as India insisted that it would not accept the Treaty unless a timetable was agreed for the abolition of all nuclear weapons. Other countries – including Britain – joined in the disruption by saying that the Treaty should not come into force unless the three non-declared nuclear weapons states of India, Pakistan and Israel signed it.[27] In spite of the obstacles, however, the Treaty eventually came into existence. The

Australian government took it directly to the UN General Assembly for endorsement in September 1996, where it was approved by 158 votes to 3.

The NPT Review Conference 1995

During the intense campaigning against the tests, throughout 1995, the Nuclear Non-Proliferation Treaty Review Conference and the Hiroshima Anniversary had made their marks. Under the leadership of Chair Janet Bloomfield, a committed Quaker peace activist, CND had worked hard both in the run-up to the NPT conference – through lobbying, local meetings and campaigning of all sorts – and at the event itself, to put British nuclear weapons policy under massive pressure. With intensified campaigning, popular support was now in CND's direction, 'with opinion polls from Gallup and Mori showing over 50 per cent of the British public opposed to nuclear weapons for the first time.'[28] Indeed, in the run up to the conference, the *Independent* reported that CND's policy of opposition to Trident was attracting worldwide support.

The NPT had come into force in 1970, and had provided for a 25-year Review Conference to decide on the future of the Treaty. So the conference, which took place from 17 April to 13 May 1995, was required to decide whether the Treaty should be extended, and if so, for how long. Anti-nuclear campaigners, fearing endless prevarication by the nuclear weapons states, wanted to have a 10-year deadline by which to complete its goals. But as was expected, the nuclear weapons states did not wish to be restrained in this way, and aimed for indefinite extension. In fact, this was the first NPT conference in which all five declared nuclear weapons states participated – China and France had only signed up in 1992. That was in itself an achievement. The conference also managed to reach three other agreements: the NPT was to be indefinitely extended; a set of principles and objectives on non-proliferation was to be adopted; and an improved review process was to be set up.[29] A number of countries, in particular South Africa, Mexico and Sri Lanka, worked hard to achieve these agreements, and other issues were also addressed, including the universality of the Treaty and nuclear weapon-free zones. It was also agreed that preparatory committees would meet in the three years prior to the five-yearly review conference, to try to exert greater pressure on the nuclear weapons states to make some progress towards disarmament.

Of course, what the conference failed to deal with was how to bring about disarmament: how to set a realistic timetable for the nuclear weapons states to comply with Article VI (ie pursuing nuclear disarmament), and thus end the NPT stand-off (where the nuclear weapons states have a massive military advantage over the non-nuclear weapons states, perpetuating a morally indefensible situation that can be used to their own political advantage). As a result of their disappointment at the indefinite extension of the NPT, activist organisations working for the global abolition of nuclear weapons got together to found Abolition 2000, a worldwide network focusing on the demand for a treaty on the phased elimination of all nuclear weapons by the year 2000. Around 400 organisations were involved more or less from the start and, although their goal was not achieved in 2000, the network continues to play a positive role, particularly in campaigning around the NPT process. Former CND Chair Janet Bloomfield, who did so much to help the development of Abolition 2000, remains active in its leadership.

The World Court Project

There was one more positive development for the movement in the mid-1990s, before the situation began to go rapidly downhill. This was over the question of the legality of the use of nuclear weapons. In 1993, anti-nuclear activists from around the world, working together as the World Court Project, persuaded the World Health Organization to get an advisory ruling from the International Court of Justice (also known as the World Court). Campaigners had collected over 100 million signatures worldwide on the Appeal from Hiroshima and Nagasaki, and 170,000 Declarations of Public Conscience, which were presented to the Court. In Britain, this task was spearheaded by George Farebrother, who worked tirelessly to collect signatures. This was the first time ever that citizens had brought a case.[30] In the face of major opposition by the nuclear weapons states, in 1994 sympathetic countries in the UN General Assembly backed up the Project. They put a resolution to the General Assembly to ask the Court for an advisory opinion, and it received overwhelming support. The question they asked the Court was, 'Is the threat or use of nuclear weapons in any circumstances permitted under international law?'

The Court gave its opinion, in 1996, that the use of a nuclear weapon is 'unlawful'.[31] It also took the view that the threat of use of a nuclear weapon is illegal. Within the team of judges there was some difference of view over the implications of the right to self-defence enshrined in Article 51 of the UN Charter. Nevertheless, 10 of the 14 judges came to the conclusion that the existing body of international law governing the conduct of armed conflict would make the use or threat of use of nuclear weapons illegal. With reference to the existing body of humanitarian law, the judges made these points in their opinion:

The cardinal principles contained in the texts constituting the fabric of humanitarian law are the following. The first is aimed at the protection of the civilian population and civilian objects and establishes the distinction between combatants and non-combatants; states must never make civilians the object of attack and must consequently never use weapons that are incapable of distinguishing between civilian and military targets. According to the second principle, it is prohibited to cause unnecessary suffering to combatants: it is accordingly prohibited to use weapons causing them such harm or uselessly aggravating their suffering. In application of that second principle, states do not have unlimited freedom of choice of means in the weapons they use . . . In conformity with the aforementioned principles, humanitarian law, at a very early stage, prohibited certain types of weapons either because of their indiscriminate effect on combatants and civilians or because of the unnecessary suffering caused to combatants, that is to say, a harm greater than that unavoidable to achieve legitimate military objectives. If an envisaged use of weapons would not meet the requirements of humanitarian law, a threat to engage in such use would also be contrary to that law.[32]

The Court gave 'no opinion' on whether the use of nuclear weapons might be legal in a situation of extreme self-defence where the existence of a state was threatened. The judges differed in their views on this, in a scenario, for example, where a state is under attack from weapons of mass destruction. Three judges considered nuclear weapons to be unlawful regardless of Article 51, because a state so defending itself would be in open violation of the cardinal principles of international law. 'A nuclear weapon launched against an urban centre of an aggressor state by a defending state would make the defending state the source of "immeasurable suffering" to the civilian population within the territorial borders of the regime instigating the aggression. The potential annihilation of millions of innocent noncombatants as a "defensive act" would be inherently unlawful, constituting a gross violation of humanitarian and other international law'.[33]

Lawrence Wittner describes the World Court ruling as a limited victory, which it was, but it was also true that, although there was a loophole for nuclear use, it was a very small one – much smaller than the one the nuclear weapons states wanted.[34] Despite its limitations, the ruling has been of considerable help to anti-nuclear activists since, particularly in arguing against nuclear first-strike policies and the development of a new generation of nuclear weapons designed for first use.

The nuclear club expands

The second half of the 1990s, which included the carrying out of nuclear tests by first India and then Pakistan in May 1998, was a downward spiral for peace and disarmament. CND mounted immediate protests, whilst also highlighting the hypocrisy of the nuclear weapons states, which used the same arguments to justify keeping their own nuclear weapons as India and Pakistan used to justify getting them. Right wing Prime Minister Atal Bihari Vajpayee, whose party, the BJP, had supported Indian nuclear weapons since 1964, declared that the tests would 'silence India's enemies and show India's strength'. In the month of the test, 91 per cent of Indians polled supported the bomb, but five months later support had slumped to 44 per cent, with the realisation that Pakistan was now in a position to nuke them.[35] So now, together with the five declared nuclear weapons states and Israel, there were eight known nuclear powers. This was a terrible and dangerous development, but the realisation of this came home so strongly to a number of states that it triggered a really remarkable initiative, which has inspired hope amongst anti-nuclear activists ever since.

In June 1998, Brazil, Egypt, Ireland, Mexico, New Zealand, Slovenia, South Africa and Sweden issued a declaration entitled: 'Towards a Nuclear Weapons-Free World'. Working together as the New Agenda Coalition (NAC), these countries demanded that the nuclear weapons states commit themselves to the elimination of their nuclear weapons and work on practical steps towards their elimination. Slovenia withdrew from the NAC under pressure from NATO, but the rest of them vigorously pursued their goal in the face of major opposition from the nuclear weapons states, and received strong support within the UN General Assembly. The NAC states came to work closely with the Middle Powers Initiative (MPI), a network of major civil society organisations brought together by the Canadian senator and former Disarmament Ambassador, Douglas Roche. The MPI sought to persuade middle-power nations to press for nuclear abolition, so the goals of the two groups coincided in a positive way, with the MPI bringing campaigning groups into the equation. It was the work of the NAC states that was to result in the adoption of the '13 practical steps' at the NPT Review Conference in 2000. At this Conference, the nuclear weapons states gave an 'unequivocal undertaking to accomplish the total elimination of their nuclear arsenals', and agreed to 'Thirteen Steps' to achieving this goal. These included the ratification of the Comprehensive Test Ban Treaty, the commencement of negotiations for a Fissile Material Cut-Off Treaty (which would prevent states from producing fissile material for weapons) and the preservation and strengthening of the ABM Treaty. The strength of public feeling worldwide that contributed to the achievement of the Thirteen Steps was clearly demonstrated at the NPT Review Conference, when Abolition 2000 presented a petition calling for abolition to the chairman of the conference. There were 13.4 million signatures on the petition.[36]

CND's campaigning initiatives

CND conducted a range of anti-Trident campaigning initiatives in the late 1990s, in the run up to the NPT Review Conference. The election of a Labour government had not brought any advance for the anti-nuclear movement, in spite of the fact that a number of members of the government had in the past been members of CND. CND produced a detailed submission for the new government's Strategic Defence Review, containing recommendations that could be implemented immediately. But as the CND Annual Report of 1997 pointed out: 'It's just a shame that, despite the election result, Labour spokespeople still trot out the lie that no savings can be made by scrapping Trident as the money has already been spent.'[37] Events such as the Traffickin' Trident tour attempted to raise public awareness of the ongoing dangers of the Trident nuclear weapons system. A massive 20-foot long 'missile' was transported from Faslane, Scotland to Downing Street over two weeks in May 1997, being seen by tens of thousands of people en route and receiving considerable media coverage. Other actions involving numerous local activists continued, such as the monitoring and obstruction of nuclear warhead convoys, the maintenance and support of peace camps – such as the longstanding and courageous Faslane peace camp – and opposition to nuclear power and the transportation of nuclear waste, particularly in areas housing nuclear power stations and suffering the waste transports.

Activists' reports

The monitoring group Nukewatch was very active during the late 1990s, as is shown by the following report given for the first six months of 1998:

> *Seven convoys containing Trident warheads left AWE Aldermaston for the final assembly plant at AWE Burghfield. On 15 June, a convoy of Trident warheads left AWE Burghfield for Scotland. Meanwhile, seven convoys have brought the last WE-177s and the first of the Chevaline warheads for disassembly from East Anglia to AWE Burghfield. Special Nuclear Materials convoys continue to go from the AWEs to Rolls Royce Nuclear, Derby and to AEATech, Harwell. AWE Nuclear Waste goes by road to Drigg [Cumbria], AEATech, Harwell, Winfrith [Dorchester] and Rechem in Southampton. (It also goes by pipeline into the Thames and Silchester Sewage Works and out of the stacks into the atmosphere.) These are the realities which the SDR [Strategic Defence Review] does not make clear. If you SEE or HEAR of a convoy . . . please ring us urgently.*[38]

Extracts from CND regional reports from this time also give a flavour of the range of activities undertaken:

> *We marked CND's 40th anniversary with a wonderful social event, 'Marching Through the Decades', bringing together old and new members and setting the tone for an active year ahead. During the Iraq crisis, we set up demos and public meetings, and joined the Greater Manchester Coalition Against War in the Gulf. We've had public meetings on MOX [fuel made out of uranium and plutonium, produced at the Sellafield Thorp nuclear reprocessing*

plant] and on the Global Nuclear Trade and organised our second successful Abolition 2000 Citizen's Forum . . . We're co-ordinating the Walk for Disarmament, Traffickin' Trident in our area, Hiroshima Day/Anti-testing actions and organising visits to Faslane with the new group 'Manchester Anti-Nuclear Direct Action'. And, of course, organising the Hague Peace Day and helping to co-ordinate this [CND annual] Conference.

Greater Manchester and District CND

A major feature of this year's work has been nuclear transport campaigning. The discovery that MOX flights could be over-flying the region, added to the regular trains bound for Sellafield and radiation convoys, resulted in us producing a 'Nuclear Crossroads' briefing pack for local politicians and journalists. This has led to city council discussions of the issues we raised. Land-based nuclear transport is observed and logged and gains publicity. We have also been heavily involved in the MOX seminars organised in Carlisle by Nigel Chamberlain, and have lobbied Sellafield and Westminster on transport safety issues, in addition to writing a submission in response to the PA Consulting report on the financial case for MOX.

West Midlands CND

Our grant from National CND has made possible the biggest change in our own history; the establishment of a CND workspace (desk, computer, files, etc) in The Greenhouse, where up to now we have merely perched. We organised a gathering of about 50 at the Peace Pillar in central Norwich on Remembrance Sunday, at which we read poems and songs about peace. Our white poppy sales (in local shops and cafes) caused a bigger than usual stir in the local press. In December we did the giant Christmas card to T Blair . . . a useful and heartening street action. During the Gulf crisis we had a letter in our local press co-sponsored by about a dozen Norwich groups. In April we helped King's Lynn CND mount a Chernobyl exhibition in their library. We joined the annual John Bugg walk on the public footpath through Lakenheath US Air Base.[39]

Norwich CND

Campaigning against Star Wars

Meanwhile, progress on disarmament between the US and Russia had ground to a halt. The Russian parliament refused to ratify START II and so strategic nuclear arsenals remained at the levels agreed in START I in 1991. In March 1997, Boris Yeltsin and Bill Clinton met at Helsinki and arrived at a 'framework agreement' for a START III, but they also agreed it was not possible to make any progress on it until the Russian parliament ratified START II. Finally this did happen under the leadership of Vladimir Putin (Yeltsin's successor) in April 2000, but by the end of Clinton's term of office, Russia and the US between them still had around 34,000 nuclear warheads.[40] The Comprehensive Test Ban Treaty, which had been such a great advance, ran into a brick wall in the US in 1998. Since the US elections in 1994, the US Congress was dominated by Republicans, and there was significant opposition to the Treaty. President Clinton backed the ratification of the Treaty, campaigners worked vigorously for it and public opinion was overwhelmingly in favour, but the Republicans in the Senate killed it off in October 1999.

The situation also deteriorated over National Missile Defense, the 1990s version of Reagan's SDI, or Star Wars. The Republicans were extremely keen on this, while the Democrats opposed it on the basis of its cost, its dubious reliability and the likelihood that it would cause a new nuclear arms race. Under pressure from the Republicans, in 1996 Clinton agreed to its development. In March 1999 its deployment was endorsed by Congress, even though a workable system did not yet exist. Massive campaigning then followed and in September 2000, Clinton announced that he would not authorise deployment of the system. He had decided to leave that decision to his successor. Unfortunately that turned out to be George W Bush.

Campaigning against the US's National Missile Defense system and for the maintenance of the ABM Treaty was a major area of work for CND during this period, in particular opposing British participation in the scheme. In May 2000, on the 30th anniversary of the signing of the ABM Treaty, local CND groups sent giant postcards to Prime Minister Tony Blair protesting against US National Missile Defense plans. Bruce Kent and Jeremy Corbyn MP, CND Council member and MP for Islington (where the CND offices are located), sent the postcard from National CND. A clear focus for the campaigning was the Fylingdales and Menwith Hill bases in Yorkshire, both intended to have functions within the National Missile Defense system. In 2000, the Point the Finger campaign aimed to expose the nuclear collaboration between Britain and the US, and in particular attempts to use the Yorkshire bases for the system. The campaign began at the annual 'Independence Day from America' action at Menwith Hill, organised by the Campaign for the Accountability of American Bases (CAAB). A four-day walk from Menwith Hill to Fylingdales concluded with an action at Fylingdales, attended by around 300 people. From there, the campaign focused on Aldermaston, before concluding on Nagaski Day with protests at both Downing Street and the US Embassy.

Leading members of CND who were also activists at the Yorkshire bases – Dave Webb, a distinguished scientist, and Helen John, a former Greenham woman and founder of the Womenwith Hill women's peace camp – joined the board of the Global Network against Nuclear Power and Weapons in Space, a campaigning network initiated in the US. Yorkshire CND pioneered strong links internationally to campaign against National Missile Defense and played a leading role in initiating CND's work in this area.

The Hague Appeal for Peace Conference

The Hague Appeal for Peace Conference in May 1999 marked the centenary of the Hague Peace Conference of 1899, from which the foundations had been laid for the International Court of Arbitration (which eventually became the International Court of Justice). The International Peace Bureau, together with International Physicians for the Prevention of Nuclear War, the International Association of Lawyers Against Nuclear Arms, and the World Federalist Movement, organised an international conference that attracted around 10,000 people from across the world – of which over 2,000 were under 25 years old – to discuss peace and nuclear disarmament. Those attending included Nobel Prize winners – the nuclear physicist Joseph Rotblat had won the Nobel Peace Prize in 1995 – and the UN secretary general. Bruce Kent reported on the Conference for *CND Today*, describing it as a success beyond all expectations: 'Archbishop Tutu was the star of the opening ceremony. If we could get rid of apartheid why shouldn't we get rid of war? . . . The Conference was also the launch pad for several international campaigns and notably the campaign for the ratification of the treaty setting up the international criminal court, and the international campaign to stop the use of child soldiers.'[41] The conference issued a 50-point Agenda for the Future, of which one was to: 'Negotiate and ratify an international treaty to eliminate nuclear weapons.' But the Hague Conference did not get the scale of publicity that it might otherwise have done because it coincided with the illegal NATO war on the Federal Republic of Yugoslavia, which had begun on 24 March 1999, continuing for 79 days until 10 June.

The NATO war on Yugoslavia

1999 was also the year when the world saw the true meaning of NATO's expansion eastwards with the NATO intervention and bombing of Yugoslavia. Through the 1980s, the International Monetary Fund (IMF) had demanded neo-liberal economic reform as a condition for loans. This had devastated the Yugoslav republics and fuelled rising tensions between the richer and poorer regions and republics. Important forces in the wealthier republics, such as Slovenia and Croatia, began to believe that they should hold on to more of their wealth instead of subsidising poorer republics and regions such as Kosovo. Their ultimate goal became secession to join the German and Austrian economic zone to their north. The economic crisis also exacerbated tensions within Serbia over the constitutional status of the autonomous provinces, most notably that of Kosovo. Germany and Austria intervened rigorously to support Croatian and Slovenian separatism. The problem with this approach was that the 11 per cent of Croatia's population who were Serbs would wish to stay in Yugoslavia with their fellow Serbs. For Bosnia, the secession of Slovenia and Croatia would inevitably set off a three-way conflict between its Muslim, Croatian and Serb communities.

Britain had a tradition of good relations with Yugoslavia, and particularly Serbia, resulting from its stand against Nazi Germany in World War II. Many regretted the break-up of what had been a progressive and open socialist society that had found a federal and peaceful solution to the complex diversity of communities in the south Slav state. In the early 1990s, a number of MPs, in particular Alice Mahon, Tony Benn and Tam Dalyell, set up the Committee for Peace in the Balkans, to advocate and support negotiated political solutions in Yugoslavia. Given the strong leadership given by Labour MPs (although others were also involved), the CND specialist section Labour CND gave active support to the Committee; CND itself also participated in the Committee from the start. The Committee mounted a No Bombing campaign when NATO bombed the Bosnian Serbs in 1995, but it played a hugely more important role in leading the opposition to the NATO attacks on the Federal Republic of Yugoslavia (now composed only of Serbia and Montenegro) in 1999.

The NATO war on Yugoslavia in 1999 was of considerable significance, not just for the communities involved, but in the wider political context. It was a precursor to the Iraq War, in that it was an illegal intervention into a sovereign state that had taken no offensive action against NATO. Legitimate grievances of the Kosovan Albanians were manipulated and violence provoked within the province of Kosovo to justify what was presented as a 'humanitarian' war.[42] But it was clear that the air offensive against Yugoslavia was neither lawful nor humanitarian. The UN charter prohibits the use of force except in self-defence. This was clearly not a question of self-defence for NATO, and the bombardment did not take place under the authority of the UN Security Council; two of its permanent members, Russia and China, were opposed to the attacks. The US bypassed the Security Council and took action through NATO, claiming that it was bombing in accordance with humanitarian principles. As the British Foreign

Office had observed some years previously: 'The overwhelming majority of contemporary legal opinion comes down against the existence of a right to humanitarian intervention.'[43] But whatever the legality of the issue, the argument that the war was a moral one – to protect the Kosovan Albanians from Serb brutality and ethnic cleansing – also had very shaky foundations. Official reports from the run-up to the war show that the extremist Kosovan Albanian KLA was deliberately seeking to provoke outside intervention. In fact the UN Secretary-General's report covering the period January to mid-March 1999 showed that the resumption and continuation of hostilities in this period was initiated by the KLA and not by the Serbs. The report accepted the statement of the Organization for Security and Co-operation in Europe (OSCE) about 'persistent attacks and provocations by the Kosovan Albanian paramilitaries.'[44] (The OSCE had sent a mission of 1,000 verifiers to Kosovo in October 1998 to oversee the withdrawal of government troops, so were well-placed to observe what was taking place on the ground.)

During the 79 days of bombing, NATO made 37,000 bombing sorties but, although it was labelled a NATO attack, in fact it was overwhelmingly a US effort. As Peter Gowan describes: 'The US flew over 80 per cent of the strike sorties, over 90 per cent of the electronic warfare missions, fired over 80 per cent of the guided air weapons and launched over 95 per cent of the cruise missiles.' He also notes that command structures and decision making were in US hands, so that whilst European NATO allies had a great symbolic significance in the conflict, the overwhelming US control had considerable political significance within Europe.[45]

The Committee for Peace in the Balkans led a No Bombing campaign, which CND, under the leadership of Chair Dave Knight (who succeeded Janet Bloomfield in 1996), supported from the outset. Polls showed that almost a third of the population consistently opposed the NATO bombing and the Committee built a broad campaign with some significant support. The Labour left was divided on the issue and the TUC general council supported a European TUC statement backing the bombing. However, a number of trade unions did oppose the bombing; these included the National Union of Journalists (NUJ), which took a strong position against media bias over the war and the targeting of Serbian television by NATO bombers. The public service union UNISON, the Fire Brigades Union (FBU), and the university and college lecturers' Union, NATFHE, also opposed the bombing. Journalist and film maker John Pilger, playwright Harold Pinter and actress Maggie Steed were prominent campaigners with the Committee. The Serbian community in Britain organised a permanent 24-hour picket opposite Downing Street for the duration of the war, attracting up to 3,000 people at the weekends. The Serbian protestors popularised the target symbol, which was held up by Yugoslavs as they acted as human shields trying to protect their bridges from NATO bombing. Three demonstrations were held against the bombing, on 11 April, 8 May and 5 June. The attendance on these was 10,000, 25,000 and 20,000 respectively. Regional demonstrations also took place up and down the country, along with numerous well-supported public meetings, with local CND activists playing a major role.

NATO's boast of the pinpoint accuracy of its bombing led many to believe that many of the 'errors' in which civilians were killed were in fact deliberate. These included: the striking of a passenger train in Serbia, killing 20 civilians; the bombing of a convoy of Kosovan Albanian refugees, killing 73 civilians; the bombing of the Chinese Embassy in Belgrade, killing 3 Chinese citizens; and the bombing of a hospital and

of a prison. In the case of the bombing of the Serbian television studios in Belgrade, this was an entirely deliberate
attempt to prevent Serbs from hearing an alternative point of
view, killing journalists and others in the process. NATO
forces used cluster bombs and depleted uranium weapons.
The latter was linked with cancers and birth defects in Iraq,
and with Gulf War Syndrome in US troops. US jets launched
31,000 depleted uranium warheads and shells during the
bombing of Yugoslavia – and around 10,000 in Bosnia – in
spite of the fact that the UN Human Rights Commission had
condemned the use of radioactive projectiles. The US insisted
that there was no link between depleted uranium and health
problems but others disagreed. A UN team that visited Bosnia
and Kosovo found low-level radiation at 8 of the 11 sites
sampled. Team Chairman Pekka Haavisto recommended the
fencing off of contaminated areas, expressing concern about
the spread of radioactive materials: 'People had collected
radioactive shards as souvenirs, and there were cows grazing
in contaminated areas, which means the contaminated stuff
can get into milk.'[46] Despite US assurances of the safety of
depleted uranium weaponry, however, the EU ordered a
formal inquiry into the health risks, following a number of
cancer deaths of soldiers who had recently returned from the
Balkans.

The bombardment of Yugoslavia ended on 10 June with the
adoption of UN Resolution 1244, with the agreement to withdraw all Yugoslav forces from Kosovo and the entry to Kosovo
of an international security force. In fact, the Yugoslav
government had been prepared to accept this position at
Rambouillet earlier in the year. What it had opposed was the
US demand in Appendix B of the agreement: that the whole
of Yugoslavia should be open to NATO forces. No government
would willingly accept a clause giving hostile foreign troops

free rein throughout its territory. At the end of the war, Appendix B was not even mentioned, so it begged the question as to what the war was really for, as nothing more was achieved after the war than was already on offer through peaceful means before.[47] In September 1999, CND Conference overwhelmingly voted to support the position that NATO states should pay for the damage that bombing had inflicted on the civilian infrastructure and environment of Yugoslavia, that Britain should support the lifting of economic sanctions against Yugoslavia, that it should provide financial assistance for the reconstruction of the civilian infrastructure, clean up the environment and provide humanitarian aid on a non-discriminatory basis.[48]

The expansion of NATO

The Conference also highlighted another important issue – that of NATO expansion. Not only had NATO waged this illegal attack on Yugoslavia, it had also undergone a major expansion, immediately prior to the attack. In March 1999, Hungary, Poland and the Czech Republic, all former members of the Warsaw Pact, had all now become full members of NATO. Other former Warsaw Pact members were lined up to join in a future round of expansion. In addition to this, NATO also undertook some other changes. The war on Yugoslavia had been launched outside the terms of NATO's own Charter, which specified that military action could only be taken in defence of its own member states. NATO moved, while the war was actually going on, to change its remit to include such wars. At the 50th anniversary meeting of NATO leaders in Washington DC on 24 April 1999, a new 'Strategic Concept' was agreed. Drafted by the US, this committed NATO to 'out of area' – that is, offensive – operations in a geographical area extending far beyond the borders of the military alliance's

member states. It said that the future field of NATO operations would extend to the whole of western Europe, eastern
Europe and the former Soviet Union. This was a major challenge not only to Russia and other former Soviet republics,
but also to the authority of the UN because, even if NATO had
changed its remit, such actions would not be legal without
UN agreement. A suggestion, reportedly by France, that such
operations should require the authorisation of the UN was
rejected.[49] It was not surprising, then, that CND Conference
voted for 'NATO's immediate withdrawal from the NATO
nuclear alliance and the latter's dissolution.'

Into the new millennium

The new millennium opened to increasingly gloomy prospects
for world peace and nuclear disarmament. Nuclear weapons –
and even National Missile Defense – scarcely featured in the
US presidential elections of 2000. But the two main candidates
did have distinct positions. Republican George W Bush
wanted the National Missile Defense system to be built as soon
as possible and was willing to withdraw from the ABM Treaty
if Russia opposed the system. He was also opposed to the
Comprehensive Test Ban Treaty. Democrat Al Gore wanted a
smaller National Missile Defense system with delayed deployment and was vague about the ABM Treaty. But he favoured
ratifying the Comprehensive Test Ban Treaty.[50] Although Gore
received more votes than Bush, the Supreme Court gave the
Presidency to Bush amidst accusations of voting irregularities,
including the disenfranchisement of Democrat voters. The
Republicans had won control of both houses of Congress,
which was not a good development for nuclear disarmament.
As Lawrence Wittner describes it: 'Within a short time, the
victorious Republicans set about scrapping nuclear
constraints. Jettisoning the Comprehensive Test Ban Treaty,

they pressed forward instead with plans for national missile defense, the system they believed would guarantee US security and, thus, make arms controls unnecessary – at least for the United States.'[51] The terrorist attacks on the US on 11 September 2001 stripped away any lingering obstacles to Bush's increasingly aggressive foreign policy, and the next few years were to show a huge re-emphasis by the US leadership on nuclear weapons.

7

Campaigning since September 11

A decade ago, public concern about nuclear weapons had dropped away. The end of the Cold War made everyone feel much safer. In fact, many people believed that nuclear weapons had somehow disappeared. But in recent years that false sense of security has started to be eroded. The increasing tension of the late 1990s, the expansion of NATO into eastern Europe, the bombing of Yugoslavia and Washington's decision to create a National Missile Defense shield have alarmed a number of key countries – above all China, whose Embassy was bombed during the war on Yugoslavia. In the new millennium we have seen an increasing unilateralism on the part of the US, a rejection of international law and treaty frameworks and a steady course towards nuclear weapons as a usable part of the US military arsenal. The logic of this is simple; as the US economy becomes less competitive it increasingly uses its military pre-eminence to impose its interests. However, US military casualties risk provoking the kind of opposition that eventually emerged against the war in Vietnam. Nuclear weapons pose a way of cowing all possible opponents into submission. But to make the threat effective, the US knows it has to be prepared to actually carry it out. The British government has been complicit in these policies and has meekly followed the same path as Bush, irrespective of the price it has paid in the domestic political sphere.

One piece of arms control legislation has taken place, but it is of little genuine significance. In May 2002, the US and Russian governments signed the Strategic Offensive Reductions Treaty, intended to reduce deployed strategic nuclear warheads by nearly two thirds by 2012. In fact, the warheads were not required to be destroyed, but could be placed in storage instead. This obviously meant that they could fairly easily be redeployed if so desired. In addition, there was no ban on upgrading and improving actual deployed warheads, and no restrictions on tactical nuclear weapons. In effect, this appeared to be a rather cosmetic exercise.[1]

But just five years into the 21st century, the situation is radically different to that of the late 1990s, even though the US administration was already increasingly orientated towards more aggressive military policies. Whereas nuclear weapons had slipped right down the agenda in the 1990s, that is certainly no longer the case. But the context in which people now understand nuclear weapons is very different to the way it has been in the past. Through most of CND's existence, there were two nuclear-armed superpowers. Almost all discussion around nuclear weapons focused on superpower disarmament. The focus has now shifted, and it has been manipulated in a very specific way. We are told that the nuclear threat comes from 'rogue states' proliferating and developing nuclear weapons. It has even been deemed necessary to wage war on Iraq on suspicion that it may have been trying to develop nuclear weapons. These 'new threats', we are told, are the new great danger – third world countries that will try to nuke us. This is the reason given for the maintenance of our so-called nuclear deterrent, and the justification for the development of new nuclear weapons. This is what has brought nuclear weapons up the political agenda once again.

As a result of the war on Iraq, virtually everyone in Britain has heard of nuclear weapons and 'weapons of mass destruction'. WMD have even become the punch line in humorous advertising campaigns – a buzz word for the early 21st century. Of course everyone now knows – and nearly everyone in power admits – that there were no nuclear weapons in Iraq. But the possibility that Iraq possessed WMDs and supposedly had the capacity to deliver them far afield was used as an excuse to go to war on Iraq. A similar case seems to be under construction at the moment against Iran, with the US suggesting that Iran's civilian nuclear power programme is actually being misused to produce nuclear weapons. As yet, no evidence has been produced to show that the Iranians are doing what the US is accusing them of. But this has not stopped the US's war-like rhetoric against Iran. So this is why nuclear weapons are such a big issue at the moment; they are being used to justify wars. But is there a real danger presented by nuclear weapons, and if so, where does it lie?

To understand this we need to look first at the global political situation. The tragic events of 11 September 2001 – the terrorist attacks on the US – have had a massive impact on international relations and have reshaped the concerns of everyone about safety and security. But it would be a mistake to see the increasing global tensions and dangers solely as a result of September 11, as some would like to suggest. As we have seen, the US approach for decades has been to seek to use weapons, both conventional and nuclear, in a variety of military and political ways to secure its goals.

What is actually going on in the world?

President Bush and his supporters like to give the impression that the world today is a more dangerous place because evil terrorists, supported by rogue states, are attacking civilisation, freedom and democracy. President Bush makes out that his role is to defend these values by rooting out and destroying, by whatever means necessary, those responsible for the attacks upon them. In this crusade he does not allow himself to be inhibited by namby-pamby considerations such as international law or public opinion. But this interpretation of events is far from the truth. The Bush administration certainly has its own agenda, which is not merely responsive to world events. Documentary evidence from the US suggests that this is an agenda for US global military domination. So let us consider some of the basic features of US policy and strategy and how CND conducts its campaigns against them.

Some of the dominant figures in US political life subscribe to the ideas of an organisation called the Project for the New American Century (PNAC). PNAC was set up in 1997, supposedly as a non-profit educational organisation, whose goal is to provide US global leadership. In fact it is a neo-conservative think-tank with US Vice-President Dick Cheney, Defense Secretary Donald Rumsfeld and Deputy Secretary of Defense Paul Wolfowitz in its leadership, all firm advocates of decisive military action. PNAC is not at all secretive about its goals and clearly outlines on its website what it describes as 'fundamental propositions':

- That US leadership is good for both the US and the world
- That such leadership requires military strength, diplomatic energy and commitment to moral principle

- That too few US political leaders are making the case for global leadership.

Founded during the Clinton administration, PNAC was clearly aimed at winning hearts and minds within the US for a more aggressive foreign policy. But PNAC's vision is also consciously a throw-back to the past, in particular to the Reagan period. Indeed, PNAC's founding Statement of Principles calls for a Reaganite policy of military strength and moral clarity.[2] But the general approach of PNAC seems to be that US leadership means that other countries must subscribe to the US's world view, and its own concept of politics and economics. Thus in effect it seems that US leadership means US domination, and countries that do not accept, and comply with, the US framework are labelled rogue states. Increasingly it seems that where countries do not succumb to political or economic pressure to comply with US behavioural norms, they are subjected to military pressure. Just why the US increasingly turns towards military solutions is an interesting question, and the answer probably lies in weaknesses in the US economy.

Although the US seems to be at the height of its power – unchallenged as the single global superpower – it does have some fundamental economic problems. Whilst it has undoubted military supremacy in the world, it also has a massive balance of payments deficit, and this has affected the way in which the US relates to the rest of the world. Between World War II and 1974, the US had a favourable economic relationship with the non-socialist world; it was able to put money into other countries, it exported capital and was able to win widespread acceptance of its dominant role in the world. But the US suffered a major economic crisis in 1974, and since then the relationship has changed. The US has become a debtor nation in relative economic decline. Flows of money are now going into the US to support its economy, notably from the East Asian economies.

So the US now uses its military pre-eminence to compensate for its relative economic decline; it cannot secure global domination economically any more, so it is attempting to secure it militarily, in the process securing resources and strategic assets. Given the significance of US military policy for the rest of the world, CND has followed it very carefully. What we have found is of great concern; to call developments in US military policy alarming would be a considerable understatement. There are very explicit military plans for global domination.

Full Spectrum Dominance

In May 2000, the US Department of Defense issued a document entitled Joint Vision 2020, which spelt out how the US will achieve 'full spectrum' dominance by the year 2020. Full spectrum dominance means 'the ability of US forces, operating unilaterally or in combination with multinational and interagency partners, to defeat any adversary and control any situation across the full range of military operations.'[3] This dominance will operate in all domains: land, sea, air, space and information. Joint Vision 2020 addresses full spectrum dominance across a range of conflicts from nuclear war to major theatre wars, from regional conflicts to smaller-scale contingencies. This is a pretty comprehensive vision, but one of the most worrying aspects is the emphasis on the domination of space, bringing with it the spectre of the introduction of weapons – and perhaps even nuclear weapons – in space. US Space Command describes its own role as 'dominating the space dimension of military operations to protect US interests and investment. Integrating Space Forces into war-fighting capabilities across the full spectrum of conflict.'[4] Already many of the supposedly civilian communications and satellite systems in space can be – and have been – used for military purposes. In fact, they were used in the recent war on Iraq. The danger is the possibility of a move towards actual weapons being there.

The US has already made progress with a new so-called defence system, the US National Missile Defense system, the technologies of which lay the groundwork for these developments. NMD is often called 'Star Wars', as it is more or less an update of Reagan's SDI or 'Star Wars' of the 1980s.

One of the specific problems facing Britain, as well as the worldwide issues National Missile Defense presents, is that two bases in Yorkshire are being used for this system. RAF Fylingdales houses a ground-based early warning radar that will track missiles, and RAF Menwith Hill will deal with information concerning missile launches. This will of course put Britain in the line of fire between the US and any future military opponent with this type of capability. CND has opposed ABM systems ever since they were first suggested, and in particular since the early 1980s. Since its resurgence as a realisable project in the 1990s, it has been one of CND's key campaigns and we have been working hard over the past few years to raise public awareness of these developments and to pressurise the government to withdraw its consent for the use of British bases for the system.

In early 2001, CND organised a speaking tour for Rear Admiral Eugene Carroll, from the US Center for Defense Information, an outspoken opponent of National Missile Defense who had been a strong peace campaigner for many years, also speaking out against the neutron bomb and cruise missiles. As he came from a high-level forces background, his visit provoked considerable press interest and also helped to boost the campaign. His visit to Whitby stimulated the formation of a local action group against Fylingdales and its part in the system. In addition to local campaigning, CND also placed considerable importance on international co-operation against NMD. In May 2001, Yorkshire CND, working with local groups and the Global Network Against Weapons and Nuclear Power in Space, hosted an international conference to exchange information and coordinate international campaigning with participants from 20 countries. In Easter 2002, the national CND demo from Hyde Park to Trafalgar Square was on the theme of opposition to Star Wars. But the worst scenario occurred on 13 June 2002, when the US withdrew from the ABM Treaty in order to proceed with the system. CND marked the occasion with a press conference in the House of Commons. The type of ongoing campaigning against NMD is exemplified by the work of Yorkshire CND. Here is a sample of its activities during 2002:

In March we carted more people down to the major national star wars demo in London, Alice Mahon MP launched a Yorkshire CND-inspired Early Day Motion in parliament [calling for MPs to oppose Missile Defence] and we celebrated St George's Day by holding a street stunt dressed as St George Bush and Tony Blair. In May we were represented at the Global Network Conference in San Francisco and we held the first of two Days of Dance (a major fundraiser for us). In June we held the biggest ever demo at Fylingdales and did some fundraising at Glastonbury festival. In August we held a letter-writing lobby of MPs based on Alice Mahon's EDM [Early Day Motion] and supported the mass trespass of Fylingdales. October saw the Yorkshire CND International conference on missile defence, a successful blockade of Menwith Hill, and the second Day of Dance.[5]

In June 2003, a national 'No Star Wars' tour was organised, travelling the length and breadth of the country, holding public meetings, petitioning and raising public awareness that the government has signed a Memorandum of Understanding with the US that gives them permission to use Fylingdales for the system without consultation with parliament or the people. In 2004 a detailed briefing was produced on this subject and has been targeted at MPs. Actions have continued around the country, and at Fylingdales and Menwith Hill, and the issue of 'keeping space for peace' has become a significant one in spite of government attempts to avoid the discussion. Results from a public opinion poll that CND commissioned in 2004 show that the vast majority of people oppose the Star Wars system and weapons in space.[6] But the government has ignored us, and no debate has been allowed in parliament about British participation in this system, even though it presents grave dangers for all of us. From 2005, Yorkshire CND has produced a regular Missile Defence Bulletin to provide information on recent developments.

The development of war-fighting capacity in space is deeply worrying. The Star Wars system involves interceptor missiles being fired through space, with the development of new space lasers and the expansion of spying and monitoring systems and the probable 'weaponisation' of space. War in space may seem like something out of a science-fiction fantasy to us, but that is certainly not how the US military sees it. The budgets for the US military space projects are vast – already billions of dollars have been spent. US Space Command has also been explicit about its approach. As former Commander in Chief General Joseph W Ashy stated, 'Some people don't want to hear this . . . but – absolutely – we're going to fight in space. We're going to fight from space and we're going to fight into space.'[7]

These developments around Star Wars and weapons in space are clear examples of the US administration's contempt for international treaties and a multilateral approach to problem solving. We have already seen this with the dismissive US attitude towards the 1997 Kyoto Agreement (on reducing greenhouse emissions), towards the Comprehensive Test Ban Treaty and towards the International Criminal Court, set in action by the UN in 2002 to prosecute people accused of genocide, crimes against humanity and war crimes. The US has not ratified the International Criminal Court statute and therefore is not subject to its jurisdiction. It is also demonstrated by US withdrawal from the ABM Treaty, and its scorn for the spirit of the Outer Space Treaty, which came into force in 1967. This Treaty states that, 'Space belongs to all humankind, should benefit everyone and should be explored peacefully to promote international co-operation and understanding.' Instead the US plans to put military bases on the moon!

According to a US Congressional budget released in spring of 2005, the US Missile Defense Agency aims to spend nearly $675 million from 2008 to 2011 developing an 'experimental constellation of space-based missile interceptors', for launch in 2012. The Agency's director states that whilst there are no firm plans to deploy these interceptors in an operational capacity, the potential is 'worth evaluating'. On 1 March 2005, US Defense Secretary Rumsfeld signed a new National Defense Strategy paper that said the use of space 'enables us to project power anywhere in the world from secure bases of operation'. One of the chief aims of the new Strategy is 'to ensure our access to and use of space and to deny hostile exploitation of space to adversaries.'[8]

Not surprisingly, Russia and China are strongly opposed to space weapons and have recently pressed for a new treaty at the Conference on Disarmament in Geneva. China's ambassador to the Conference stated, 'It is urgent to stop the weaponisation of outer space and maintain it for the peaceful use of all humankind.' A Russian representative stated that it was vital, 'to start working out a legally binding instrument [treaty] ... to prohibit the deployment of any kinds of weapons in space.' But the US was not at the Conference. It insists that there is no need for a treaty because no country currently has weapons in space.[9]

US Nuclear Posture Review

The full range of operations outlined in Joint Vision 2020 includes conflicts involving the use of nuclear weapons. So what exactly is the US position on nuclear weapons and their use in war?

It is quite clear that nuclear weapons are a part of the Bush administration's drive towards global military dominance. In December 2001, the US Defense Department produced a report, mandated by Congress, laying out the direction for US nuclear forces over the next five to ten years.[10] This document, the Nuclear Posture Review, outlined a new strategy for US nuclear forces that is extremely dangerous and destabilising. In particular the Nuclear Posture Review marks a definitive break with the idea that nuclear weapons are basically there to deter other countries from using them against you because you can fire them back and destroy the other country too (a notion known as mutual assured destruction during the Cold War). Instead, the Nuclear Posture Review is up front about using nuclear weapons in a first-strike capacity, developing 'offensive strike systems', developing new nuclear weapons and reducing the time required for the US to resume nuclear testing. The Nuclear Posture Review has a nuclear 'hit list' of those countries with which the US thinks it might enter into a 'contingency' (in other words result in a nuclear attack by the US). Those countries are North Korea, Iraq, Iran, Syria, Libya, China and, possibly in the future, Russia. Taken together with the US's increasingly aggressive, unilateralist approach – which as we have seen in Iraq includes illegal pre-emptive war – embracing the possibility of nuclear first strike is appalling.

It is also worth noting that in addition to the US nuclear policies laid out in the Nuclear Posture Review, the Bush administration has outlined its new approach in a document entitled 'National Strategy to Combat Weapons of Mass Destruction'.[11] This asserts that the US has the right to use nuclear weapons pre-emptively – in peacetime and on its own authority – to stop states from acquiring nuclear, chemical or biological weapons. What's next? Pre-emptive nuclear war?

Nuclear proliferation and nuclear hypocrisy

These developments expose the hypocrisy of the US and UK governments. When they recently went to war on Iraq, the reasons given were Iraq's suspected possession of weapons of mass destruction, and supposed non-compliance with disarmament resolutions. In fact, neither of these was true. However, both the US and UK possess weapons of mass destruction and have never complied with their obligations to disarm under the NPT. This is double standards. It is worth understanding a bit about the NPT, because it is being used by the US to police countries suspected – genuinely or not – of trying to develop (proliferate) nuclear weapons. The recent issues around Iran's nuclear power programme spring to mind here.

The NPT entered into force in 1970 and was a deal between nuclear weapons states and non-nuclear weapons states. Those states with nuclear weapons agreed to get rid of them, whilst those without agreed not to get them. States party to the Treaty are entitled to the development of nuclear power for peaceful purposes. There are three 'pillars' to the treaty: disarmament, non-proliferation and peaceful use of nuclear power. In fact, remarkably little proliferation has taken place; 8, possibly 9 countries have nuclear weapons, even though round about 40 have nuclear power capabilities. But the five nuclear weapons states that signed the treaty – the US, Russia, UK, France and China – have made no progress whatsoever towards disarmament, as required in Article VI. The other countries known to have nuclear weapons – India, Pakistan and Israel – never signed up to the Treaty. North Korea has withdrawn from the Treaty. From time to time, the nuclear weapons states make great play of what is effectively tidying up their nuclear stockpiles, or developing more accurate weapons, but there is no disarmament and no abolition. This failure by the nuclear weapons states to comply with Article VI naturally leads other states to believe that they need nuclear weapons.

Not only that, but if the US and UK governments are developing new nuclear weapons, which CND believes to be the case, then they are themselves proliferating nuclear weapons. So it is clearly a case of 'Do what we say, not what we do'!

New nuclear weapons
It is clear from the Nuclear Posture Review that the US is planning to develop new nuclear weapons. British policy is also moving in this direction. Since 1950, Britain's atomic bomb factory has been located in Aldermaston in Berkshire, which is why many CND marches have focused on Aldermaston over the years. Massive government investment has taken place at Aldermaston recently, suggesting that new research and development is planned or already taking place.

The Atomic Weapons Establishment at Aldermaston is responsible for most of Britain's nuclear research activities, as well as developing weapons designs and producing nuclear weapons components. It is the home of Trident warhead production (Britain's nuclear weapons), maintenance, research and development. CND believes it is currently equipping itself to build new nuclear weapons; a new range of facilities is planned at the huge cost of around £2 billion. Building started in May 2005. A big increase in the workforce – possibly as many as 300 further scientists – is also planned. The new recruits, new laboratories, supercomputers and a laser to simulate the testing of nuclear weapons all add up to the possibility of Aldermaston being equipped to build or contribute to new nuclear weapons.

Over the last few years, campaigning against a new generation of nuclear weapons has been a major focus for CND. In the autumn of 2003, we launched the No New Nukes petition and campaign pack, and held a public meeting in parliament, entitled 'No New Nukes – No Pre-emptive War' and emphasising the purpose of the new nuclear weapons – to be used in a first-strike capacity in forthcoming wars. In 2004, CND worked with the Aldermaston Women's Peace Camp and local group Slough for Peace to organise a march from London to Aldermaston over the Easter weekend, with the specific goal of raising public awareness about the new developments and the dangers they bring. Hundreds of activists marched the whole distance, many of whom were young and new to the campaign. Here are some of the marchers' experiences:

Aldermaston WMDs are 50 miles from my house. My mates challenged me to a fitness test: a four-day protest march to the nuclear base. Kids living closer can expect higher cancer levels: at least I'm still fit enough to walk. £2 billion of taxes should buy real security, like health and education. Children shouldn't live under a nuclear shadow. Strangely when I photographed a policeman protecting the base he asked me to shoot his better side and posed. Think you can hold it up for 50 miles? Show your 'better side' and get fit! I challenge you: march next year.'

Neela Dolezalova, aged 19, London

Blisters, sun stroke, samba drums playing and queuing up for food with hundreds of people in a field by the side of an A road, by day three, somewhere between Slough and Reading, all this had become routine. The support from the people we passed was immense and overwhelming at times. The temples and churches that opened their doors to us were a sweet reminder that people still care. When we arrived, a bit late, a bit tired and very relieved at the rather ugly and nondescript nightmare that is AWE Aldermaston, the people cheered and music started and it was all worthwhile. What better way to draw attention to a new generation of nuclear weapons than to lead people to Britain's bomb-making factory.

Rachel Anderson, Nottingham[12]

CND is currently supporting the Block the Builders initiative of the Aldermaston Women's peace camp, which is mobilising in opposition to the building work that started at Aldermaston in May 2005.

Non-proliferation and counter-proliferation

In 2004, at the regular international conference to discuss progress on the NPT, the US representative did not refer to disarmament once. Indeed, recent reports indicate that at the 2005 NPT Review Conference (a five-yearly big assessment of progress towards disarmament), the US will seek to invalidate the Thirteen Steps to disarmament agreed in 2000, describing it as a historical document, and rejecting the 'unequivocal undertaking' to accomplish nuclear disarmament. They claim that a new document is needed that reflects the drastic changes in international security conditions, including the September 11 attacks in 2001. The reality is that the US and UK are researching new weapons and would be prepared to use them even against a non-nuclear weapons states, as well as developing weapons for confrontation with more powerful states such as Russia or China. This is the real driver of nuclear proliferation, together with US determination to make Israel the only nuclear weapons state in the Middle East.

The new jargon is 'counter-proliferation'. Preventing new countries getting nuclear weapons is the focus, and disarmament by the states that have nuclear weapons is completely ignored. The Non-Proliferation Department of the Foreign Office has been renamed the Counter-Proliferation Department. In 2003, British government minister Geoff Hoon even suggested that Britain has a legal right to nuclear weapons under the NPT. This is a profoundly wrong re-interpretation of the NPT; all we are legally entitled to do is to progress towards their abolition.

Trident is Britain's own nuclear weapons system and so is the central focus for CND's work, in a number of ways. CND works with Scottish CND and Trident Ploughshares at the Faslane and Coulport bases in Scotland. Major annual blockades take place: in 2004, the blockade was the mass action Carry on up the Clyde, in August. In 2005, the blockade will take place in the week of the G8 summit in July at Gleneagles in Scotland, making the links between militarisation and poverty. CND also works with the Nuclear Free Coalition in

Plymouth to oppose the ongoing refit of the Trident submarines taking place there in the Devonport Dockyards. Together with local groups, CND continues to highlight the environmental and health hazards of the refit – massively increased levels of radioactive pollution in the River Tamar, for example. CND's goal is for the UK to scrap Trident and comply with Britain's disarmament obligations. We argue for decommissioning, not recommissioning. Over the past few years CND has also organised and supported a number of demonstrations in Plymouth. In 2005 it is supporting the Trident Ploughshares Disarmament camp. Trident Plough-shares is a remarkable direct action organisation that campaigns against Trident. Here is a sample of its activities:

> *During 2004 many Trident and Trident-related sites were invaded, blockaded and decorated: Devonport: another camp, with the MoD admitting that recent campaigning activity had put back, by five years, the relationship between the city and the dockyard; Faslane and Coulport: small blockades throughout the year, a big blockade in August with 70 arrests, and lots of intrusions, by land and sea, during the two-week camp at Penton Wood; Aldermaston: some fine and meaningful artwork on buildings inside the fence; Burghfield: a break-in to give leaflets about war crime to base personnel; the Lockheed Martin HQ in London: a sit-in and repeated attention throughout the year; Northwood: a Citizen's Inspection to mark the release of Mordechai Vanunu.*[13]

CND also campaigns to prevent the development of a replacement for Trident. The 2003 Defence White Paper stated that UK nuclear weapons are 'likely to remain a necessary element of our security', and it has been announced that a decision will be made during the life of the parliament after the 2005 general election.[14] On being questioned about the Trident replacement during the election campaign, Tony Blair responded: 'Well, we've got to retain our nuclear deterrent, and we've had an independent nuclear deterrent for a long time. Now that decision is for another time, but in principle I believe it's important to retain our own independent deterrent.'[15] CND opposes any replacement for Trident and this will be the subject of urgent campaigning both inside parliament and in wider society.

International Law

So the US and UK have the plans and the policies; they are abandoning their obligation to nuclear disarmament and they are developing the wherewithal to conduct their new type of pre-emptive nuclear wars. However, they do face a few small problems, not least international law. Firstly, if the US and UK are planning to use nuclear weapons, is it legal? As we know from the World Court judgement in 1996 (see Chapter six), it is generally not. The legality of the use or threat of use of nuclear weapons has to be decided in accordance with the UN Charter and the law of armed conflict. Article 2(4) of the Charter prohibits the threat or use of force by any state against the territorial integrity or political independence of any other state. The exception is the right to self-defence but, even in this case, force has to be necessary and proportionate and must not violate international humanitarian law. In other words, given these requirements, the use of nuclear weapons is almost certainly always illegal. In any of the circumstances in which the UK has recently said that it would consider their use, it is definitely illegal. Within this, both indiscriminate attack and the causing of unnecessary suffering are outlawed. It is worth also reiterating the real legal situation with regard to nuclear weapons; we are legally obliged to get rid of them. This was reaffirmed as recently as December 2004, when the UN Secretary-General's High Level Panel produced a report entitled, 'A more secure world: our shared responsibility'. It stated that the nuclear weapons states must take steps towards restarting disarmament: 'They must honour their commitment under Article VI of the Treaty on the Non-Proliferation of Nuclear Weapons to move towards disarmament and be ready to undertake specific measures in fulfilment of those commitments; they should reaffirm their previous commitments not to use nuclear weapons against non-nuclear weapon States.'[16]

Secondly, if the US and UK are planning to wage further pre-emptive wars, will they be legal? The answer is a very clear No. Pre-emptive war is illegal under international law, as is war for regime change. But not only is it clear that the US and UK are no respecters of international law – they broke it waging war on Yugoslavia and Iraq – it is also clear that they are looking to change international law so that they can legally wage war on whom they like. British Prime Minister Tony Blair has made some running on this. In March 2004 he made a speech in his constituency in Sedgefield, where he made a fundamental attack on international law. Blair said that he was reaching for a different philosophy of international relations, breaking with the traditional notion that you did not interfere in a country unless it threatened you. The problem with Blair's new philosophy is that it could easily enshrine in law the right of the powerful to intervene anywhere in the world they choose. It is a recipe for a new colonialism. It may be that international law could be improved, but if changes are made they must be agreed by the whole of the international community, not just by two or three of the world's most powerful nations that want to impose their will.

At the moment, law is on our side, on the side of peace, and we must try to utilise it in our campaigning. CND has so far made a number of attempts to do this. In the autumn of 2002, we made a legal challenge to the UK government, arguing that it would be illegal to go to war against Iraq under UN Security Council Resolution 1441. In November, working together with the comedian Mark Thomas and Public Interest Lawyers, CND Chair Carol Naughton, who succeeded Dave Knight in 2001, served letters on Prime Minister Tony Blair, Secretary of State for Defence Geoff Hoon and Foreign Secretary Jack Straw. We asked them to clarify the government's position by a particular date, and if they hadn't replied by then we would take them to court. CND had commissioned a legal opinion from Rabinder Singh QC of Matrix Chambers on the question. His opinion was that the government could not legally go to war on the basis of United Nations Security Council Resolution (UNSCR) 1441. Firstly it contained no clear instruction that if Iraq failed to comply with the weapons inspectors then member states could take action and wage war. Secondly the phrases used in previous UN resolutions to indicate the use of force (such as 'all necessary means' and 'the severest consequences') were not present in 1441. In fact, the US and UK had fought and lost the battle to get them included. The government did not respond to our enquiries by the deadline, so our papers were lodged at the High Court. In the end, the judges ruled that the case could not be put because a British court could not rule on matters of high foreign policy, and that it was not in the public interest.

A further case followed on from this. In 2003, together with other organisations, CND took a legal initiative to bring Tony Blair, Geoff Hoon and Jack Straw to the International Criminal Court (ICC) for war crimes and crimes against humanity. Before the war started they were warned that if the conduct of the war violated international humanitarian law, then CND and others would take steps to hold them accountable before the ICC prosecutor. In November 2003, Peacerights (a group set up to promote peaceful conflict resolution), organised a tribunal of legal experts to determine whether international law had been violated during the war and occupation of Iraq. Included in this was the use of cluster bombs and depleted uranium munitions during the attack on Iraq. Both of these are indiscriminate in their impact; they can, and do, kill innocent civilians, including many children. This gives us a strong case, because discrimination and proportionality are central tenets of humanitarian law. The tribunal found that international law had been violated, and the results of the enquiry were sent to the attorney general, asking him to take action. He refused, so the case was taken to the ICC prosecutor. ICC Prosecutor Luis Moreno Ocampo has described the war crimes allegations as 'one of the most significant' cases he has seen, and has said that the allegations are being given 'deserved weight' by his investigators.[17] When the attorney general's advice on the legality of the war was finally published by the government on 28 April 2005, it was clear that there was a lot of overlap between his concerns and those of CND. Furthermore, he referred to both the CND challenge over UNSCR 1441, and our warning to the government on war crimes charges, in his opinion.[18] We are now giving support to the demand made by the families of servicemen killed during the Iraq war and occupation for an independent public inquiry into the legality of the war against Iraq.

The anti-war movement

The demonstrations in the UK against the war on Iraq were enormous and included, on 15 February 2003, the largest ever demonstration in British history. Up to 2 million people demonstrated in London on that day, tens of thousands more across Britain, and tens of millions across the world. The scale of this mobilisation showed the incredible public feeling against attacking Iraq. It also showed a new level of international co-ordination of peace campaigning that is crucial if we are to be successful in our demands for peace. In an increasingly globalised world, CND feels strongly that we must link and work internationally, not only within the peace movement itself, but also with other campaigns and movements. There is a clear link, for example, between war and poverty, war and human rights abuse, and we must work together with others to raise our demands in every arena.

One of the ways in which CND has pursued international links and co-operation is through the World Social Forum movement, which has the slogan – coined by the great Indian peace activist Arundhati Roy – 'Another World is Possible'. The social forum movement brings together a massive range of campaigning organisations, NGOs, civil society organisations, trade unions – huge numbers of people – to discuss new ways of solving problems, new alternatives for society, based on the values of peace and social justice. CND has been actively involved in both the European Social Forum (ESF) and the World Social Forum (WSF) since 2002. In October 2004, CND played a major role in the organisation of the ESF in London. The event attracted over 25,000 people, and one of the highlights was CND's organisation of a live telephone link-up with nuclear whistle-blower Mordechai Vanunu in Israel. The positive role of the ESF in linking up organisations and movements was very clearly shown when it was from the ESF in Florence in 2002 that the call came for a global Day of Action against war on 15 February to mobilise public opinion worldwide against a war on Iraq.

So already we have seen the scale of mobilisation that can take place if we cooperate internationally. But what about the anti-war movement in Britain? Britain is famous throughout the world for having a huge anti-war movement, and people watch our demos on television as far afield as Japan and the Philippines. The pulling down of the Bush statue, constructed by the anti-nuclear theatre group Theatre of War, on the occasion of Bush's visit to London, was beamed around the world. How has this movement come about?

After the attacks on the US on 11 September 2001, President Bush declared a 'war on terror', and it rapidly became clear that he was hell-bent on war against Afghanistan. Bush suspected the Taliban government there of harbouring and giving support to Osama Bin Laden and the Al Qaeda network, the chief suspect in the terrorist attacks. CND strongly supported the aim of capturing and bringing to justice those suspected of the crimes of September 11. CND's 2001 Annual Conference took place just a few days after September 11 and the conference was overwhelmingly united in condemning the terrorism, but also united in condemning all forms of terrorism, by states too, not just by non-state actors. We were also united in the view that war was not the answer and that war against a whole nation – Afghanistan was emerging as the likely target at this time – would undoubtedly result in many civilian casualties and was completely wrong. Even if Bin Laden was guilty and was hiding in Afghanistan we did not believe it to be right. If a murderer hides in a block of flats, you don't blow up the block of flats. You take all necessary steps to capture the murderer and bring him or her to trial. Many people in Britain and around the world shared the same view. Shortly after this, a new movement was initiated by the left – including a number of far-left organisations. This was the Stop the War Coalition (STWC), committed to stopping Bush's 'war on terror' and resolving the world's problems through peace and justice. CND nationally did not join the STWC – although many CND groups and regions have – but has worked closely with it to oppose the war on Iraq and to end the occupation of that country. STWC very rapidly won massive and broad support, and CND members throughout the country were centrally involved in many local STWC groups. Concerns by some CND members that the left-wing leadership of STWC would take extreme positions that would alienate its broad support proved to be unfounded. There were differences, but the calls for action are always based on the broadest possible appeal, in order to be as inclusive as possible, and CND's participation helped ensure that this was the case. Numerous trade unions give their support, together with MPs from a range of parties, celebrities, religious figures and an enormous cross-section of British society. A number of CND members opposed CND's involvement in anti-war campaigning, particularly with the STWC, but the overwhelming majority supported it, as demonstrated by regular votes at National Council meetings and CND conferences.

At CND's Annual Conference in 2003, I was elected as chair of CND, specifically on the position of furthering CND's anti-war campaigning, continuing to work with STWC and taking CND's anti-nuclear issues out into the wider movement. I also stood for making a priority of strengthening our links with the trade unions, which had been greatly weakened some years earlier by the agreement that CND and its trade union section should separate. I believed that the trade unions should be an integral part of CND and I set about restoring links with the trade unions and encouraging them to affiliate directly to CND. My own anti-nuclear activity dated back to the 1980s. I went on the big anti-cruise demonstrations and held hands round Greenham, but I had never been a CND activist until the late 1990s. The illegal war on Yugoslavia in 1999, coupled with NATO expansion and the US drive towards developing the Star Wars system, rang big alarm bells for me, and I decided to get properly involved. My first post was as chair of London Region CND, then I became a vice-chair of CND in September 2001, just days after the terrible events of September 11. That tragedy set a new framework for world politics, within which CND has a great role to play. My goal as chair of CND is to bring its issues centre-stage; as we have seen throughout the previous chapters, CND cannot allow itself to be outside the mainstream of popular concerns on issues of war and peace, especially at a time when nuclear weapons are so central to war-fighting policies.

CND and the STWC have also worked with the Muslim Association of Britain (MAB) on these same issues. MAB helped to develop the largest mobilisation of Britain's Muslim community ever in the anti-war movement. It proposed, and it was agreed, to include freedom for Palestine in the slogans of the anti-war movement. This highlighted the feeling of injustice when Iraq was invaded without the authority of the UN, while Israel ignores UN resolutions requiring its withdrawal from the Palestinian territories it has occupied since 1967. Together the three organisations have organised all the major anti-war demonstrations and have been a tripartite alliance for peace. The unity of the anti-war movement has been remarkable. We have worked together for a number of years now and we have all recognised the need for cooperation to keep the movement strong because we know we will face further challenges – not only the ongoing occupation of Iraq, but the danger of attack on Iran. There have been areas of disagreement, but these have been resolved through discussion. Immediately after the invasion of Iraq in March 2003, there was a discussion over the slogans for the demonstration that was being organised. A majority of the STWC steering committee favoured 'Blair must go', but CND argued against that as a joint official slogan because we felt that it would make it difficult for trade unions and many Labour party members who opposed the war to participate. We wanted the broadest possible support for the demo. In the event, the slogan was not an official slogan of the march. The scale of participation in the great anti-war demonstrations, particularly prior to the war, far exceeded the expectations even of the organisers. Andrew Murray, chair of the STWC, makes the following observation:

> *The anti-war movement from 2001 onwards, and especially in early 2003, represented the biggest such mobilisation of public opinion in British history. At the heart of it was a three-way alliance between the Stop the War Coalition, the Muslim Association of Britain and CND. Each organisation brought unique contributions to the overall development of a movement, which came within a hair's-breadth of stopping Tony Blair backing Bush's war. Each mobilised people the others would have had difficulty reaching. CND particularly brought not just its universally recognised identity as Britain's historic peace movement but its wealth of support among liberal, Christian, environmental and pacifist activists. Without that support, the overall movement could not have reached as far as it did into the mainstream of public opinion. This sort of unity is the guarantee of the continuing vitality of the anti-war movement, and our ability to stop not just further wars of aggression but also to achieve the world of peace and justice which has always been CND's objective.*[19]

The diversity of the movement has also been remarkable. This has been the first time that the Muslim community in Britain has been involved in such a campaign in a major way. Over the months and years since September 11, Muslims have often been under attack in a racist backlash – often being portrayed by the media as potential terrorists, linked to the September 11 attacks. Anti-war campaigners have united to oppose this absurd caricature that has had a terrible impact on the lives of innocent people. We also work together to oppose attacks on civil liberties and the increasing incursions upon the right to protest. There has also been, almost from the start, a real awareness of how so many issues are linked together.

Going back to 2001, the first big demonstration against the war on Afghanistan, with around 50,000 participants, took place in October. Our second demo, which was planned for November, actually took place about a week after the fall of Kabul, the capital. Many people at the time said that no one would come, that we should call off this demonstration; but ultimately it was larger than the first, with 80,000 people on it. There was a noticeable change in this demonstration, because for the first time there was a huge diversity amongst the marchers. On the first demonstration there were mostly peace activists and anti-war campaigners; the second demonstration included campaigners against globalisation, against oppression in the occupied territories, against debt, against the arms trade and much more. It was as if a sudden realisation had occurred, of how all these events and problems in the world are actually linked together and are part of a huge process. In a way it was like a spontaneous occurrence of the social forum movement process – bringing together and linking the issues and making us all stronger by being and working together. Many long-standing peace activists commented on the diverse nature of the movement at this point and strongly welcomed it. It is this linking of issues again that takes CND to the G8 summit in 2005, as part of both the Make Poverty History Alliance and G8 Alternatives to link the issues of weapons, war and poverty. CND is an organisation focused on campaigning against nuclear weapons and wars in which they might be used, whilst cooperating and debating with movements addressing the vast range of related issues. This linking of issues is widely accepted by CND members, both new and longstanding. Here is Bruce Kent, on the significance of this for CND today and for its future campaigning:

Since its foundation in 1958, CND has been one of the most significant, controversial and often the largest of pressure groups in Britain and perhaps even in the world. History moves on. The challenges of 2005 are not the same as those of 1958. Then there was a reasonable hope that nuclear renunciation by Britain might have created a climate in which the two major powers of the day would have started on a process of nuclear weapon elimination. Today at least eight countries have nuclear weapons and, if there is no change of direction, it will not be long before some group, not based on territory, gets a crude nuclear bomb. The nuclear weapons states have shown no interest in the abolition of their nuclear weapons. Abolition, if discussed at all, is mentioned as a pious hope or a utopian dream out of the range of practical politics.

In the world of 2005 threats to our planet and its inhabitants are better understood than they were 50 years ago. Climate change, the gap between rich and poor, health crises like the aids epidemic, and the vulnerability of major military powers to terrorist attack are now public issues. It is also becoming clear to many that war and the preparations for war are major causes of world poverty and environmental damage. There is a growing sense of partnership between pressure groups working on such issues.

Problems, once seen as separate, are now seen to connect. Security, once thought of as only a military matter, is now understood in much wider terms. Nuclear weapons are, for most of the world, seen to be a cause of global insecurity. It is the right time to press through the UN for negotiations on an international treaty abolishing all nuclear weapons worldwide. A draft treaty has already been prepared. As we deliver the message that British nuclear weapons are illegal, immoral, expensive and far from independent, we must give equal force to efforts to move internationally towards a treaty aimed at the elimination of all nuclear weapons everywhere.[20]

It has to be said that the scale of mobilisation against the war – especially on 15 February – surprised even those of us who organised it, even though we had reports in advance of the numbers of coaches and trains booked from every part of the country. The mobilisation on that day was like a cross-section of British society, and a true indication of the real breadth of the anti-war movement. There were people on that demonstration who were seasoned campaigners with 50 years or more experience; there were people who had never been on a demonstration before in their lives; there were senior citizens and babies in pushchairs; there were Muslims, Jews, Christians and atheists; there were pacifists and anti-imperialists; trade unionists and also the unemployed; people from a whole range of political parties and people who had never even voted. In short, all of life was there – all of life, that is, that wanted a peaceful resolution to the problems of Iraq, that wanted an end to lies, that wanted to prevent a barbarous war.

But the government didn't listen. Tony Blair persisted in his claims about the imminent danger presented by Iraq and about the evidence of Iraqi possession of weapons of mass destruction. We said at the time that there was no evidence and we were right. Even the US has now declared an end to the search for WMD in Iraq. Yet Blair has consistently dodged responsibility for the trumped-up charges and the illegal war; we have seen two Inquiries that have passed the buck away from the prime minister. The results of the general election on 5 May 2005 clearly indicate that the war and the lies have had a big impact on the electorate. But what we also have to be clear about – and what we need to convey to the British public at large – is that all the evidence shows that Iraq is not a one-off event and that worse is yet to come.

Taking the movement forward

The war on Iraq was illegal and immoral. It has already resulted, according to a US scientific survey, in the deaths of 100,000 Iraqis, of which over half are probably women and children.[21] Many thousands more are suffering from, and continue to die from, preventable diseases. More continue to die, or face amputation and disability when they lose limbs, as a result of cluster bombs. Untold numbers more face cancers, especially leukemia, and birth defects for years to come as a result of radiation poisoning from depleted uranium munitions. An obscene feature of the occupation of Iraq is that the occupation authorities – the US and British governments – do not even bother to count the deaths of Iraqi civilians. This demonstrates an extraordinary moral bankruptcy. This was also a war in which the invading countries had said that nuclear weapons might be used. In the run-up to the war on Iraq, it was made clear that the aggressor nations now see nuclear weapons as part of a useable arsenal. US Defense Department documents indicate the intention to develop a new generation of nuclear weapons for easy use on the battle-field.[22] Whatever governments may say, whatever excuses they may come up with, this is a qualitative shift in nuclear policy. Now is the time for us to be aware of it, and not later – not during or after the next illegal war, during or after a nuclear attack.

When it comes to President Bush's war drive for global domination, the issues of war and nuclear weapons cannot be separated out. The US and UK governments have brought those nukes in there, centre-stage. But let us be clear that it is US and UK nuclear weapons that are the problem, not the mythical weapons of states in line for US-imposed regime change and enforced compliance with the Bush interpretation of freedom and democracy. That is why CND campaigns both for the abolition of nuclear weapons and the prevention of wars in which they may be used. That is the demand of the anti-nuclear movement today. That is why we take our anti-nuclear campaigning into the heart of the anti-war movement.

There is an even more fundamental reason for under-standing this relationship. The US fought a Cold War for more than 40 years against its only serious military challenger, the Soviet Union. That conflict is over. But US policy is clear, as shown by the Project for the New American Century and Full Spectrum Dominance: it will act to prevent the emer-gence of any power or combination of powers capable of challenging it. It will act against any power or combination of powers that is not subordinate to the US becoming dominant in any continent of the world, in particular Europe or Asia. It will act to ensure it is the dominant power in the Middle East. It will act against any attempt of any other power to become dominant in Latin America. Those are a lot of potential causes of world war.

Are there any potential candidates for such conflict? The answer is yes. The number one strategic concern of Washington today is the rise of China. Starting from a very low level of output per head, China has enjoyed the fastest economic growth in the world for more than 25 years. There is no sign of any slackening in that extraordinary performance that has increased the well-being of more people in a shorter time than ever before. If China's growth continues at this pace, at some point the size of its economy will exceed that of the US. Washington has no intention of allowing that to happen – not least because, for all of the market reforms and economic opening of the last 25 years, the core of China's economy remains under the control of the state. The US did not devote billions of dollars to defeating the Soviet Union only to see another superpower rival emerge. US moves to put weapons in space, to develop a national missile defence shield and to develop a similar shield with Japan in Asia can all be seen as the beginning of a nuclear arms race against China – with the same goal of maximising military superiority and simultaneously forcing China to stall its economic growth by devoting more and more resources to arms. China is a nuclear power, but of very limited capacity, and is certainly incapable at the present time of destroying the US.

Washington also has its sights on Russia. Its goal is to steadily advance NATO and US military bases to Russia's borders. This is an economic and military threat to Russia, whose citizens watched with horror NATO bombs falling on Belgrade in 1999. Russia remains a nuclear power. In the longer perspective still, both Japan and Germany are likely at some point to conclude that if they really want to be independent of the US they need to develop their own nuclear weapons.

We live in a rapidly changing world. At present US wars are against small, weak nations, to achieve objectives such as dominance over Middle East oil supplies. But the US opposition to the rise of China poses altogether larger issues of the re-emergence of nuclear superpower conflict. That is why CND is as relevant today as at the time of its foundation. Without the vigilance of world public opinion informed by organisations such as CND, it is possible that 'low-yield' nuclear weapons could have been used to minimise US casualties in Iraq. It is also likely that computer simulations of a nuclear war with China are already running.

The challenge facing us is enormous and we have to work in every way at every level to change these policies of war and destruction.

Changing public awareness is central to our goals: peace education aimed at children and young people is an increasing part of our work. In 2005, the 60th anniversary of the atomic bombings of Hiroshima and Nagasaki, our peace education pack has been well-received. Launched at the National Union of Teachers conference, it has been sent to all secondary schools in London, with a letter of recommendation from the Mayor of London. Ken Livingstone has been supportive of the peace movement for many years and has signed up to the Appeal from the Mayors of Hiroshima and Nagasaki, as a Mayor for Peace supporting the global abolition of nuclear weapons.

To educate young people – future citizens and future leaders of our communities and countries – in the reality of nuclear weapons and war is fundamental to achieving our goals. Without this knowledge, we cannot bring about the changes in policy that are so vital to secure the future of the human race.

For CND to be effective and ultimately successful, we have to build alliances for change at every level within society, in every walk of life. That is why we work broadly, linking with other organisations and movements, re-forging our relations with the trade union movement, working with institutions as well as with activists, cooperating internationally, basing our work on the principles of unity and diversity. This is the course of action that can bring a sea-change in popular attitudes in Britain and around the world, and build the kind of movement that governments will not be able to resist: for a world of peace and social justice, free from the fear of nuclear annihilation.

REFERENCES

1 The origins of our nuclear world

1   A detailed breakdown of the death toll is to be found in Anzai Ikuro, 1975, *Nuclear War and the Earth*, Iwasaki Shoten, Japan.
2   For more information on the effects of the atomic bombing, visit CND's website www.cnduk.org.
3   Kai Bird and Lawrence Lifschultz (eds), 1998, *Hiroshima's Shadow*, The Pampleteer's Press, Stony Creek, Connecticut, pp 417–28.
4   These children's testimonies are taken from Arata Osada, 1959, *Children of the A-bomb*, by Arata Osada; reprinted 1982, Midwest Publishers, Ann Arbor, Michigan, USA.
5   Ibid.
6   From *Nuclear War and the Earth*, opcit.
7   www.cnduk.org.
8   This and other accounts are to be found on the CND website.
9   This statement from the Dean of St Albans was passed to me by Bruce Kent, vice-president of CND and a former catholic priest.
10 Quoted in *Hiroshima's Shadow*, opcit, p xviii.
11 Ibid, pp xix–xx.
12 The best work to read on this subject is *Hiroshima's Shadow* (see Note 3). Published in 1998, it is a collection of writings by distinguished historians and writers – including six Nobel laureates – on the history and politics of the decision to use atomic weapons on Hiroshima and Nagasaki.
13 Quoted in *Hiroshima's Shadow*, opcit, p lxiv.
14 Ibid, p 15.

15 *Hiroshima's Shadow*, opcit, p lxiv.

16 Gar Alperowitz, 1966, *Atomic Diplomacy: Hiroshima and Potsdam*, Secker and Warburg, London, p 109.

17 Quoted in *Hiroshima's Shadow*, opcit, p xxxiv.

18 An interesting account of this is to be found in JK Galbraith, 1981, *A Life in Our Times: Memoirs*, Houghton Mifflin, Boston.

19 For more information on Churchill's perspective on the bombing, see his wartime memoirs: Winston S. Churchill, 1954, *The Second World War: Volume Six: Triumph and Tragedy*, The Reprint Society Ltd, London, p 514.

20 This term gained popular currency after the publication of Gar Alperowitz's book (see Note 16) of that name in the 1960s.

21 *Hiroshima's Shadow*, opcit, p lvi.

22 Rosalie Bertell, 1985, *No Immediate Danger*, The Women's Press, London, p 137.

23 Ibid, pp 139–42.

24 Lawrence S Wittner, 1993, *The Struggle Against the Bomb: Volume One: One World or None: A History of the World Nuclear Disarmament Movement Through 1953*, Stanford University Press, Stanford, California, p 17.

25 Fred Roberts, 1999, *Sixty Years of Nuclear History: Britain's Hidden Agenda*, Jon Carpenter Publishing, Charlbury, Oxford, p 33.

26 Memo from the prime minister in the Cabinet Office, 28 August 1945, entitled 'The Atomic Bomb', from paragraphs 12 and 13.

27 *The Struggle Against the Bomb: Volume One*, opcit, pp 85–86.

28 *Sixty Years of Nuclear History*, opcit, p 34.

29 Kathleen Lonsdale, 1957, *Is Peace Possible?* Penguin Books, Harmondsworth, Middlesex, Foreword.

30 Caroline Moorhead, 1987, *Troublesome People: Enemies of War 1916–1986*, Hamish Hamilton, London, pp 203–04.

31 Quoted in *Hiroshima's Shadow*, opcit, pp 485–86.

32 *The Struggle Against the Bomb: Volume One*, opcit, p 97.

33 Ibid, p 84.

34 Ibid, p 41.

35 Ibid, p 84.

36 Christopher Driver, 1964, *The Disarmers: A Study in Protest*, Hodder and Stoughton, London, p 18.

37 Letter from John Cox, 31 March 2005.

38 *The Disarmers*, opcit, p 18.

39 *The Struggle Against the Bomb: Volume One*, opcit, p 311.

40 Interview with Pat Arrowsmith, 19th Februaury, 2005.

41 Bertrand Russell, 1961, *Has Man a Future?*, Penguin, Harmonds-worth, Middlesex.

42 *The Struggle Against the Bomb: Volume One*, opcit, p183.

43 Quoted in ibid, p283

44 John Minnion and Philip Bolsover (eds), 1983, *The CND Story: The First 25 Years of the CND in the Words of the People Involved*, Allison and Busby, London.

45 *The Disarmers*, opcit, p 20.

46 Jeremy Isaacs and Taylor Dowling, 1998, *Cold War: For 45 Years the World Held Its Breath*, Bantam Press, London, p149.

47 *No Immediate Danger*, opcit, pp 71–72.

48 John Cox, 1981, *Overkill: The Story of Modern Weapons*, Penguin Books, Harmondsworth, Middlesex, pp 422–23.

49 Chris Busby, 1995, *Wings of Death: Nuclear Pollution and Human Health*, Green Audit Books, Aberystwyth, pp 111–12.

50 Letter from Tony Benn, 11 April 2005.

51 Lawrence S Wittner, 1997, *The Struggle Against the Bomb: Volume Two: Resisting the Bomb: A History of the World Disarmament Movement 1954–70*, Stanford University Press, Stanford, California, p 29.

52 Letter from Sue Davis, 17 March 2005.

53 *The Struggle Against the Bomb: Volume Two*, opcit, pp 44–45.

54 *The CND Story*, opcit, p 13.

55 *The Struggle Against the Bomb: Volume Two*, opcit, p 31.

56 *The Disarmers*, opcit, p 38.

57 Peggy Duff, 1971, *Left, Left, Left: A Personal Account of Six Protest Campaigns 1945–65*, Allison and Busby, London, p 119.

58 Letter from Tony Benn, 11 April 2005.

59 Quoted in *The Disarmers*, opcit, p 39.

60 *Left, Left, Left*, opcit, p 121.

61 Ibid, p 124.

62 Quoted in *The Disarmers*, opcit, p 47.

2 Aldermaston and the early radicalism

1 *Look Back in Anger*, 1958, directed by Tony Richardson, screenplay by John Osborne, GB; *A Taste of Honey*, 1961, directed by Tony Richardson, screenplay by Shelagh Delaney, GB.

2 Jeff Nuttall, 1968, *Bomb Culture*, MacGibbon and Kee, London, p 51.

3 *Left, Left, Left*, opcit, p 129.

4 CND Annual Report, 1959, CND Archive, British Library of Political and Economic Science.

5 *The Struggle Against the Bomb: Volume Two*, opcit, p 182.

6 Ibid, p 183.

7 *The CND Story*, opcit, p 15.

8 *Left, Left, Left*, p 167.

9 Ibid, p 167.

10 *The CND Story*, opcit, p 15.

11 Ibid, p 25.

12 Article I: 'Each nuclear-weapon State Party to the Treaty undertakes not to transfer to any recipient whatsoever nuclear weapons or other nuclear explosive devices or control over such weapons or explosive devices directly, or indirectly; and not in any way to assist, encourage, or induce any non-nuclear weapon State to manufacture or otherwise acquire nuclear weapons or other nuclear explosive devices, or control over such weapons or explosive devices.'

13 *Overkill*, opcit, p 199.

14 *Left, Left, Left*, opcit, p 12.

15 Ibid.

16 *The Disarmers*, opcit, p 55.

17 *The Struggle Against the Bomb: Volume Two*, opcit, p 90.

18 Letter from John Cox, 31 March 2005.

19 *The CND Story*, opcit, p 27.

20 Ibid, p 49.

21 Lawrence S Wittner, 'A Hot Day at the PRO', in *Peace and Change*, Vol. 26, No. 2, April 2001, p 244. Many thanks to Dr Sheila Jones, CND archivist, for pointing this article out to me.

22 Ibid.

23 Letter from Dr DA Hunt to Peggy Duff, 18 November 1959, CND Archives, British Library of Political and Economic Science.

24 *Left, Left, Left*, opcit, p 127.

25 Ibid, p 166.

26 Ibid, pp 166–67.

27 *Overkill*, opcit, pp 205–06.

28 *The Struggle Against the Bomb: Volume Two*, opcit, p 186.

29 *Overkill*, opcit, p 201.

30 *The Struggle Against the Bomb: Volume Two*, opcit, p 186.

31 *The CND Story*, opcit, p 19.

32 *Left, Left, Left*, opcit, p 187.

33 *The Struggle Against the Bomb: Volume Two*, opcit, p 186.

34 Letter from Tony Benn, 11 April 2005.

35 *The CND Story*, opcit, p 57.

36 Ibid.

37 Lawrence Freedman, 1980, *Britain and Nuclear Weapons*, Macmillan, London and Basingstoke, p 31.

38 *The CND Story*, opcit, p 49.

39 Ibid, p 20.

40 Interview with Pat Arrowsmith, 10 May 2005.

41 *Left, Left, Left*, opcit, p 168.

42 Ibid.

43 *Left, Left, Left*, opcit, p 169.

44 Minutes of CND Co-ordinating Committee, 13 May 1959, CND Archive, British Library of Political and Economic Science.

45 CND Annual Report, 1959, CND Archive, British Library of Political and Economic Science.

46 Ibid.

47 Ronald W. Clark, 1975, *The Life of Bertrand Russell*, Penguin Books, Harmondsworth, Middlesex, p 720.

48 *The CND Story*, opcit, p 21.

49 *The Life of Bertrand Russell*, opcit, p 717.

50 Ibid.

51 Ibid, p 718.

52 Ibid, p 719.

53 Letter from John Cox, 31 March 2005.

54 Quoted in *The Struggle Against the Bomb: Volume Two*, opcit, p 391.

55 *The CND Story,* opcit, p 52.

56 *Left, Left, Left,* opcit, p 174.

57 *The Life of Bertrand Russell,* opcit, p 738.

58 *The Struggle Against the Bomb: Volume Two,* opcit, p 190.

59 Canon Collins' resignation letter, 1964, CND Archive, British Library of Political and Economic Science.

60 Quoted in *Overkill,* opcit, p 209.

61 Canon Collins' resignation letter, opcit.

62 Letter from Pat Allen, 10 April 2005.

63 *The CND Story,* opcit, p 25.

64 Ibid.

65 *The Struggle Against the Bomb: Volume Two,* opcit, p 191.

66 *The CND Story,* opcit, p 22.

67 Adam B Ulam, 1974, *Expansion and Coexistence: Soviet Foreign Policy 1917–73,* Holt, Reinhart and Winston, Inc, New York, p 620.

68 Ibid, p 620.

69 Ibid, p 655.

70 Draft Annual Report, April 1961–May 1962, CND Archive, British Library of Political and Economic Science.

71 Ibid.

72 *Cold War,* opcit, p 182.

73 Interview with Pat Arrowsmith, 13 March 2005.

74 *Cold War,* opcit, 190.

75 Quoted in *Cold War,* opcit, p 232.

76 *The Struggle Against the Bomb: Volume Two,* opcit, p 392.

77 *Expansion and Coexistence,* opcit, p 675.

78 Interview with Pat Arrowsmith, 13 March 2005.

79 For a full account of this expedition see Pat Arrowsmith (ed), 1972, *To Asia in Peace: The Story of a Non-Violent Action Mission to Indo-China,* Sidgwick and Jackson, London.

80 *The CND Story,* opcit, p 57.

81 *The Struggle Against the Bomb: Volume Two,* opcit, p 357.

3 From the Vietnam War to the neutron bomb

1 *Cold War*, opcit, p 205.

2 Quoted in ibid, p 206.

3 http://en.wikipedia.org, accessed 12 May 2005.

4 *Cold War*, opcit, p 218.

5 See *Overkill* for more discussion on this; opcit, pp 214–16.

6 1961 Report from the CND General Secretary, on a number of important issues, for the consideration of the Executive Committee of CND. CND Archive, British Library of Political and Economic Science.

7 *Overkill*, opcit, p 216.

8 *Left, Left, Left*, opcit, pp 245–47.

9 Ibid, p 248.

10 Ibid, pp 252–53.

11 *Overkill*, opcit, pp 217–18.

12 Letter from Michael Kustow, 2 May 2005.

13 CND Annual Conference Resolutions 1966, CND Archive, British Library of Political and Economic Science.

14 Report from CND General Secretary October 1965, CND Archive, British Library of Political and Economic Science.

15 Letter from Duncan Rees, 5 May 2005.

16 CND Conference Resolutions 1968, CND Archive, British Library of Political and Economic Science.

17 CND Annual Conference Report 1968 (supplement for September/October); CND Executive Minutes, 15 February 1969, CND Archive, British Library of Political and Economic Science.

18 *Overkill*, opcit, p 218.

19 Minutes of CND National Council Meeting 11–12 May 1968, CND Archive, British Library of Political and Economic Science.

20 'Students and CND', Report to CND National Conference 1969, CND Archive, British Library of Political and Economic Science.

21 *Cold War*, opcit, p 224.

22 *To Asia in Peace*, opcit.

23 Fred Halstead, 1978, *Out Now!: A Participant's Account of the American Movement Against the Vietnam War*, Monad Press, New York, p 729.

24 *The Struggle against the Bomb: Volume Two*, opcit, p 439.

25 *The CND Story*, opcit, p 31.

26 CND Annual Conference 1968, Report of Work, CND Archive, British Library of Political and Economic Science.

27 *CND Into Action* Bulletin, May/June/July 1966, CND Archive, British Library of Political and Economic Science.

28 *Cold War*, opcit, p 238.

29 Valerie Flessati, 1997, *Waking the Sleeping Giant: The Story of Christian CND*, Christian Campaign for Nuclear Disarmament, London, pp 25–26.

30 *Cold War*, opcit, p 244.

31 *The Struggle Against the Bomb: Volume Two*, opcit, p 433.

32 Ibid.

33 Ibid.

34 Ibid, p 343.

35 *Out Now!*, opcit, pp 710–11.

36 *The CND Story*, opcit, p 77.

37 Lawrence S Wittner, 2003, *The Struggle Against the Bomb: Volume Three: Toward Nuclear Abolition: A History of the World Nuclear Disarmament Movement, 1971 to the Present*, Stanford University Press, Stanford, California, p 22.

38 *The CND Story*, opcit, p 101.

39 *Overkill*, opcit, p 222.

40 *The CND Story*, opcit, p 105.

41 Ibid, pp 32–33.

42 Conversation with Duncan Rees, 17 April 2005.

43 Letter from Duncan Rees, 5 May 2005.

44 *The Struggle Against the Bomb: Volume Three*, opcit, p 4.

45 *Overkill*, opcit. pp 99–100.

46 Quoted in *The Struggle Against the Bomb: Volume Three*, opcit, p 4.

47 Conversation with Duncan Rees, 17 April 2005.

48 Response on behalf of the Director General of the BBC about the decision not to screen *The War Game*, from JA Norris to Mrs E Barker, 25 March 1968. CND Archives, British Library of Political and Economic Science.

49 *The CND Story*, opcit, pp 73–74.

50 *The Struggle Against the Bomb: Volume Three*, opcit, p 46.

51 Ibid, pp 22–23.

52 Ibid, p 49.

53 United Nations Special Session on Disarmament, 1978, Final Document, part III, section 47, reproduced in Ron Huzzard and Christopher Meredith (eds), 1985, *World Disarmament: An Idea Whose Time Has Come*, Spokesman, Nottingham, p 64.

4 Campaigning against cruise missiles

1 Thomas R Rochon, 1988, *Mobilizing for Peace: The Anti-Nuclear Movements in Western Europe*, Adamantine Press, London, p 3.

2 Owen Greene, 1983, *Europe's Folly: The Facts and Arguments about Cruise*, CND Publications, London, p 27.

3 *Mobilizing for Peace*, opcit, p xvi.

4 *Europe's Folly*, opcit, pp 9–10.

5 Government publication, *Cruise Missiles: A vital part of the West's Life Insurance*, undated.

6 For more on this issue, see Kate Hudson, 2000, *European Communism since 1989: Towards a New European Left?*, Palgrave, Basingstoke, pp 28–29.

7 Quoted in *Cold War*, opcit, p 334.

8 Fred Halliday, 1983, *The Making of the Second Cold War*, Verso, London, p 162.

9 Quoted in *Cold War*, opcit, p 333.

10 Malcolm Chalmers, 1984, *Trident: Britain's Independent Arms Race*, CND Publications, London, p 13.

11 Ibid, p 14.

12 *The CND Story*, opcit, p 34.

13 Bruce Kent, 1992, *Undiscovered Ends: An Autobiography*, Harper-Collins, London, p 171.

14 Phil Bolsover, undated, *Civil Defence: The Cruellest Confidence Trick*, CND, p 7.

15 EP Thompson, 1980, *Protest and Survive*, CND pamphlet, London; EP Thompson and Dan Smith (eds), 1980, *Protest and Survive*, Penguin Books, Harmondsworth, Middlesex.

16 *Protest and Survive* (Penguin book), opcit, back cover.

17 Ibid, p 224.

18 *The CND Story*, opcit, p 83.

19 Ibid, p 84.

20 Ibid, p 35.

21 Ibid.

22 *Overkill*, opcit, p 229.

23 *Undiscovered Ends*, opcit, pp 171–72.

24 Lawrence S Wittner, 'The Transnational Movement against Nuclear Weapons, 1945–1986: A Preliminary Survey', in Charles Chatfield and Peter Van Den Dungen (eds), 1988, *Peace Movements and Political Cultures*, University of Tennessee Press, Knoxville, p 278.

25 *The CND Story*, opcit, p 96.

26 Letter from Rae Street, 26 April 2005.

27 *The CND Story*, opcit, p 38.

28 *Undiscovered Ends*, opcit, p 175.

29 *The CND Story*, opcit, p 90.

30 *Nuclear-Free Zone Campaign Manual*, undated, CND Publications, London, p 1.

31 *The CND Story*, opcit, p 93.

32 *You Can't Kill the Spirit (Yorkshire Women Go To Greenham)*, 1983, Bretton Women's Book Fund, Wakefield, p 26.

33 *The Struggle Against the Bomb: Volume Three*, opcit, p 134.

34 *New Statesman*, 18 March 1983, p 8.

35 *The CND Story*, opcit, p 38.

36 *Troublesome People*, opcit, p 312.

37 *Waking the Sleeping Giant*, opcit, p 30.

38 *The Struggle Against the Bomb: Volume Three*, opcit, p 135.

39 Ibid, pp 28–32.

40 *New Statesman*, 30 March 1984, p 10.

41 *The Struggle Against the Bomb: Volume Three*, opcit, p 253.

42 *Undiscovered Ends*, opcit, p 180.

43 Ibid.

44 Quoted in *The Struggle Against the Bomb: Volume Three*, opcit, p 282.

45 Ibid, p 314.

46 *Cold War*, opcit, p 342.

47 EP Thompson (ed), 1985, *Star Wars: Self Destruct Incorporated*, Penguin Books, Harmondsworth, Middlesex, p 24.

48 Ibid, pp 25–26.

49 Quoted in *Cold War*, opcit, p 342.

50 Interview with Michael Foot, 16 May 2005.

51 *The Struggle Against the Bomb: Volume Three*, opcit, p 138.

52 *Undiscovered Ends*, opcit, p 193.

53 Interview with Michael Foot, 16 May 2005.

54 Walter Wolfgang, 'Labour and unilateral nuclear disarmament', in *Britain and the Bomb*, 1996, Labour Action for Peace, London, p 8.

55 Ibid.

56 Ibid, p 9.

57 *The Struggle Against the Bomb: Volume Three*, opcit, p 138.

58 Ibid, p 281.

59 *Cold War*, opcit, p 347.

60 Ibid, pp 347–49.

61 Quoted in *The Struggle Against the Bomb: Volume Three*, opcit, p 279.

62 Ibid, p 319.

5 Towards the end of the Cold War: the Gorbachev era

1 Quoted in Mikhail Gorbachev, 1987, *Perestroika: New Thinking for Our Country and the World*, Collins, London, p 212.

2 Haralambos Athanasopulos, 2000, *Nuclear Disarmament in International Law*, MacFarland and Company, Inc, Jefferson, North Carolina, p 85.

3 Quoted in Stephen White, 1993, *After Gorbachev*, Cambridge University Press, Cambridge, p 194.

4 *The Struggle Against the Bomb: Volume Three*, opcit, p 385.

5 *Cold War*, opcit, p 359.

6 Ibid, p 363.

7 *Nuclear Disarmament in International Law*, opcit, p 86.

8 *After Gorbachev*, opcit, p 196.

9 *Perestroika*, opcit, p 219.

10 Ibid, p 221.

11 *Sanity*, September 1990, p 31.

12 EP Thompson et al, undated, *Exterminism and Cold War*, Verso, London, p 20.

13 Ibid, p 289.

14 Ibid.

15 *The Struggle Against the Bomb: Volume Three*, opcit, p 335.

16 *Campaign!*, June 1985, p 3.

17 *The Struggle Against the Bomb: Volume Three*, opcit, p 336.

18 Ibid.

19 *Nuclear Disarmament in International Law*, opcit, pp 87–88.

20 *The Struggle Against the Bomb: Volume Three*, opcit, p 337.

21 Martin Baxendale, 1991, *Cruisewatch*, Silent But Deadly Publications, Stroud, un-numbered page.

22 CND Conference Report, 1988.

23 *Schools Against the Bomb*, undated, Information Handbook, London.

24 *Campaign!*, June 1985, p 10.

25 Ibid, p 13.

26 *Campaign!*, August 1985, p 5.

27 *Campaign!*, July 1985, p 2.

28 *Wings of Death*, opcit, p 91.

29 Ibid, p 92.

30 *The Struggle Against the Bomb: Volume Three*, opcit, p 350.

31 Conversation with Rae Street, 9 April 2005.

32 *Perestroika*, opcit, pp 235–36.

33 Ibid, p 239.

34 *Cold War*, opcit, p 364.

35 *Nuclear Disarmament in International Law*, opcit, p 94.

36 Quoted in *The Struggle Against the Bomb: Volume Three*, opcit, p 400.

37 *Britain and the Bomb*, opcit, p 9.

38 Quoted in *The Struggle Against the Bomb: Volume Three*, opcit, p 378.

39 Ibid, p 379.

40 CND Conference Report 1987.

41 Quoted in *The Struggle Against the Bomb: Volume Three*, opcit, p 402.

42 Quoted in *Cold War*, opcit, p 372.

43 Quoted in *Cold War*, opcit, p 402.

44 CND Conference Report 1989, p 5.

45 *Guardian*, 4 August 1990.

46 *The Times*, 14 August 1990.

47 CND Defence Briefing, 1991/1.

48 For further information on the Committee, visit its Archives at Warwick University.

49 Quoted in the *Guardian*, 25 September 1990.

50 *Sixty Years of Nuclear History*, opcit, p 161.

51 CND Annual Report 1991.

6 The post-Cold War world

1 CND Conference Booklet 1993, p 28.

2 CND Conference Booklet 1992, p 8.

3 *CND Today*, Summer 1994, p 7.

4 CND Conference Booklet 1993, p 36.

5 Ibid, p 23.

6 *CND Today*, Summer 1992, p 4.

7 Conversation with Marjorie Thompson, 14 April 2005.

8 CND Conference Booklet 1992, p 6.

9 CND Conference Booklet 1993, p 24.

10 *Nuclear Disarmament in International Law*, opcit, p 100.

11 *The Struggle Against the Bomb: Volume Three*, opcit, p 434.

12 *Nuclear Disarmament in International Law*, opcit, p 118.

13 Ibid, p 117.

14 *The Struggle Against the Bomb: Volume Three*, opcit, p 442.

15 *Nuclear Disarmament in International Law*, opcit, pp 122–23.

16 *CND Today*, Summer 1992, p 11.

17 *CND Today*, Summer 1993, p 10.

18 Ibid, p 11.

19 CND Annual Report 1993, p 7.

20 *Sixty Years of Nuclear History*, opcit, p 166.

21 CND Conference Booklet 1993, p 8.

22 *CND Today*, Summer 1994, p 10.

23 *The Struggle Against the Bomb: Volume Three*, opcit, p 449.

24 Ibid, p 461.

25 Ibid, p 462.

26 CND Conference Report 1995.

27 *The Struggle Against the Bomb: Volume Three*, opcit, p 464.

28 CND Conference Report 1995.

29 *Sixty Years of Nuclear History*, opcit, p 166.

30 *The Struggle Against the Bomb: Volume Three*, opcit, p 455.

31 Quoted in *Hiroshima's Shadow*, opcit, p 565.

32 Ibid, pp 565–66.

33 Ibid, p 567.

34 *The Struggle Against the Bomb: Volume Three*, opcit, p 455.

35 Ibid, p 472.

36 Ibid, p 476.

37 CND Annual Report 1997.

38 CND Conference Report 1998, p 12.

39 All from CND Conference Report 1998.

40 *The Struggle Against the Bomb: Volume Three*, opcit, p 465.

41 *CND Today*, August 1999, p 6.

42 For a fuller account of this, see Kate Hudson, 2003, *Breaking the South Slav Dream: The Rise and Fall of Yugoslavia*, Pluto Press, London.

43 Quoted in Mark Littman QC, 2000, *Neither Legal nor Moral. How NATO's war against Yugoslavia breached international law*, Committee for Peace in the Balkans, London, p 3.

44 Ibid, p 15.

45 *Labour Focus on Eastern Europe*, 64/1999, p 25.

46 *International Herald Tribune*, 6–7 January 2001.

47 *Breaking the South Slav Dream*, opcit, p 135.

48 CND Conference papers, 1999.

49 *Breaking the South Slav Dream*, opcit, p 217.

50 *The Struggle Against the Bomb: Volume Three*, opcit, p 480.

51 Ibid.

7 Campaigning since September 11

1　*The Struggle Against the Bomb: Volume Three,* opcit, p 481.
2　See PNAC's website, www.newamericancentury.org.
3　www.defenselink.mil/news, accessed 10 October 2003.
4　United States Space Command, *Vision for 2020,* undated.
5　CND Annual Review, 2002.
6　Results of an ICM/CND opinion poll of 1008 people conducted October 2004.
7　See CND's information briefing, 'Keep Space for Peace', www.cnduk.org.
8　Missile Defence Bulletin, Yorkshire CND, No. 2, April 2005.
9　Ibid.
10　www.globalsecurity.org/wmd/library/policy, accessed 10 October 2003.
11　www.whitehouse.gov/news/releases/2002, accessed 25 May 2005.
12　Both from *Campaign,* No. 2, 2004, p 8.
13　CND Annual Report, 2004.
14　See the British American Security Council's briefing on the Citizens' Inquiry into the Legality of Trident, www.basicint.org/nuclear/legalnc.htm.
15　Quoted in CND's briefing paper for the NPT Review Conference, 2005, 'Rejecting the logic of counter-proliferation'.
16　Quoted in *New World,* Jan–March 2005, p 9.
17　CND Annual Report, 2004.
18　See text of Attorney General's Advice on the CND website www.cnduk.org.
19　Letter from Andrew Murray, 27 April 2005.
20　Letter from Bruce Kent, 24 April 2005.
21　In October 2004, the *Lancet* published research by scientists from the Johns Hopkins Bloomberg School of Public Health in Baltimore, US, which concluded that poor planning, air strikes by coalition forces and a 'climate of violence' have led to more than 100,000 extra deaths in Iraq. www.news.bbc.co.uk, accessed 25 May 2005.
22　See US Nuclear Posture Review, 2002.

INDEX

ABOUT THE AUTHOR

Kate Hudson is Chair of the Campaign for Nuclear Disarmament, a post she has held since September 2003. She is also Head of Social and Policy Studies at London South Bank University, teaching Russian and East European politics and history. She is author of *European Communism since 1989* and *Breaking the South Slav Dream: The Rise and Fall of Yugoslavia,* and editor of the international journal *Contemporary Politics.*